CAMBRIDGE LIBRARY

Books of enduring schol

History

The books reissued in this series include accounts of historical events and movements by eye-witnesses and contemporaries, as well as landmark studies that assembled significant source materials or developed new historiographical methods. The series includes work in social, political and military history on a wide range of periods and regions, giving modern scholars ready access to influential publications of the past.

New Zealand's First War

Thomas Lindsay Buick (1865–1938) became interested in New Zealand history while working as a political journalist in Wellington, and became an influential figure in the field. He wrote twelve books and numerous pamphlets on the early history of the country and was elected Fellow of the Royal Historical Society in 1914. This book, first published in Wellington in 1926, describes one of the most significant conflicts in nineteenth-century New Zealand, the Flagstaff War (1845–6), in which European settlers and their Maori supporters fought those Maori who were resisting colonial encroachment. A key figure during the war was the Nga Puhi chief Hone Heke, from the Bay of Islands, who famously refused to acknowledge British sovereignty and repeatedly felled the British flagpole in Kororareka. Buick's account probes the complex relationships among the warring factions, describes the individual phases of the war, and explains how peace was eventually restored.

Cambridge University Press has long been a pioneer in the reissuing of out-of-print titles from its own backlist, producing digital reprints of books that are still sought after by scholars and students but could not be reprinted economically using traditional technology. The Cambridge Library Collection extends this activity to a wider range of books which are still of importance to researchers and professionals, either for the source material they contain, or as landmarks in the history of their academic discipline.

Drawing from the world-renowned collections in the Cambridge University Library, and guided by the advice of experts in each subject area, Cambridge University Press is using state-of-the-art scanning machines in its own Printing House to capture the content of each book selected for inclusion. The files are processed to give a consistently clear, crisp image, and the books finished to the high quality standard for which the Press is recognised around the world. The latest print-on-demand technology ensures that the books will remain available indefinitely, and that orders for single or multiple copies can quickly be supplied.

The Cambridge Library Collection will bring back to life books of enduring scholarly value (including out-of-copyright works originally issued by other publishers) across a wide range of disciplines in the humanities and social sciences and in science and technology.

New Zealand's First War

Or, the Rebellion of Hone Heke

T. LINDSAY BUICK

CAMBRIDGE
UNIVERSITY PRESS

CAMBRIDGE UNIVERSITY PRESS

Cambridge, New York, Melbourne, Madrid, Cape Town,
Singapore, São Paolo, Delhi, Tokyo, Mexico City

Published in the United States of America by Cambridge University Press, New York

www.cambridge.org
Information on this title: www.cambridge.org/9781108039987

This edition first published 1926
This digitally printed version 2011

ISBN 978-1-108-03998-7 Paperback

CAPTAIN ROBERT FITZROY, R.N.

Governor of New Zealand, December, 1843, to November, 1845.

NEW ZEALAND'S FIRST WAR,

OR

THE REBELLION OF HONE HEKE.

BY

T. LINDSAY BUICK, F.R.Hist.S.,

Author of
" *Old Marlborough,*" " *Old Manawatu,*" " *An Old New-Zealander,*"
" *The Treaty of Waitangi.*"

Published under the auspices of the Board of Maori
Ethnological Research.

WELLINGTON.
W. A. G. SKINNER, GOVERNMENT PRINTER.
—
1926.

Dedication.

TO THE MEMORY OF

THOMAS MORLAND HOCKEN, M.R.C.S., F.L.S.,

WHOSE PATIENCE AND INDUSTRY IN COLLECTING THE
EARLY RECORDS OF THE DOMINION HAS MADE
THE WRITING OF THIS ACCOUNT OF NEW
ZEALAND'S FIRST WAR POSSIBLE,

I GRATEFULLY DEDICATE THIS BOOK.

PREFACE.

THE genesis of this book is to be found in a request I received on the eve of the Great War, to collect such facts as were then available regarding the activities of the 96th Regiment during the time it was stationed in New Zealand. The idea was that when these facts had been collected and put into narrative form they were to be included in a history of the Manchester Regiment, then being prepared in England, the 96th having in recent years been embodied as the 2nd battalion of that unit of the King's forces. I was able to devote some furtive hours to this work, and I hastily put together such facts as I could find in the limited time at my disposal. Then the Great War broke out, and I never heard whether the manuscript reached England, or whether it was ever published. It is more than likely that in the world welter which took place between the years 1914 and 1918 it was either lost or forgotten. Since then I have had other opportunities of adding to the incomplete details which formerly fell under my notice. I therefore began to amplify them; but as the story developed I discovered that it would become somewhat disproportionate if the 96th Regiment was put upon a pedestal, while other regiments, whose detachments were of greater strength and equally heroic, were left on the ground-level. I therefore decided to change the plan of the work, and, while giving all credit to the 96th Regiment, enlarge it to a history of Heke's war, in the later phases of which the 96th took no part. And here the extended story is given to such as may feel an interest in it.

THE AUTHOR.

5 Boston Terrace,
    Wellington, New Zealand.

NOTE OF ACKNOWLEDGMENT.

T HE story of this book has been compiled from official records of the Dominion, contemporary newspapers, and from private letters written by Governor FitzRoy. Where European sources have failed to explain events from the native point of view I have utilized the account of the war related by an old Nga-Puhi chief to F. E. Maning, and published by him as " The War in the North." Carleton's " Life of Henry Williams " has been drawn upon as a mine of curious information, and especially helpful have been some notes on the war left by Colonel Despard, as well as the published diary of the Rev. Robert Burrows, the representative of the Church Missionary Society at Waimate, and Coleman's Memoir of the Rev. Richard Davis, the resident Church missionary at Kaikohe. The unpublished diary of Major Cyprian Bridge, and some letters written by the missionaries at the Bay of Islands, copies of which I found in the Hocken Collection at Dunedin, and from which I was kindly permitted to make copious extracts, have also been extensively used.

A number of the illustrations have likewise been obtained from the same generous source, the Governors of the Collection freely placing their pictures at my disposal.

For the photograph of the Rev. Mr. Burrows I have to thank his granddaughter, Miss Erina S. Edgcumbe, of Parnell, Auckland.

For several of the illustrations I am also indebted to Mr. James Cowan and Mr. J. McDonald.

I have likewise to thank the Hon. Sir Maui Pomare, M.P., Mr. Tau Henare, M.P., Mr. Elsdon Best, Mr. H. M. Stowell, Mr. Horace Fildes, and Mr. H. R. H. Balneavis for much valuable assistance and for kindly suggestions.

CONTENTS.

LIST OF ILLUSTRATIONS.

CHAPTER I.

INTRODUCTION.

PRIOR to 1840 New Zealand was internationally a
"No Man's Land." At a period still undefined some
Polynesian navigator sailing or drifting in his canoe
had sighted its shores, and subsequently his race had peopled
its fertile and forest-clad lands, unknown to and unknowing of
the great world beyond the Pacific. Then came Abel Janszoon
Tasman, the Dutch explorer, who in 1642 stumbled upon
its coast and left it again unconscious of what he had
really seen and found. For more than a century after
that no civilized sailor ventured near its shores, until
Captain James Cook, the greatest navigator of them all,
rediscovered for Britain in 1769 a treasure which Holland
by her lack of enterprise had lost. At various points
he took possession of the country for and in the name
of King George III, but beyond these formal precautions
Britain was as negligent of her new-found possession as
were her Dutch neighbours. No systematic occupation of
the territory followed, nor were any other steps taken
which would serve to confirm her right to exclude other
nations from the colonization of the Islands. Failure to
enforce her claim was not, however, the only feature which
characterized the policy of Britain, for by several direct
executive acts she had proceeded to divest herself of even
the slender rights she once possessed. These acts of
renunciation culminated in 1834 when Lord Aberdeen, on

1—First War.

behalf of the Government of King William IV, definitely recognized as an independent nation a confederation of chiefs in the northern portion of the northern Island, and presented them with a national flag as the symbol of their independence.*

It is true that in the previous year the Government had appointed a British Resident in the person of Mr. James Busby, but he had and could have no real power, since he was unsupported by physical force of any kind. He was therefore of more service as a butt for the cynics than to his own countrymen or to the native people whose interests he was supposed to protect. The necessity for this appointment lay in the fact that the spirit of adventure and enterprise in the British people was not so lethargic as their Government officials. As the result of the wide publication of the accounts of Cook's voyages and the growth of the whaling industry in the southern seas many persons of robust British birth were finding their way to these antipodean islands, where the free life and bracing climate proved an irresistible attraction. There was thus growing up at several centres—notably at the Bay of Islands—an ungoverned and to some extent an ungovernable white population, many of whom by their lawlessness were creating a social problem which could not be ignored, while others by their industry were building up commercial interests, for the conservation of which the British Government was constantly being solicited to take effective measures. To do this, British

---

* The pole upon which this flag was flown was destined to play an important part in New Zealand history. It was made from a kauri spar grown upon the land of Hone Heke, and was given by that chief to Mr. Busby, the British Resident, who erected it in front of his house at Waitangi. When British sovereignty over the country was declared, the staff was taken down and removed to the opposite side of the harbour, where it was erected on Maiki Hill, above the town of Kororareka. Here it was used primarily to signal ships entering the Bay of Islands, but when not so employed the Union Jack was flown at its peak, a proceeding which angered the anti-British element at the Bay, and at the same time served materially to mystify the Maori, who was slow to comprehend its true meaning. The misunderstandings—intensified by mischievous Europeans—which centred round the staff, led to its being cut down by Hone Heke in 1844, and so brought on the war described in these pages.

statesmen of all parties were distinctly disinclined. There was a feeling that Britain had colonies enough, and that the existing responsibilities of the infant Empire were as much as the parent country could bear. There was then no vision of a world-wide confederation of peoples, embracing men of all races and all religions, who were to find a common bond in the justice and freedom which the British Constitution affords.

If, however, British statesmen were loath to interfere with such members of the race as were then residing in New Zealand, and if they hesitated to accept the responsibility of protecting the increasing trade of those Islands, they were unable successfully to maintain this attitude of indifference when, in 1839, the question of colonizing this country began to be actively canvassed, especially in England. The first big factor which then materially influenced British policy was the fear of French intervention, and the second was her own social stress at home. However well- or ill-founded the fear of French aggression may have been, there could be no question as to the pressure of the social unrest. The industrial and agricultural condition of the British Isles was truly deplorable, propagating a feeling which Carlyle described as the "sullen, revengeful humour of revolt against the upper classes."

To the study of how best to alleviate the prevailing political sores there came a body of young men whose almost revolutionary spirit longed to break the bonds of English conservatism, and who because of their advanced views became known as the "Philosophic Radicals." To their aid came a small band of philanthropic Tories, who were gravely concerned at the alleged "overpopulation" of the British Isles. These men busily propounded the doctrine of colonization as the cure for Britain's social and industrial woes, and when searching for a field in which their scheme might find fulfilment they selected New Zealand as the country offering "the most profitable investment for British capital and the highest prospects

1*

for employment and opportunity for England's idle labour."

This agitation passed through several phases and many vicissitudes, but was ever insistent, and at last, when its promoters believed they were unable to induce the Government to act in the direction they desired, the movement became so practical that its leaders despatched the smart-sailing brig *Tory* with an advance party to form a colony of their own somewhere on the shores of Cook Strait. That the British Government would sooner or later have taken measures to consolidate the British position in New Zealand is tolerably certain, but the act of the New Zealand Company in rushing their vessel off to begin the work of systematic colonization was a new and vitalizing influence which stirred up the dry bones of Downing Street in a manner most surprising. Rapidly a decision was reached that the Government must now intervene ; that they must despatch an Agent of their own, invested with Consular powers and with instructions to negotiate a treaty with the native chiefs for the cession of their sovereignty to the Queen. The choice of an officer to fill this position fell upon Captain William Hobson, R.N., who had previously been in New Zealand in the *Rattlesnake*, and who had reported upon the most advisable method of controlling and safeguarding British interests there.

The plan of the Imperial authorities was that if Hobson succeeded in his mission New Zealand was to be attached as a dependency to New South Wales, and that in matters of importance Hobson was to take his directions from Sir George Gipps, the Governor of that colony. Hobson left England in H.M.S. *Druid*, and after a brief stay in Sydney, where he assembled his staff of civil officers and received his final instructions, he reached Kororareka, in the Bay of Islands, on the 29th January, 1840. Kororareka is caustically described at this date by one of Hobson's staff as " a miserable place, composed of some twenty houses and native huts, standing on a narrow shingly bank which separates the beach from a morass forming the background of the 'town' as it is called; immediately behind which the hills rise steep and abrupt, clothed with coarse fern and dwarf cyprus scrub. The soil is very sterile, and the whole appearance of the place wretched in the extreme." Still, it was the largest settlement of Europeans in the country, and on the day after his arrival Hobson proceeded to the little Mission Church, and there announced by Proclamation that he had been appointed Lieutenant-Governor over such territory, the sovereignty of which the natives were willing to cede to Her Majesty Queen Victoria.

This announcement created a distinct flutter in the local dovecote. It gladdened the hearts of those who were anxious to see some system of regular government established in the country, just as it deeply aggrieved those who desired to continue their land-sharking or to pursue their loose and irresponsible mode of living. But, whether he was welcomed or contemned, Hobson's arrival laid down a definite milestone in the history of New Zealand, for, as events proved, he had come to stay.

Before he left England Captain Hobson had received specific instructions that any concessions the natives might make to Her Majesty must be of a purely voluntary character, and that they must be accompanied by a *quid pro quo* in the shape of some definite guarantee of Her Majesty's good will. He was therefore not to seize the country, but to endeavour to persuade the chiefs to cede their sovereignty under a fair and equitable treaty. These reservations were made because the spirit of Britain at that day revolted against the practices of former times, under which native peoples had been ruthlessly despoiled of their possessions and so reduced to a state of moral and physical degradation. Beyond these general outlines Hobson appears to have had but little to help him in formulating the terms of the treaty. With, however, the assistance of several local gentlemen, notably Mr. James Busby, who was now superseded in his position as British Resident, he devised a document at once terse and simple in its terms, but none the less a storm-centre of conflicting interpretations for many years. This treaty provided,—

(1.) That the native chiefs should cede their sovereignty to the Queen of Great Britain.

(2.) That the lands, forests, fisheries, and food-places of the natives should remain theirs inviolate, but that the right of pre-emptive purchase of their lands should vest in the Crown.

(3.) In return for these concessions Her Majesty would afford the native race her Royal protection and impart to them all the rights and privileges of British subjects.

The draft of the treaty was first promulgated at a large meeting of representative natives at Waitangi on the 5th February, 1840. The debate involving its acceptance or rejection lasted with fluctuating fortunes all day, and was then adjourned to permit of private discussion. On the 6th February forty-five chiefs put their signatures to the document, and from that moment New Zealand virtually, if not actually, became a dependency of the British Empire, over which Captain Hobson proclaimed himself Lieutenant-Governor. The full status of a British colony was not, however, reached until the 17th June, 1840, on which day Major Bunbury declared the Queen's sovereignty over the South Island by virtue of the signatures he had received to the treaty from the southern chiefs. Between the 5th February and the 17th June the procuration of signatures was actively pursued by the Lieutenant-Governor and his accredited agents, the majority of whom were the Protestant missionaries then labouring in the country. Not all the chiefs were asked to sign, nor did all who were so asked comply with the request ; but most of the accessible portions of the Islands were visited, and with few exceptions the influential chiefs became parties to the pact, the conditions of which they and their people were able to grasp with a remarkable degree of clarity. On the whole, then, the canvass for signatures was fairly comprehensive, and the signatories were reasonably representative of the race.

The work which Captain Hobson was sent to do was thus progressing with apparent success until it received a severe check in his own sudden and complete prostration by illness. On Sunday, the 1st March, while on a visit to Waitemata, he was stricken by paralysis, which incapacitated him from work of any kind. Never a robust man, this illness was due to physical exhaustion and mental anxiety arising from the strain of his new responsibilities, accelerated by irritating differences with Captain Nias, who commanded H.M.S. *Herald*, and with whom he was compelled to travel. Both captains were Irishmen, but evidently not of that genial type which Erin's Isle so frequently produces.

When thus stricken and lying helpless in his cabin Hobson's first impulse was to resign his Governorship and return to Sydney. From this course he was dissuaded by the Rev. Henry Williams, head of the Anglican Mission, who promised him care and attention at the Waimate Mission Station, together with assistance in his administrative duties. To these solicitations Hobson yielded, and for some weeks he lay suffering in body and wracked in mind while the urgent task of formulating his administrative plans remained in complete abeyance. His protracted illness necessarily exercised an injurious influence upon the interests of the colony by retarding the development of governmental schemes and depriving the Executive of all life and energy. The Government was, in fact, a mere mockery, for, except that a Police Magistrate and two or three constables were stationed at Kororareka, political and social conditions remained in much the same state as formerly. The authority of the Government was frequently derided, even despised, by both its own subjects and by foreigners. Thus from the unfortunate circumstance of Captain Hobson's illness the movement to establish constitutional rule in New Zealand received at its inception a check from which it made but slow recovery.

Before he left Sydney certain gentlemen had been allocated by Sir George Gipps to Captain Hobson as the personnel of his civil staff. Lieutenant Willoughby Shortland, R.N., was appointed to the office of Chief Police Magistrate ; Mr. George Cooper came as Treasurer and Comptroller of Customs ; Mr. Felton Mathew as Surveyor-General ; and Mr. James S. Freeman as Acting Colonial Secretary. Between these gentlemen and Hobson there, unfortunately, did not develop that *esprit de corps* so essential to the harmonious working of an infant Government. Justly or unjustly, Hobson refused to repose any measure of confidence in his officers. Public business was therefore stagnated while he was an invalid, and when he was convalescent he insisted upon giving every transaction his personal attention. He thus unnecessarily vexed himself and irritated his staff, who resented what they regarded as his petty interferences. There was as a consequence clash and friction instead of smooth working in official circles, with a resultant loss in executive efficiency and delay in administrative progress.

Hobson's illness had, amongst other things, rendered impossible the determination of a site for the capital of the new colony, and when he was sufficiently recovered to transact public business one of his first acts was to select a spot for the temporary headquarters of the official establishment, the idea being that the locality chosen would prove a desirable site for a town when the Government should be removed to the capital. The opinion of the Surveyor-General on this point being required by the Lieutenant-Governor, that officer's advice was that Kororareka, which already contained a white population of between three hundred and four hundred souls, should be taken possession of by the Government, and that all parties claiming land therein as purchased from the natives should be compensated in a manner subsequently to be determined. Hobson did not, however, read his instructions as wide enough to bear him out in such a measure. He also foresaw difficulties in adjusting matters with the land claimants, who were not likely to act in a conciliatory spirit towards a Government which they regarded as an intruder and which for the most part they despised. The idea of making Kororareka the official centre was therefore rejected, as, indeed, most of the official recommendations were.* The Surveyor-General was instructed to report upon the next most eligible site for a settlement and future town. To comply with the known views of the Lieutenant-Governor an area of land at the junction of the Kawakawa and Waikare Rivers was suggested. This property was owned by a Mr. J. R. Clendon, who was at that time acting as Consul for the United States. Upon it he had erected an excellent house, extensive stores, and outbuildings, which appeared to provide the Lieutenant-Governor with all that he required for a temporary establishment. As a result of negotiation it was agreed that the Government should purchase the property for the sum of £15,000. Outside official circles this was considered an overlarge price to pay. The transaction was severely criticized, and proved ultimately as embarrassing to the Government as it was unpopular with the public. Hobson's justification was that time was pressing. The storeship *Westminster* was daily expected from Sydney with the whole establishment of the Government, a number of mechanics, and a large quantity of stores. It was necessary to make some immediate arrangements for their disposal. In the state of his health it was impossible to leave the Bay of Islands, and no other property at the Bay with the same advantages presented itself. He therefore closed the bargain, and saddled himself with an obligation which proved unexpectedly irksome to him and equally unsatisfactory to Mr. Clendon.†

* Major Bunbury states that Hobson was very jealous of his authority, and obstinate, particularly as disease made encroachments upon his frame and intellect.

† Owing to the breakdown in Hobson's finance, he was unable to pay the price agreed upon in cash, and the affair was, after protracted delay, finally settled by granting Mr. Clendon 10,000 acres of land within twelve miles of Auckland.

Having settled these initial details at the Bay of Islands, Captain Hobson now seriously turned his attention to the larger question of selecting the permanent site for the capital of the colony.   In this he was greatly influenced by the advice and advocacy of the Rev. Henry Williams. On the 30th January, 1840, Henry Williams was at Waimate, having reached that mission station on his return from the south, whither he had gone with Tamihana te Rauparaha and Matene te Whiwhi to install the Rev. Octavius Hadfield in his charge at Otaki.   Late that night the missionary received a note from Captain Hobson — of whose arrival he was unaware—telling him of the British Government's intentions with regard to New Zealand. In these proposals Hobson invited the co-operation of the missionary, with whom he begged the pleasure of an interview at the earliest possible moment.   They met next day, and one of the many subjects discussed was the purchase of a site for the proposed colonial capital.   In this connection the missionary's geographical knowledge was invaluable.   He was an ex-officer of the British Navy and had a keen appreciation of a good harbour.   Moreover, he had travelled up and down the Island by land and sea, and was better informed than almost any other white man in the colony as to the relative values of the northern sites.   When asked for his opinion he immediately pronounced solidly against the Bay of Islands, where, he contended, the land was too circumscribed for a potential city.   He was, however, enthusiastic about the isthmus at Waitemata, as being unoccupied by natives and possessing topographical advantages far in excess of any other known site.

It was therefore for the dual purpose of inspecting this promising locality and of meeting the natives in the vicinity of Waitemata that Captain Hobson and Mr. Williams left the Bay of Islands in H.M.S. *Herald* on Friday, the 21st February.   With them they took Mr. Felton Mathew, the Surveyor-General, upon whom devolved the duty of advising the Lieutenant-Governor whether the recommendation of the missionary was or was not sound. One has only to read the rough diary which Mr. Mathew has left us to realize that he was a man wholly unsuited to the task allotted to him. He was a man apparently without vision, without enterprise, without the spirit of the pioneer, and he had not been in New Zealand many weeks before he became undisguisedly disgruntled at what he regarded as a quixotic attempt at colonization. On the 24th February he began his inspection of the isthmus, but without any enthusiasm for its potentialities. It is therefore not surprising to find him telling us that—

After a week's examination our efforts are unsuccessful. The northern side of the harbour and river of Waitemata present a fine anchorage, but the land is precipitous and the position unfavourable. The south side of the harbour is shoal, and the shores, though undulating flats of moderate elevation, are destitute of wood and water, and present not one single advantage which could render them eligible as the site for a town.

This may have been Felton Mathew's opinion, but it was not Hobson's, who during the most of this week was busy holding meetings with the natives in the interests of the Treaty of Waitangi, and on Sunday, the 1st March, he had that paralytic seizure which necessitated his immediate return to the Bay of Islands, and which, as already narrated, was to incapacitate him for the discharge of public business for many weeks. By the middle of April, however, Hobson had sufficiently recovered to take the matter again into consideration, and, acting under his instructions, the Surveyor-General, on the 18th of the month, left the Bay in the revenue cutter *Ranger* to resume his interrupted investigations. After a careful and minute examination of the coast during the next two months he was forced to concede that the isthmus was the most suitable locality ; and he favoured Tamaki as the most eligible site for the capital. Before accepting this recommendation, however, Captain Hobson decided to make a further personal examination of the district, and towards the end of

June, accompanied by Mr. George Clarke, Protector of
the Aborigines, and Captain Rough, he went down in
the *Ranger* and promptly rejected the Surveyor-General's
advice, because from the sailor's point of view the channel
was inadequate for the volume of shipping he anticipated
would soon be arriving in that part of the colony.

He next visited the upper reaches of the Waitemata
Harbour, but here again the water access was unsatisfactory.
In the meantime, however, Captain Rough* had been
exploring in another direction, and returning to the ship
with a report that excellent soundings had been taken on
what is now the Ponsonby side of the harbour, Captain
Hobson at once decided to adopt the advice of Henry
Williams and establish the capital on the shores of
Waitemata Harbour,† leaving the determination of the
actual spot until a later date.

This was ultimately fixed by Mr. Felton Mathew, and
negotiations were entered into with the chiefs of the
Ngati-Whatua tribe‡ for the purchase of 3,000 acres, more
or less, the price paid being the usual collection of
miscellaneous articles, including pipes, pots, and blankets,
together with £50 in cash.   The deed was signed on the
20th October, and in the following month the site was
formally taken possession of with some little ceremony
by a number of Government officers.   The Lieutenant-
Governor did not, however, officially enter the capital
until the 14th March, 1841, and there he died on the
10th September in the following year.

In a despatch to the Secretary of State for the
Colonies, dated 10th November, 1840, Hobson indicated
that he proposed to call the new capital "Auckland."
This was done by way of compliment to Lord Auckland,

* Captain Rough was appointed first Harbourmaster at Waitemata
in August.

† In a despatch dated 15th October, 1840, Captain Hobson details
to the Secretary of State for the Colonies the reasons which induced him
to select this site.

‡ The representatives of the Ngati-Whatua tribe had already waited
on Captain Hobson and invited him to found the capital at Waitemata,
and their friendly attitude may have had some influence with him.

OFFICIAL BAY, AUCKLAND, 1844.

After the drawing in the Hocken Collection, Dunedin.

then Governor-General of India, but who while at the Admiralty had befriended the unemployed Hobson by giving him the command of the *Rattlesnake* in which he first came to New Zealand.

While these events were in process of development at Auckland things were going but indifferently with Hobson at the Bay of Islands. A not unimportant part of his schemes there was that the land surrounding the new official quarters should be laid off as a township, from the sale of which it was anticipated a large sum of money would be derived with which to carry on the administration of the country. To the surprise of every one, and the especial annoyance of the Lieutenant-Governor, the sale of town lots in what was to have been the settlement of Russell* was vetoed by Sir George Gipps, and by this interdiction Hobson's financial schemes were brought with a crash to the ground. He was thus unable to give effect to one of the essential provisions of the Treaty of Waitangi—viz., the pre-emptive clause under which native land must be purchased from its owners not by private individuals, but by the Government.

Unaided by finance from Home and deprived of the opportunity of raising sufficient funds within the colony, Hobson found his land policy—the thing that mattered most — completely thwarted. It followed that no new land was being settled, which angered the natives, who were anxious to sell land, while the decision to investigate and revise the titles of all land already purchased from the natives irritated to even a greater extent the white population. Because settlement was at a standstill production was reduced, and trade diminished almost to vanishing-point. There was a consequent unrest which manifested itself in various ways : one of the most pronounced, and at the same time most disquieting, was the frequent quarrels between the white and brown races. To provide against such a contingency the Lieutenant-Governor had no resources. On leaving Sydney he had in

* So named after Lord John Russell. This name was subsequently transferred to Kororareka.

his retinue four members of the New South Wales Mounted
Police, but these men had come as a bodyguard to the
Governor rather than as guardians of the public peace.
Their numbers were wholly inadequate to the exigencies of
the case. The critical state of the public peace was thus
an additional source of anxiety to Hobson, and in his
despatches to the Home Government and in his reports
to Sir George Gipps he repeatedly pointed out the
necessity for some military force to support him in his
dangerous isolation.*

On the 16th April, 1840, the *Buffalo*, a Government
storeship, arrived from Sydney at the Bay of Islands with
a detachment of 100 officers and men of the 80th Regiment,
under the command of Major Thomas Bunbury.† This
small augmentation of his means of asserting his authority
was very welcome to Hobson, as may be judged from the
following statement of the position by a then resident at
the Bay :—

> The presence of the soldiers was greatly required to overawe
> the natives, who were at this time much excited in consequence
> chiefly of a barbarous murder committed by a native on a
> shepherd employed by the Rev. Henry Williams. The murderer
> was seized and given up by his countrymen, but owing to the
> impossibility at that time of establishing a Court of criminal
> jurisdiction he could not be tried. The natives, not under-
> standing the necessity for delay, became dissatisfied and would
> have executed the man after their own fashion. This, of course,
> could not be allowed, hence their anger and unrest. The man
> was kept in prison awaiting his trial. He several times escaped,
> but was always retaken by his countrymen, and after many
> months of protracted suffering died a victim to confinement and
> anxiety.

Almost before the men of the 80th had landed,
certainly before they were properly quartered on shore,
their Commander received a request from the Lieutenant-

* Sir George Gipps, Governor of New South Wales, was authorized
by Lord John Russell, Chief Secretary for the Colonies, to send 100 men
to aid Captain Hobson if he should require them when he assumed the
title of Lieutenant-Governor of New Zealand.

† Major Bunbury carried with him a commission as Acting Lieutenant-
Governor, which he was to use in the event of Hobson's death.

Governor to proceed in H.M.S. *Herald* to secure the signatures of the chiefs in the South Island to the Treaty of Waitangi. Though loath to leave his men in a state of transition, the Major felt he could not refuse the obligation, seeing that Hobson's health was so precarious and that he had specially stressed his unwillingness to again sail with Captain Nias.* The detachment was therefore placed in charge of Captain Lockhart, the Major proceeding to the South.

The presence of the soldiers did not, however, altogether mend the social order, and Hobson was ere long compelled to appeal for a still larger force.† In describing a disturbance between some European sailors and the natives he wrote to Lord John Russell on the 15th June, 1840 : —

> The inference to be drawn from these occurrences is that an augmentation of the military is absolutely necessary. It must never be overlooked that the native population are a warlike race, well armed, and ever ready to use those arms on the slightest provocation.

This passage is but typical of the many appeals to the Home authorities which Hobson was constrained to make in his despatches of that time, and although both Lord John Russell and his successor, Lord Stanley, treated his requests with the utmost courtesy, they were wont to emphasize their grave disinclination to grant the required aid in view of the wide demands upon the British Army at that important period of Imperial expansion.

In this respect the policy of the British Ministers was meagre in spirit and narrow in vision, and to those shortcomings must be attributed many of the colony's early misfortunes. Once they had determined that New Zealand

---

* Sir George Gipps told Major Bunbury that Hobson and Nias were both Naval officers of the same rank, equally violent in temper, and that he would find it very difficult to decide between them.

† One of the difficulties in the way of securing an increase in the military was an order from Lord Hill, Commander-in-Chief, to the Australian authorities not to increase the New Zealand force beyond the men under Major Bunbury's command.

must be colonized, and that the military were necessary to the settlers' protection, it became their duty to see that the country was provided with a force at least sufficient in strength to overawe the natives, of whose warlike propensities they could not have been ignorant. Major Bunbury had already reported that when he and his men of the 80th arrived, and for some time after, the natives had " an almost superstitious dread of encountering the military."* But he was shrewd enough to see that " the least check would dissolve the charm." To attempt more than his small force could successfully accomplish would be but to invite disaster, a possibility which, to him, was becoming more and more imminent, since the efforts of the Government and the missionaries were tending to eliminate the jealousies of the tribes, only perhaps to unite them against the settlers.

This extreme peril of the colony had been pressed upon the two great Secretaries of State with a reiteration bordering on the painful, but the fact is New Zealand was as yet of small importance in the Empire. Her necessities and wants were not understood by men whose minds were occupied by larger things — or things which seemed larger because they were not diminished by the glossing effect of extreme distance. How nearly this failure to visualize the clamant needs of the infant colony came to rendering bankrupt the moral effect of British power in the eyes of the New Zealand natives the incidents which are hereafter recorded may serve to demonstrate.

In September, 1840, a second detachment of the 80th arrived from Sydney, some of whom were posted to do garrison duty at Wellington, where there was also the simmering of native trouble. The tension was further relieved in the following year by Sir Eardley Wilmot, Governor of Van Diemen's Land, who sent over a

* One of the earliest things which bewildered the natives after the arrival of the soldiers was the bugle. When they first heard its notes at Kororareka and saw the soldiers obeying its calls they wonderingly asked, " What is this they have which speaks at so great a distance ? "

detachment of the 96th Regiment.* This much, at least, is certain. Major Bunbury tells us in his " Reminiscences " that when he was ordered to proceed to Tauranga to punish the chief Taraia for an attack he had made upon his neighbours his little force was "joined by the detachment of thirty men from Port Nicholson, who were relieved by a detachment of the 96th Regiment from Van Diemen's Land."

In September, 1842, Major Bunbury reported to Acting-Governor Shortland, who had succeeded to the Administration after Captain Hobson's death, that the force under his immediate command consisted of 2 Captains, 1 Subaltern, 1 Assistant Surgeon, 5 sergeants, 2 drummers, and 96 rank and file, including the sick in hospital and men employed by the Ordnance Department. In reply to a further inquiry as to whether he considered this force sufficient to meet the contingency of a native rising, Bunbury strongly recommended that the force should be increased to at least 200 bayonets, and that it should be concentrated at Auckland.†

In compliance with this recommendation the detachment of the 96th, under Captain Eyton, was withdrawn from Wellington, so that when Major Bunbury returned from Tauranga he was able to report: " We have now

* The question may be asked, " What were these regiments doing in Australia, where there was neither native nor foreign troubles ? " The answer to this query is at once simple and interesting The policy of establishing convict settlements in Australia was one which reacted upon the British Army in numerous and important ways, the history of several regiments being considerably influenced by the fact that they were despatched to the Antipodes to act as escorts on board the convict ships, or as guards at the convict settlements in New South Wales, Van Diemen's Land, and Norfolk Island. Among the regiments selected for this particular duty was the 96th, which between the months of July, 1839, and August, 1841, proceeded from England to the southern colonies in twenty-six separate detachments. These sections of the regiment were employed in the above capacities as circumstances directed, the major portion of them being stationed in Van Diemen's Land, one detachment at Norfolk Island, one at Adelaide.

† Major Bunbury states that one of his greatest difficulties was in preventing the Governor dissipating his force by dividing it into small detachments.

quartered in the barracks the Grenadier Company of the 96th, with two companies of the 80th."

These two bodies of men, armed with the old-fashioned muskets of the flintlock type, continued to perform the functions pertaining to garrison duty at Auckland for something like two years without any more exciting incidents to relieve the monotony of their exile than the false report of a Maori rising, which not infrequently stirred the fears of an excitable populace.

Being at the seat of Government the tedium of the soldiers' life was, of course, relieved by the ceremonies, functions, and junketings connected therewith. The arrival of a ship-of-war was always the occasion of not a little relaxation, and if it happened to be a French frigate the flood of hospitality was not less generous. Shortly after the return of the troops from the abortive expedition to Tauranga Major Bunbury mentions that a French frigate anchored in the Auckland Harbour. The Frenchmen entertained the officers of the garrison at a dinner, the compliment being returned in the evening by a ball given to the visitors in the barrack-room.

" I was greatly amused," relates the Major, " at the singular effects of champagne at the Frenchmen's dinner party. None of the officers of my detachment spoke French, and very few of them understood it. A few of the Frenchmen spoke English, the Captain and one or two others. The consequence was that the party was somewhat formal and heavy, and on my expressing my regret to him that none of our officers or those of the 96th could speak the French language, he said : ' Wait a bit, you will see how soon they will pick it up and understand one another. All they want is a few more bottles of champagne. I have always found it an excellent teacher of languages.' He spoke the truth," continues the Major, " for almost immediately the prescription took effect, and the whole company seemed to understand one another, and were as garrulous as a flock of geese. Even the reserve of the Captain of the Grenadiers of the 96th, who hates Frenchmen and everything French, forsook him, and he, too, seemed as much excited and as noisy as the rest of the party."

As a result of Major Bunbury's policy of concentrating
the military at Auckland there was necessarily no force
at the southern settlement of Wellington when on the
17th June, 1843, the conflict took place between the Europeans, led by Captain Wakefield, and the natives, under
Te Rauparaha, on the fringe of the Wairau Valley. This
constituted one of the grievances of the southern settlers
against the Government, and immediately the news of the
catastrophe reached Wellington the residents requisitioned
the Mayor to call a public meeting to protest and petition
against being left in this unprotected state.* The meeting
was held at the Town Hall on the following day at
1 o'clock, amongst the resolutions agreed to being one
affirming,—

That an address be prepared to Her Majesty's Government
setting forth our defenceless condition, and that the same be
transmitted to the Secretary of State for the Colonies, through
the local Government at Auckland, and that a similar statement
be forwarded to the Governor of New South Wales.

In obedience to this resolution a copy of the address
was despatched to Sir George Gipps by the ship *Vanguard*,
which sailed from Wellington on the following Thursday—
22nd—and the original, numerously signed, was sent to
Acting-Governor Shortland, at Auckland. Amongst other
appeals, the memorial begged for some military support :—

Amidst the dangers which thus environ and daily deepen
upon us and our families, the document stated, the storm of
which may suddenly burst upon and destroy us, we look around
for protection and assistance, and we find none. We have
neither military aid to rely upon nor force of any kind to
interpose between ourselves and possible destruction ; nor have
we here any authorized person to receive our complaints, direct
our movements, or even to sanction the means which at this
moment we are driven to adopt for our preservation.

* The people of Nelson also memorialized Sir Eardley Wilmot, Governor
of Van Diemen's Land, who promptly despatched the *Emerald Isle*
with 100 soldiers ; but Captain Nicholson, the officer in charge of the
troops, had orders not to disembark them unless he found the settlers in
actual collision with the Maoris. This not being the case, the troops
returned immediately to Hobart Town.

The Colonial Secretary replied on the 10th July, intimating that he had received and laid before His Excellency the citizens' memorial, and stated that in order to secure the tranquillity of the town a detachment of the 96th Regiment, quartered at Auckland, was under orders to proceed in the Government brig to Port Nicholson. " A measure which it is hoped will relieve the memorialists from any apprehension and restore that confidence between the natives and the Europeans which hitherto existed."

In consequence of these instructions the Government brig *Victoria* entered Wellington Harbour on the 24th July, bringing with her Major Matthew Richmond, a former officer of the 96th, who was to act as Chief Magistrate, several other Government officials, and Lieutenant R. E. Bennett, of the Engineers, who was in command of a modest company of fifty-three men. Pending the erection of Government barracks the men were quartered in premises lent by Colonel Wakefield, probably the building at Thorndon close to the Wadestown Road and long known as the " Red House."

It is now a matter of history that no serious trouble with the natives occurred after the affair at Wairau. The tactfulness of the Rev. Mr. Hadfield kept the Ngati-Toa in check, and the conciliatory policy of the Magistrates and of Wi Kingi Rangitake calmed the Ati-Awa, whom Te Rauparaha sought to rouse. In these circumstances there was little for the 96th to do beyond maintaining a general air of authority, which they did with every credit to themselves, until they were relieved in the following year by a company of the 58th.

As the term of service of the 80th Regiment was about to expire a further detachment of the 96th was sent from Australia in March, 1844, to relieve them. This company, which was under the command of Bt. Lieut. Colonel William Hulme, consisted of four officers and 105 other ranks, and upon arrival in New Zealand was stationed at Auckland. Lieut.-Colonel Hulme, who now succeeded Major Bunbury in command of the New Zealand

Forces, was an officer of some experience, having served as Captain in the famous Pindari campaign. He commanded the flank companies in the general action on the 21st December, 1817, for which he received the brevet rank of Major, and again commanded them at the storming of the Fort of Fulnair on the 27th February, 1818. He is said to have been an alert and intelligent man, endowed with a good measure of common-sense, and a strongly marked characteristic for always appearing smartly dressed. It was this portion of the 96th Regiment, commanded by Lieut.-Colonel Hulme, which during the anxious months of 1845 and the early part of 1846 was constantly engaged with the natives in the northern and southern districts of the colony, losing nearly half its strength in killed and wounded, the gaps being filled by reinforcements from Van Diemen's Land.

In May, 1841, New Zealand became an independent colony, Captain Hobson being raised to the status of a Governor. The country was still, however, a Crown colony, but free from the tutelage of New South Wales. The charter of independence defined that in the event of the Governor's death the duties of that officer should be taken up by the then Colonial Secretary and not by the Officer Commanding the Military. Consequently when Captain Hobson's end came on the 10th September, 1842, Lieutenant Shortland, who had been acting as the Governor's chief Executive officer, took over the administration of the colony. In education, experience, and temperament he lacked all the qualifications necessary to success in so difficult a post, and had he proceeded to govern the country according to his own whims and limited ideals he would certainly have made confusion worse confounded. Fortunately, he decided to do nothing, or next to nothing. He at one time was vain enough to entertain hopes that the Governorship might be conferred upon him, but the opposition in the colony to this course was so strong that to have done so would have surely wrecked a position already none too secure.

He was therefore informed that his tenure of office could only be of a temporary nature, and thereupon he appears to have decided that his safest policy was simply to mark time. While, then, he sometimes consulted his Executive Council, no meeting of the Legislative Council was called, and no legislation was passed designed to meet the accumulating difficulties. Further, he is charged with a prodigal expenditure of what little public money was available. Extravagance thus tended to deepen his political complications and to increase the public resentment already roused by his departmental deficiencies, his pompous and unpropitiatory manner.

Hobson's successor in the Governorship of the colony —Captain Robert FitzRoy, R.N.—arrived in Auckland in December, 1843. By this time the country from the most northerly to the most southerly settlement was seething with discontent. The northern settlers and their native neighbours were angry because the land was being locked up under the Government's pre-emptive right of purchase, and trade was, in consequence, stagnant. The southerners were excited and alarmed because of the tragic occurrence at the Wairau in the previous June, while the natives were no less restive under what they regarded as an unwarrantable attempt by the New Zealand Company to seize their lands. Without money to satisfy the earth-hunger of the Europeans, or soldiers to quell the simmering insurrection among the natives, FitzRoy was given an almost impossible task. The whole atmosphere was charged with distrust and uncertainty. The one sure thing was that a storm was about to burst, but whether it would first break in the north or in the south no one could tell.

CHAPTER II.

HONE HEKE.

THE causes which bred the discontent referred to in the previous chapter were, as may be judged, political rather than military. There was, however, in them something more than the mere question of the Government buying land from the natives and selling it to the Europeans. They were, in fact, largely the outcome of that inherent conflict which must ever wage between the forces of barbarism and those of civilization : the inevitable fear and apprehension of the savage at the breaking-down of his old customs by the introduction of civilized law. This fear, aggravated by the forces of envy, of national jealousy, and all uncharitableness inseparable from the founding of a colony such as New Zealand, if persisted in, could have but one result and but one remedy—an appeal to arms. As we have seen, the principal European settlement in the country when Hobson landed in 1840 was at Kororareka, a straggling township on the shores of a sheltered inlet at the Bay of Islands. The population was for the most part composed of whalers and persons engaged in trading with whalers and natives—men of all nations and all degrees of probity, some moral, some immoral, and some unmoral. Among these people there had always been a half-lawless, half-civilized system of trading carried on, which the natives were partly obliged and partly prepared to accept, being gratified with a lucrative business which left their supremacy intact while their customs were never seriously interfered with. In these circumstances the natives were willing enough to have the *pakeha* settled in their midst, foreseeing as they did substantial advantages from the white man's presence, his intercourse, and his trade.

Four years later the majority of the Maori race was probably of the same opinion, though this state of mind was by no means unanimous. Even a superficial observer might ere this have discovered a widespread feeling of distrust among them, for there were of necessity certain economic changes taking place as the result of the establishment of constitutional Government, the reason for which the primitive mind of the Maori could but dimly comprehend, and no great pains appear to have been taken by the authorities to explain the political mystery to them. This altered order of things as it appealed to the natives in the northern districts has thus been cogently stated by one of their own chroniclers :—

After the first Governor came the second Governor, but the towns and the numerous *pakeha* traders we expected did not come. We heard of a town at Waitemata (Auckland) having been built, and others farther south ; but in our own part of the country—the Bay of Islands—there were no new towns, and the *pakehas* did not increase in number, but, on the contrary, began to go away to the town at Waitemata, to be near their chief, the Governor, who lived there, and many of us had no one left to sell anything to as formerly. Tobacco began to be scarce and dear ; the ships began to leave off coming to the Bay of Islands, Hokianga, and Mangonui. We inquired the reason of this, but the few *pakeha* traders left amongst us told us different stories. Some said the reason tobacco was scarce and dear was because the Governor would not let it be brought on shore until he was paid a large price for it, besides what was paid to the people of the ship, who were the right owners of it. This we, at first, did not believe, because you (*pakehas*) all said you were not slaves, not one of you, but all were free men. Others said the reason ships did not come as frequently as formerly was because the Governor made them pay for coming to anchor in the ports. Some said all the evil was by reason of the flagstaff which the Governor had caused to be erected on Maiki Hill, above Kororareka, as a *rahui*,* and that as long as it remained there things would be no better. Others, again, told us the flagstaff was put there to show ships the way into the harbour; others that it was intended to keep them out; and others said that it was put up as a sign that this Island had been taken by the Queen of England, and that the nobility and the independence of the Maori were no more.

But this one thing, at least, was true : we had less tobacco and fewer blankets and other European goods than formerly; and we saw that the first Governor had not spoken the truth, for he told us that we should have a great deal more. The hearts of the Maori were sad, and our old *pakeha* friends looked melancholy, because so few ships came to bring them goods to trade with.†

To lose their trade was in itself a serious matter, but this was not all. Immense pains had been taken by certain mischievous interests to induce the natives to believe Her Majesty's Government was not sincere when it promised them security under the British Crown. Unfortunately, the previous Administrations had frequently held out threats towards offenders which had never been executed, and promises were made to victims of rapacity or violence which had never been fulfilled. This failure on the part of the authorities to live up to their professions lent some colour to the allegations of their detractors, and was no small factor in sapping confidence in both the justice and the generosity of the Government. Contempt for law and order was, as a result, fostered among the younger men, who were rapidly becoming impatient of restraint, an impatience which the diminished influence of the chiefs was unable to check or the impotent Government to punish.

Many, too, of the older people, who had welcomed the first few white settlers, were now becoming alarmed at the rapidity with which the Europeans were flocking into the country, and were veering to the opinion that a mistake

* A reserve. Used in this sense as a sign to warn off strangers or intruders.

† For a number of years the receipts from furnishing supplies to whalers, &c., averaged about £45,000, but by 1845 the trade was practically extinct.

had been made in admitting them on such favourable
terms — if, indeed, they should have been admitted at
all.* Some had even passed beyond the stage of doubt
and had reached a definite concurrence in the Pathan's
view of British penetration :—

First comes one Englishman to shoot birds or beasts ; then
come two Englishmen to map ; and then comes an army to
take possession of the country.   It is better to kill the first
Englishman.

Among the Europeans the sense of insecurity and discontent was no less evident.   The prosperity which they
had been led to expect had not attended the colonization
of the country, because their land-titles were being challenged and production had been checked while their claims
went through the slow and tortuous process of investigation.   The vanishing trade — most acutely felt at the Bay
of Islands — was an increasing source of uneasiness to the
white traders, some of whom, in their extremity, adopted
the expedient of raising unfounded alarms in the hope
either that the Government would augment the naval and
military forces in the colony, or that their less experienced
neighbours would, in their panic, abandon their businesses
and leave the alarmists to monopolize the trade.   As the
days went by the native and European malcontents nursed
their grievances ; time brought recruits to their ranks, until
now Governor FitzRoy was about to reap the accumulated
crop of trouble sown for him by human passions on the
one hand and by the mistakes of his predecessors† on
the other.

Of those natives who manifestly were restless under
the changing economic and governmental conditions none
was possessed of greater social influence, of military *mana*,

* This feeling Hone Heke crystallized into one of the Maori's apt
aphorisms when he said, " One beehive is very good, but several are
troublesome."

† " Every white man in New Zealand, not excepting the officers of
the Government, must now admit that by the system pursued by Messrs.
Hobson and Shortland, from the first existence of the local Government,
the colonists and the natives were transformed from friends into jealous
rivals."—*New Zealand Spectator.*

or of a more striking personality than Hone Heke Pokai, who was destined to achieve for himself a notoriety, if not a notable name, in New Zealand history.   Heke was able to look back with pardonable pride to ancestors who came over in the original *Arawa* canoe from Hawaiki, one of whom is said to have sacrificed his son to the gods on landing, and on that account was named Te Puhi Tani-wharau ; hence, according to some authorities, arose the name Nga-Puhi, which descended from his *hapu* and was afterwards adopted by all the northern tribes.   Additional lustre was lent to Heke's social status by the fact that he was the nephew of Hongi Hika, the man of greatest renown in all New Zealand of that day.

Heke first distinguished himself as a brave at the battle of Kororareka in the year 1830, when Hengi was killed. He further enhanced his reputation at Tauranga in 1833, when Nga-Puhi, under Titore, attacked Otumoetai.   There Heke was wounded, and was sent back to the Bay of Islands lest his boldness should get the better of his discretion.   After this he fell under the influence of the missionaries and became a Christian, living for several years at Paihia in intimate family relationship with Henry Williams, by whom he was baptized and christened " John " (" Hone ").   He attended daily at the mission school, and in due course was chosen as a lay-reader in the Church.   At this time he married Ono, the daughter of Te Pahii, of Ngati-Rehia, who was indeed a great lady. She, too, accepted the Christian faith and received the baptismal name of Lydia.   During Lydia's life Heke remained quiet and studious, but upon her death he threw off the shackles of restraint and was again to the fore in 1837 when Nga-Puhi were fighting Pomare at Otuihu.   On this occasion he narrowly escaped capture by the enemy while he was daringly crossing the Bay in a small canoe with only four men.   At the close of these hostilities he retired to the district of Kaikohe, where his restless spirit ever kept the neighbourhood in a state of turmoil.   Here he made it a practice to levy toll upon all travellers passing through his domain at Puketona, which lay across the high road from the Bay of Islands to the interior, roughly handling all who sought to evade his taxation. His right to levy this impost was generally submitted to on account of his high birth. It was said of him in palliation, *He uri na Kauteawha* ("He is a worthy descendant of Kauteawha"), a man widely famed for energy and character. In Heke's veins there thus flowed the best blood of the Nga-Puhi people, and to this high birth he had again added the advantage of a second marriage with Hariata, the handsome and intelligent daughter of Hongi. By the time, then, that Captain Hobson arrived at the Bay of Islands, charged with the mission of securing the cession of the sovereignty of the country to the Queen, Heke was a man widely known, and by all the Maori standards one who was entitled to speak with authority and to be listened to with respect.

At the negotiation of the Treaty of Waitangi Heke adopted an equivocal attitude. He spoke ambiguously of the treaty, but was the first to sign it, probably because it afforded him an opportunity for a little theatrical display. A few months of British rule were, however, sufficient to convince him that his love of spectacular effect had led him further than he was willing to go. He found that his authority, hitherto undisputed, was challenged by a rival power; that his revenue from whaling-ships was intercepted by the Crown; and that, so far as he could see, there were no compensating advantages in large and frequent sales of land. Perhaps, too, he was not altogether uninfluenced by the advice given to his people — who were now Heke's people — by the great Hongi, as he lay upon his death-bed at Whangaroa, fourteen years before. After counselling his tribe to be kind to the missionaries, to have friendly intercourse with the settlers, but to resist the soldiers — "the men who wear red garments, the men who neither sow nor reap"— the dying chief closed his farewell message with these significant words :—

Children, and you my old comrades, be brave and strong in your country's cause. Let not the land of your ancestors pass into the hands of the *pakeha*. Behold! I have spoken.

Having thus delivered his last "word" to his weeping people, Hongi drew the corner of his mat across his face and passed through the gates of Ruakipouri — the gates which inexorably open only the one way. That this counsel swayed the impressionable mind of Heke and entered into his calculations in this hour of crisis can only be surmised. What we do know is that towards the middle of 1844, while Governor FitzRoy was absent in Taranaki, he began to talk boisterously and to act violently. Among the settlers at Kororareka he, unfortunately, found not a few disappointed speculators ready to urge him on in the hope that his outrages might embarrass the hated Government that had come between them and the natives. By birth and training* Heke was better qualified than most of his contemporaries to perceive the drift of national events. His survey of the daily happenings led him to the conclusion that the white tide which flowed around them was carrying his countrymen into the whirls and eddies of destruction. For his parallels he went to the Scriptures, with which he had at times an inconveniently intimate acquaintance. He likened the British Government to the Egyptian tyrants, and the Maori people to the Israelites of old, bending under the oppression of the Pharaohs.† He saw that while many Maoris were the servants of Englishmen, no Englishman was as yet servant to the Maori, which to him was proof enough of their subjection. If testimony of their degradation were required it was to be found in the fact that their clothes were now old blankets in place of native mats, and that

* Education would have made Heke an accomplished diplomatist, for his mind was of the order found in the front rank of intellectual progress.—*Thomson.*

† Sunday, 27th April.—Our native teacher was out holding service with Heke's people. On his return he reported to me that Heke had been addressing the people, comparing themselves to the persecuted children of Israel.—Vide *Rev. R. Burrows's diary.*

instead of smoking American tobacco, as they had done before 1840, they were reduced to puffing the leaves of indigenous plants.

To the adoption of these views he was helped by a temperament singularly volatile and a mind that fed upon vanity — a vanity that pictured him as the saviour of his race, purging it of every vestige of British tyranny. This combination was responsible for mental effects which caused the missionaries to believe him sometimes scarcely sane.* Rash, impetuous, and imperious, he was intolerant of all authority save his own. He was troublesome to the missionaries; he once rebuked the Bishop, of whose ecclesiastical station he was envious; and now he was on the high road to defy the Governor — to tear up the treaty he had been the first to sign.

In April, 1843, he had been engaged in a war with the Rarawa people led by Nopera Panakareao, the dispute arising out of an injudicious land-purchase made by Captain Hobson and Lieutenant Shortland.† Into the midst of the battle the Rev. Henry Williams had gone, and, with bullets flying about him, he at last succeeded in inducing the leaders to make peace. From this war Heke had returned flushed with success, and had ever since exercised an authority peculiarly his own. He kept his men together, and whenever he heard of a dispute he would appear upon the scene, hold an inquisition into the facts, deliver his judgment, and enforce it to his own enrichment. It enhanced his *mana* and ministered to

* Heke is a strange character, and, I believe, not always sane."— *Rev. R. Davis.*

† An event soon occurred which gave him an opportunity of venting his spleen against the *pakeha*. A large block of land had been purchased on behalf of the Government, at Mangonui, from Nopera Panakareao, a chief of Kaitaia. This block included land at Taipa, the property of Porirua and others, of Whangaroa, relatives of Heke, who disputed the sale by building a *pa* on the land and forbidding occupation. Panakareao came in force to oppose them. Heke, invited by Porirua to come over and help him, went over with his young men, gave battle to Panakareao, routed him, and required that the land should be resigned publicly to Porirua, which was done. This established Heke's *mana*, and he was henceforth looked upon as the leader of Nga-Puhi.—*Carleton.*

his self-esteem that he should be able thus to exercise the ancient prerogatives of a chief. For this reason he became intensely jealous of British authority, which he had sanctioned by signing the Treaty of Waitangi. The treaty was no longer " a good thing, even as the Word of God," and the Governor was no longer to be a " father " to him. Both were now regarded as dangerous rivals to his personal power, the exercise of which had grown so agreeable that it was not lightly to be laid down.

Almost the earliest manifestation of this jealousy of established authority occurred when the Government Commissioners arrived at the Bay of Islands to examine the land claims of the colonists. One of Heke's sales was amongst the first to be investigated, and he chose to regard the proceeding as an unwarrantable interference with his right to sell his own land. So deeply did he resent this prying into his dealings that he told the gentleman who was the purchaser that he was quite prepared to close the whole argument by driving such an inquisitorial authority out of the country. In this spirit of insubordination he ever after lived, and in this spirit he may be said to have died.

Two things in particular had tended to inflame him against the Government, even such a feeble Government as it was. The first of these was the hanging of the highly connected young chief Maketu for the brutal murder of Mrs. Robertson and her family on the 20th November, 1841.* The duty of maintaining law and justice clearly devolved upon the Government, but, situated as they were, the authorities were impotent if the natives chose to resist the criminal's arrest. Some counselled the surrender of the culprit, others favoured defiance. The issue thus became the first trial of native loyalty, the first test to prove whether the Treaty of Waitangi was a reality, based upon the free will of the Maori people, or

* Mrs. Robertson, a widow, residing at Motu Apohia—generally known as Robertson's Island—was murdered, together with two of her children, a half-caste child, a grandchild of the chief Rewa, and a European man servant, by a young well-connected chief, son of Ruhe.

whether it was, as the New Zealand Company alleged, merely "a device to amuse savages."

As usual, the wildest rumours were current regarding the bloodthirsty designs of the natives. In the excitement of the moment this isolated outrage was translated into the precursor of a general rising, the wholesale massacre of the settlers being gloomily predicted by some and as confidently expected by others. Though ever extremely reluctant to implicate himself in the management of these secular affairs, Henry Williams felt that in the face of such a crisis something must be done to allay the excited feelings of the natives and to calm the fears of the white population. Accordingly, at the urgent request of Tamati Waaka Nene, he summoned a meeting of Nga-Puhi chiefs at Paihia on the 16th December, when in response to his invitation upwards of a thousand people were present, every chief of note and influence attending. The discussion was long and animated, Heke being among the belligerents. In his opposition to the surrender of Maketu he gave his turbulent spirit free rein, advocating open revolt, and almost succeeding in breaking up the gathering in disorder. Fortunately, moderate counsels prevailed ; the treaty was respected ; Maketu was given up ; and Heke was, for the once, worsted.*

At this meeting the following resolutions were agreed to :—

(1.) This assembly disapproves of and discountenances the murders of Maketu at Motu Apohia.

(2.) This assembly declares that they did not know the murderous intention of Maketu towards the Europeans. His resolution was his alone. The chiefs of Nga-Puhi declare that they have no thought of rising to massacre the Europeans living in New Zealand, and their hearts are sorry because the Europeans have thought that this is the desire of the natives. This assembly declares that they will strongly protest against the murderer Maketu being brought back to the Bay of Islands.

* The disturbance arising from the arrest of Maketu was happily suppressed, but I do not hesitate to say that had not the grandchild of Rewa been one of the victims, thus bringing the Nga-Puhi tribes as auxiliaries to the Europeans in the event of war, the result would have been far otherwise.—Vide *Rev. Henry Williams.*

Hone Heke Pokai.
After the drawing in the Hocken Collection, Dunedin.

These resolutions were conveyed to the Governor in two letters signed by a large number of chiefs, who again protested their abhorrence of Maketu's conduct and their own good feeling towards the settlers. They asked that no credence be given to the disconcerting reports " which have flown about in the wind," because these reports were " falsehoods of the tongue."

For this adhesion to law and order Heke never forgave the leaders of Nga-Puhi, while he nursed his wrath against the Government which had not only robbed him of his dignity and his revenue, but now claimed the right of life and death over his countrymen.

The second event, or series of events, which excited his displeasure was the imposition of Customs duties and the suppression of smuggling at the Bay of Islands. Trade with the whalers had, in former times, constituted one of Heke's chief sources of income* and his hopes of prosperity. The imposition of fiscal restrictions had also irritated the whalers, who gradually avoided the Bay of Islands, preferring to refresh their ships in other ports where the Queen's writ did not as yet run, or was not administered with equal rigour. This was a perpetual source of annoyance to Heke, who petulantly repudiated such a Government and all its ways. The culminating-point in Heke's anger was reached early in 1844, when two American whalers were seized for smuggling, and, being convicted, were heavily fined.† The Acting American Consul at the Bay of Islands at that time was Captain

* Heke had shared with his cousin an anchor duty of £5 per vessel, levied on all ships coming to the Bay of Islands prior to 1840. Pomare, as head chief of the inner waters, collected a toll from vessels anchoring in the passage of the Kawakawa and Waikare Rivers.

† The American ships seized and fined were : The *General Jackson*, Captain Ransdale. Her master was fined £160 for not reporting some slop clothing and cigars kept on board for the use of the ship's company. The Board of Commissioners at London were memorialized in connection with the case, and the fine was remitted. The second ship fined was the *Nile*, Captain Cook. The circumstances are not known, but the fine was £600. In this case also a memorial was sent Home, and it is generally understood the fine was remitted.

2—First War.

William Mayhew.   He, too, became deeply incensed at the
severity of the fines, and told Pomare, his particular
trading chief, that if such things went on the whalers
would cease coming to the Bay altogether, and that he
himself would take the first opportunity of going elsewhere.*   Mayhew, always prejudiced against the British
Government, impressed upon Pomare that the root of all
this evil was the flagstaff which stood upon Maiki Hill
at the back of Kororareka and on which the Queen's
flag flew ; that by virtue of this flag the *whenua*—the
country—had passed to the Queen ; that, notwithstanding
anything the Treaty of Waitangi might pretend to the
contrary, the fact was the Maori had ceased to be his own
master : he was, indeed, a slave and could no longer do
as he pleased.   Pomare thought gravely upon these words,
and the poison readily sank into his soul.   He went
deeply into consultation with several of his fellow-chiefs,
for he, too, was beginning to be alarmed at the rapidity
with which the land was being bought up for ephemeral
articles of trade which gave but a momentary pleasure and
no permanent profit.   " Pots and pipes are soon broken,
but the land remains," was his summation of this rather
unequal bargaining, which was only a less graceful way
of stating the Maori proverb :   " Man is mortal, but land
is a living thing."   No definite conclusion was reached as
the result of these conferences, and active opposition was
certainly not at that moment contemplated.

In the meantime Heke had succeeded in fomenting
a quarrel with Kemara,† his cousin, which necessitated the
sending of a *taua*‡ against him.   This quarrel arose through
one of Kemara's wives having in some way misconducted
herself, and Heke, the self appointed preserver of the
peace, believed it to be his duty to impose the punishment.   When the preliminaries common to such occasions

* Captain Mayhew sailed from the Bay of Islands on the 21st April,
1844, for Tahiti in the brig *Nimrod*, via Wellington.
† Kemara was the Maori equivalent of Campbell.
‡ *Taua* = war-party.

had been completed, Kemara interposed by sending a message to Heke, through Te Haratua, who was in charge of the *taua*, pointing out the futility of spending his strength upon such an insignificant matter as the misbehaviour of a wayward woman. Why not turn his attention to the one great question of the moment—Mayhew's statement to Pomare as to the evil of the flagstaff, which alone was worthy of his quality as a warrior ?

Heke now more clearly began to see his way to enter upon larger issues. To this course he had shortly before been predisposed by Ruhe,* the father of the executed Maketu appearing before him and chanting a song full of mystical allusions, the burden of which was that his son's death should be avenged, and that Heke was the man appointed to the task :—

> I know thou art a warrior bold,
>   Rejoicing in the din of war ;
> Thy deeds, tho' left as yet half-told,
>   Have struck the foe with direful awe.
>
> I fain would link my fate with thine,
>   Enlist on Rawhirawhi's side,
> Whose star shall rise and brightly shine,
>   Whose footsteps victory shall guide.
>
> Quench not my zeal, oh long tried friend ;
>   But tread the warpath stern and bold,
> Nor fear mishap, nor doubt the end :
>   Men never wavered thus of old.
>
> There's work of moment to be done,
>   For which I name thee principal ;
> My name avails to bear you on ;
>   Then haste, at once obey the call.

As sung by Ruhe this song had sounded in the vain ears of Heke as an inspired call. To be named " principal " in such a crusade was indeed greatness ; the only question

---

* Ruhe, at the time, consented to the execution of his son, but he appears subsequently to have repented of that decision.

2*

was how to procure or provoke a *take* — a good and sufficient cause of quarrel. Here, then, in the word of Te Hu,* the flagstaff and the Queen's colour, *te kara*, as the natives called it, was the germ of a quarrel ready made, in the prosecution of which he was inspired by Ruhe and encouraged by Kemara. To cut down the flagstaff on which that colour floated was to deliver his people from the burden of oppression, and to be the deliverer of his countrymen henceforth became the purpose of Heke.†

There still, however, remained the problem as to what manner of resistance would be offered by the Government and the European settlers. He must feel his way cautiously ; he must pick his quarrel discreetly. With this intent he sought and found a pretext for a *taua* upon the white people in a circumstance of which the European residents of Kororareka were wholly innocent. It happened that a slave-girl, known as Kotiro, and over whom Heke claimed to exercise a jurisdiction, was living in the town with a European, a butcher named Lord. Heke, who by Maori custom had some colour of right to do so, determined to try the experiment of taking her away from the companionship of Lord.‡ The plan devised was that a messenger should be sent on in advance, Heke to follow with his band of young men, who were to carry the girl off, or to fight if resistance were offered. The message was delivered to Kotiro while she was in Lord's shop. She received with the utmost disdain the demand that she should return to Heke. Who, indeed, was Heke that

---

* Captain Mayhew was called by the natives "Te Hu."

† In one of his letters about this time Henry Williams says : " There is much excuse to be made for Heke and those with him. There are many Europeans and Americans who have poisoned their minds with stories of other days, impressing them with the idea that their country is gone, and they themselves sold for slaves. Heke has been represented as a patriot, until he nearly believes himself to be such.

‡ Kotiro is said to have been a native of Taranaki, taken captive in one of the Nga-Puhi raids fifteen years before and handed over to Heke as a slave. She first married a Scottish blacksmith named Alexander Gray, and subsequently became the wife of Lord. One of her children by her first husband was Sophia Hinerangi, the once well-known guide at Whakarewarewa, Rotorua, born 1827, died 1912.

he should presume to control her? Then, turning and
pointing to one of the fat hogs that hung in the shop, she,
with an angry flash of her dark eyes, exclaimed, "*Ina a
Heke*" ("That is Heke"). This surely was a *tapatapa*,
as gross an insult as could well be hurled at a chief.
To be compared to a hog was degradation indeed! No
sooner was the circumstance reported to Heke than he
made his way to Lord's shop and demanded payment*
for the hurt to his feelings and the contempt for his name.
Lord refused to make any payment, and took no pains
to be gracious about the manner of his doing it. The
natives then withdrew to the beach, where they delivered
angry speeches and danced a furious *haka*. It was during
the excitement of these proceedings, which took place on
the afternoon of the 5th July, 1844, that a half-naked
warrior, addressing the people, exclaimed as he wildly
brandished his *taiaha*: "War! War! War with the white
people!" This call to arms was the first vocal declaration of the storm that had long been brewing and which
was now about to burst upon the heads of the two races.
In support of this fervid appeal to force Heke made a
speech, full of fire and ill-concealed rebellion, during the
course of which he asked the significant question so
often quoted against him: "Is Te Rauparaha to have
all the credit for killing the Europeans?"†

For several days the followers of Heke remained in
the town, under the pretence that they were intent upon
securing some sort of reparation for Kotiro's insult, but
in reality they were feeling the pulse of the Government
and of the settlers. They swaggered through the streets,
pilfered goods from shops, bullied peaceable residents, and
in some cases behaved with the utmost impropriety towards women. Mr. Beckham, the Police Magistrate, was
powerless to check these depredations, and the position at
last became so intolerable that an appeal was made to the

* The payment demanded was a large keg of tobacco.
† A reference to the conflict at the Wairau in the previous year.

missionaries at Paihia to come over and mediate.* The
missionaries, though intensely in earnest about the civilization of the natives, and always uncompromising towards
their grosser practices, were yet men of the world enough
to know that these children of barbarism could not be
weaned from all their wild customs in a day. They
therefore looked upon some of their ways with tolerance,
and in this case ruled that Heke was justified in resenting
Kotiro's bitter taunt, and that some payment should be
made for her insult. As Lord had no tobacco to give,
a bag of rice and some sugar were substituted,† the price
being now a matter of little consequence to Heke. What
did count was the discovery that if he cut the flagstaff
down he was not likely to be met with an opposition that
would prove overpowering, and so once more " the means
to do ill deeds made ill deeds done." At daybreak on
the 8th July, 1844, the flagstaff was cut down.‡

In this act of aggression, which was a challenge
to British authority, Heke did not personally participate,
although he was the moving spirit in it and cannot escape
his due responsibility. Some days previously he had met
the Rev. William Williams, for whom he had a genuine
regard, and as the result of the reverend gentleman's
persuasions he agreed to return quietly to his home. He
therefore did not consider it consistent with his promise
to take part in the destruction of the staff, though the line
of distinction was a fine one, since he remained in his canoe
while his men, led by Te Haratua, climbed the hill and
did the deed. The issue as to whose authority was to
be supreme — the authority of the Government or the
authority of Heke — was now fairly before the country,
and this mode of testing the question was, Heke thought,

* The Rev. Henry Williams being from home, the Rev. William
Williams and the Rev. Robert Maunsell came over, accompanied by
Mr. H. Tacy Kemp, the Sub-protector of Aborigines.

† It being a stipulation by Mr. Williams, who really made the payment, that the natives would not disturb the people on the following
day—Sunday.

‡ After the staff was cut down portion of it was burned ; the signal-
balls were carried away, as were also the remaining portions of the staff.

the more justified since, as he said, the staff had neither bones nor blood and would feel no pain.*

Having achieved his object, Heke returned to his head-quarters at Kaikohe.† Thus did he precipitate the first inglorious act in what was to prove a somewhat inglorious war.

Intelligence of these happenings was at once forwarded to Auckland, where the news created a profound sensation, accompanied as it was by the usual exaggeration that a horde of native savages was marching to attack the capital. Governor FitzRoy acted with commendable promptitude. He at once despatched vessels from Auckland to Sydney and Hobart Town to appeal for military assistance. To Sir George Gipps he wrote :—

Although the utmost pains and precautions have been used by me to avert the necessity of making a hostile display, there is no longer any alternative ; and I am obliged to ask in the most earnest manner for immediate assistance, both military and naval. Either we must submit to be treated as men not only unwilling but unable to defend ourselves, to protect our women from insult, and our flag from dishonour, or we must now take such effective measures as will restore respect for our flag and ensure tranquillity in the colony . . . To make such a demonstration I now formally request such means as Your Excellency may be able to supply. I am sure you will feel with me that the greater the display—the larger the force—the more speedy, peaceful, and lasting will be the consequences.

Simultaneously, instructions were sent to the local Magistrates to re-erect the flagstaff, but to " observe temperate and conciliatory measures until assistance could

* At the time this outrage was committed the Rev. Henry Williams was absent from the Bay of Islands. He had been requested by Bishop Selwyn to take his brother's duty at Turanga (Gisborne) while that gentleman was engaged upon a revision of the native New Testament, working in conjunction with Mr. Maunsell, Mr. Hamlin, and Mr. Puckey, who were considered to be the best Maori linguists of that time. He returned from Turanga on the 16th September, 1844.

† Bishop Selwyn says : " I was at Paihia at the time, engaged in the native school, at the close of which the first words I heard were ' kua hinga te kara ' (' the colour has fallen '). I shuddered at the thought of this beginning of hostilities, so full of presage of evil for the future. Heke then crossed to Paihia, and with his party danced the war-dance in my face, after which many violent speeches were made, and they then returned to Kaikohe."

arrive, which would be with all speed." They were also to call together the principal chiefs, state to them what had happened, and request their assistance in compelling Heke to make such compensation and atonement as the Governor might deem necessary.

The missionaries vigorously protested against the re-erection of the flagstaff until sufficient force could be sent to protect it against every probable attack, but their remonstrances found no favour with the authorities at Auckland. Either from a sentimental belief—which would come natural to a sailor like FitzRoy — that failure to keep the flag flying was tantamount to surrender,* or from a mistaken estimate of Heke's fighting-qualities, the mature advice of men who were just as patriotic as they was disregarded, with the result that one disaster followed fast upon another.

An officer and thirty men of the 96th were sent to act as a garrison to the little town, but with strict orders to act solely on the defensive for the maintenance of order and tranquillity of the community. The officer was especially debarred from making any excursion into the country, and on no account was he to employ the men under his command in hostile operations, except in self-defence, or, at the written request of the Police Magistrate, in defence of the inhabitants. By the second week in August the Governor's preparations for his contemplated "hostile display" had so far advanced that the barque *Sydney* arrived at the Bay of Islands with 160 troops on board. On the 24th of the same month the Governor arrived there also with H.M.S. *Hazard* and the Government brig *Victoria*, having on board a detachment of the 96th, under Captain Bennett. The whole force was under the command of Lieut.-Colonel Hulme, the total strength disembarked being 250 men of all ranks.

---

* A sailor's view of the matter was expressed by Lieutenant Phill-potts, after the fall of Kororareka, when he wrote, "That it was a defeat I must acknowledge, as I consider losing the flagstaff in the same light as losing a ship."

The appearance of this force, imposing in the eyes of the natives, had a most salutary effect, determining many of the waverers to adhere to the cause of the Crown, whose arms were considerably augmented thereby. Being assured of a large measure of native support, it was decided to push on into the interior for the purpose of administering a wholesome check to the rebellious spirit of Heke. Boats were hired for the transport of the troops up the Kerikeri River ; but at this juncture information was brought to the Governor that many of the friendly chiefs were of the opinion that Heke might still be susceptible to conciliation, and that before force was used the effect of reason might be tried.

Only too anxious to avoid a breach with the native race, Governor FitzRoy agreed to this course, and, accompanied by Bishop Selwyn, several of the missionaries, and Lieut.-Colonel Hulme, he proceeded to Waimate, the principal mission station in the north, where on the 2nd September he met the friendly chiefs. The Governor made an eloquent and soothing speech, during the course of which, amongst other acts of conciliation, he announced the abolition of the obnoxious Customs duties :—

" I have found," he said, "that some of the regulations of the Government about ships and goods brought in them have been injurious—have done harm to those who live near the Bay of Islands. Being truly desirous of promoting the welfare of the settlers amongst you, and yourselves, I have altered these regulations, and you will in future be able to trade freely with all ships."*

This speech was followed by others† from the chiefs, in which they virtually agreed to guarantee the good behaviour of Heke, and undertook that he would not

* The Bay of Islands was immediately declared a' free port, and on the meeting of the Legislative Council at Auckland on the 19th September, 1844, His Excellency brought in a Bill, which was passed, for the abolition of Customs duties throughout the colony.

† These speeches have been partially preserved, but FitzRoy states they were so full of allegorical references, and references to ancient Maori lore, that much of them was not understood by the missionaries, who could not render them into English.

again disturb the peace. That worthy craftily abstained from attending the meeting, but he sent a letter in which he displayed no very penitent spirit. His lame apology— if it can be so appraised—and the more sincere assurances of the loyal chiefs were, however, accepted. On this occasion Waaka Nene spoke as follows :—

GOVERNOR,—If the flagstaff is cut down again we will fight for it. We will fight for it, all of us. We are of one tribe, and we will fight for the staff and for our Governor. I am sorry this trouble has occurred, but you may return the soldiers. Return, Governor. We will take care of the staff. We, the old folks, are well disposed, and we will make the young ones so also.

As an earnest of the chiefs' sincerity the Governor demanded the surrender of ten guns,* which were immediately placed at his feet, but not by Heke. To the price of his forgiveness Heke contributed nothing but the following ambiguous letter :—

FRIEND GOVERNOR,—This is my speech to you. My disobedience and rudeness is no new thing. I inherit it from my parents—from my ancestors. Do not imagine that it is a new feature of my character ; but I am thinking of leaving off my rude conduct to Europeans. Now I say I will prepare another pole inland at Waimate, and I will erect it at its proper place at Kororareka in order to put a stop to our present quarrel. Let your soldiers remain beyond the sea and at Auckland. Do not send them here. The pole that was cut down belonged to me. I made it for the native flag, and it was never paid for by the Europeans.

From your friend,
HONE HEKE POKAI.

On this basis a peace was patched up, which was to last only so long as Heke could secure no advantage from its violation. The troops then re-embarked and returned to Auckland, those from Australia being sent back to

* Heke thought the proposal made at Waimate by Governor FitzRoy to surrender guns meant the surrender of land. In his discussion with Ruhe he told that chief that he believed the Ahuahu district was to be the butt end of the guns and the Kaikohe district the barrels, the distance being about ten miles.

Sydney. Upon this settlement of the trouble becoming known in Wellington the *New Zealand Spectator*, which hated the Government and everything it did, could not resist the temptation to be facetious at Governor FitzRoy's expense by comparing his gyrating army to—

> The King of France's men,
> Who were marched up a hill,
> And then—marched down again.

Scarcely had the soldiers settled down in barracks than news of fresh disturbances began to reach the Governor. The culprits this time were the followers of Kawiti, the chief of Kawakawa, who was to some extent the rival and enemy of Heke, but who was shortly to be driven by the exigencies of war into terms of closest friendship with him. At this stage, however, there was a material difference between these belligerents. The followers of Kawiti were actuated largely by motives of robbery and plunder ; Heke, by the more — shall we say — patriotic part of ridding the country of the authority of the Queen. For the details of the incident which brought the Kawakawa natives into active hostility to the Government we must turn to those valuable " Reminiscences " which the Rev. Henry Williams* has left behind him :—

The police-boat, with the sergeant of police and four men, was ordered to Kawakawa to apprehend a European† residing by the side of the river, though not in the *pa*. The boat arrived some time after dark ; the natives say midnight—that is, some time after they had fallen asleep. The police were armed with swords and forced open the door of the *pakeha's* house. Kohu, sister of Hori Kingi Tahua, son of Whareumu, and *mokopuna* (grandchild) of Kawiti, were in the house with some other women. They were alarmed at seeing some armed white men, the light of the fire showing their swords, and attempted to rush out of the house. In the scuffle the finger of Hori Kingi's

---

* The Rev. Henry Williams was appointed Archdeacon of Waimate on the 22nd September, 1844, with jurisdiction over the whole of the northern district. This was rendered advisable on account of the Bishop's removal to Auckland.

† His name was Buvers.

sister was cut, drawing blood, which, though ever so little, is by Maori law a serious aggravation of offence. Not finding the man they were seeking, the police returned to Kororareka. The natives in the *pa*, so soon as they heard of the affair, were very indignant, denouncing the transaction as *kohuru*, coming without notice in the night, and declared had they been aware of what the police were doing they would have fired on the boat. These people had been always on the most friendly terms with the Europeans. The following day Hori Kingi, with a party of men, came to the Resident Magistrate at Kororareka for redress on account of the assault. The Magistrate treated the subject with great indifference. He said they had better put a piece of rag on the finger, and it would soon get well. Kingi demanded compensation for the assault. On being refused, he left in anger, saying that he would call again the next day. On the morrow Hori Kingi returned with a strong party; some rough language was used, but with no better success. After long discussion, Kingi observed, " This is my second demand for compensation for the assault on my sister by the police. I shall call once more, when you will attend to my demand." On the following day Kingi came again with a large party armed. The Magistrate now became alarmed, so also were the inhabitants of Kororareka. The Magistrate came over to Paihia for advice. I said that as there had been undoubtedly an assault on the part of the police the more quietly it was settled the better. I mentioned a circumstance which had occurred at Pakaraka, in the killing of a pig, for which a calf worth £10 had been given, the European being in the wrong. The Magistrate was perplexed and displeased, but there was no alternative, and a calf was given to the worth of £10, though with bad grace. This event rankled in the minds of the people and brought to issue the irritation of the natives.

As the result of this irritation a spirit of lawlessness broke loose. Eight horses were taken from Captain Wright, who was in no way connected with the affair at Kawakawa. Two of the horses were obtained by breaking open the stable, and the perpetrators threatened to shoot the Captain if he resisted. By the interference of the Chief Protector of Aborigines the horses were subsequently restored. The out-settlers at the Bay of Islands fared no better. Four horses belonging to Captain Hingstone were taken by some natives of the Kawakawa tribe, and no redress was obtained for them. Early in the year 1845 a

KAWITI.

After a drawing in the possession of the Kawiti family.

very daring outrage, robbery with personal violence, was committed at Matakana, about twenty-five miles to the northward of Auckland, which may be said to have been incited by similar acts at the Bay of Islands. On the 6th January four Europeans had their cottages broken open and plundered of everything, leaving them perfectly destitute of clothing and bedding. For these depredations three chiefs of the Kawakawa tribe — Pareoro, Mate, and Kokou — were held responsible, and a reward of £150 was offered for their arrest. " And I further proclaim," said the Governor, " that the strongest measures will be adopted ultimately in the event of these methods being found insufficient."

With what his followers were doing to assert what they believed to be their rights Kawiti had at first no sympathy and strongly advised moderation. It was only when he found, as he afterwards expressed it, " their blood was up " that he realized the day for moderation had passed and bent himself to the popular will. Kawiti was in reality a man of noble spirit and admittedly one of the pillars of the Nga-Puhi people. He came of a long line of famous chiefs, and it is suggestive of his influential station that his name appears at the head of all those who signed the Treaty of Waitangi. During the years which had passed since the negotiation of that compact he had always stoutly maintained the authority of the Queen, and up to this point had proved himself a staunch friend to the Europeans. What, then, caused his disaffection? The official explanation at the time was that, like his followers, he was actuated by acquisitiveness and cupidity, and that to rob and plunder the settlers was his sole purpose in throwing off his allegiance to the Crown. Subsequent events did not justify this theory, for throughout the war Kawiti was guilty of no act which could be said to have shown a reduced regard for the principles of honesty, nor which could tarnish his already high reputation for chivalry. Whatever may be thought of Kawiti's part in the rebellion, he was certainly not actuated by the baser motives officially attributed to him. The true explanation of his entry into the conflict is to be found in his loyalty to his own people, whom he felt bound to support in their quarrel with the Government, and in the natural combativeness of the man — in that relish for a fight which ran in the blood of the Maori.

Kawiti was in fact a born fighter, and the desire to gratify this proclivity was no small factor in inducing him to join in the opposition to a Government which seemed disposed to treat with scant respect the time - honoured customs of his people. At the close of the war he told Sir Everard Home, Captain of the *North Star*, that " he had heard of the British soldiers and he wished to see them." This was only his way of indicating that he was anxious to try conclusions with the fighting - men from overseas. This feeling had been simmering through his mind for some time, but his final decision was made somewhat dramatically and in true Maori fashion. To Kawakawa Heke came to pay a ceremonial visit to his elder tribesman, of whose feelings he was not altogether ignorant. With him he brought a small parcel carefully bound up in a covering of dressed flax. Handing the package to Kawiti, he invited him to unbind the cord with which it was tied. This Kawiti did amid the silence of the onlookers. When the folds of the covering had been unwound the contents were discovered to be a beautiful greenstone *mere*, one of the most precious possessions of the ancient Maori, smeared with human filth. No words were spoken, but to the alert mind of Kawiti the significance of the suggestion was at once apparent. The *mere* typified the Maori people, the filth the indignities that were being heaped upon them. He saw that this was Heke's method of insinuating to him that the Europeans were defiling the dignity, the prestige, the *mana* of the Maori ; that they were, indeed, depriving them of their heritage, and that unless the incursions of the white man into the land were checked the end must inevitably be the annihilation of their race. It was for Kawiti to say whether he would clean the *mere* or leave it soiled. Upon this issue so symbolically presented to him Kawiti pondered long and silently, and when at last he gave voice to his feelings he said to Heke : " You may return home. Your desire will be gratified. I will speak to my people as you desire." From that moment the die was cast. His mind was made up, and he began the immediate mobilization of his forces.

When it became known among the discontented natives generally that Kawiti was prepared to pit his skill in war against the British troops he rose immensely in their esteem. Heke then discovered that in Kawiti he had raised a frankenstein, for the Kawakawa chief was much talked about ; he became a man of the hour, and consequently in Heke's eyes a rival. The danger of being outstripped in popular favour was more than Heke's haughty spirit could brook, but he refused to emulate the followers of Kawiti in their course of plunder in order to enhance his popularity with the malcontents. So far from this being the case, these depredations upon the settlers were roundly denounced by Heke, who saw no harm in the settlers themselves. He ever did his utmost to restrain the peculation of his immediate followers, and seriously quarrelled with those, like Te Haratua, who disregarded his wishes in this respect. His *mea whawhai** was the Government and its symbol, the flagstaff ; therefore when asked to sanction the proceedings of the plunderers he stoutly answered : " No. Let us fight with the flagstaff alone." Heke, however, felt that he must assert himself in order to maintain his " place in the sun," so seriously threatened by the popular Kawiti.

In pursuit of this policy, on the night of the 9th January, 1845, he quietly marched a number of his tribe behind the sleeping town of Kororareka, and at daylight again cut down the flagstaff, but without subjecting the inhabitants to any violence. A Proclamation was accordingly issued

* His *mea whawhai* = the thing he was combating.

offering a reward of £100 for the capture of Heke, a proceeding that deeply offended him. Highly incensed, he asked : " Am I a pig that I am thus to be bought and sold ? " and promptly offered a like reward for the capture of the Governor. This, of course, did not dismay FitzRoy, who at once wrote to Lieut.-Colonel Hulme :—

There is no longer any doubt as to the necessity of employing the military in active operations at the Bay of Islands. I have exhausted every means of averting such a course, but in vain. There is a limit beyond which forbearance and peaceful conduct cannot be carried without becoming injurious to the permanent welfare of the community, and at that limit I have fully arrived.

As an immediate precaution he ordered Hulme to again despatch thirty men of the 96th Regiment to Kororareka ; he instructed Acting-Commander Robertson to return from Wellington with H.M.S. *Hazard*,* and he sent another appeal to Sir George Gipps for naval and military assistance.

In accordance with the Governor's instructions, the Government brig *Victoria* left Auckland early in the second week in January for the Bay of Islands with thirty of the rank and file of the 96th Regiment, accompanied by Dr. Sinclair, the Colonial Secretary. Upon his arrival there Henry Williams and other gentlemen who well knew the feeling of Heke towards the flagstaff entered a spirited protest against its re-erection. They argued that the policy of the Government might involve the safety of the whole settlement, and pleaded for delay until a stronger force could be sent to protect the settlers in the event of an attack upon them. Dr. Sinclair, however, would listen to none of these representations. With a fatal persistency he insisted upon a temporary pole being rigged by the crew

* When the *Hazard* first arrived in New Zealand waters she was commanded by Captain Bell. That officer subsequently fell into ill health and left the vessel at Auckland to recuperate. Failing to recover as rapidly as he would have liked, he thought a change to the Bay of Islands would benefit him, and one night in August, 1844, while on board the Government brig *Victoria* he either fell or jumped overboard. He was taken out of the water alive, but died shortly after. He was buried in the little cemetery at Russell, and was succeeded in the command by Acting-Commander Robertson.

of the *Victoria*, warmly declaring that with thirty soldiers all the powers of Maoridom could be defied. The official mind was at this period passing through the evolutionary process under which the Maori as a fighter was at first despised, then feared, then respected.* At the moment it had progressed no further than the first phase, and was accordingly arrogant and bombastic in its attitude. On Thursday, therefore, a small spar was erected and placed under an alternate guard of the soldiers and a detachment of Waaka Nene's men. Heke saw it next morning and promised himself that on the following Monday he would cut it down. This programme was interfered with by an incident which turned his next attack upon the staff into something of a personal vindication. He had heard that a number of Waaka Nene's men had spoken slightingly of him in the streets of Kororareka. They had said to some of his friends, " If Heke comes again to cut the flagstaff down we will put him in our pipes and smoke him," meaning thereby that they would arrest him, claim the Governor's reward, and with the money buy tobacco which they would put in their pipes and smoke. Heke heard this threat with a mixture of amusement and irritation, and decided to put the matter immediately to the test. Accordingly, early on the morning of Saturday, the 19th January, 1845, he arrived at the Bay, and leaving his armed men at the foot of the hill he, with amazing audacity, walked up the winding track leading to the top. There confronted by the guard of Waaka's men, whom he imperiously brushed aside, he cut the back stays of the pole, and as it fell he coolly remarked, " *Heoi ano*."† He then walked down the hill, entered his canoe, and with his jubilant followers paddled right under the stern of the *Victoria*, firing their muskets in derision as they passed.

It may be asked why, if the flagstaff was so guarded, was Heke able again to accomplish its destruction with such

---

* Heke is doubtless a bad man, but he is not the despicable foe he has been considered.—Vide *Rev. R. Davis.*

† " *Heoi ano* " ═ " That is enough."

simplicity. The answer to that question is to be found in the strength of native custom rather than in the weakness of the force by which the staff was protected. At the moment of Heke's arrival the staff was being guarded by a band of Waaka Nene's men. On Heke's approach one of them levelled his gun at him, but Heke disdainfully pushed it aside, which left the natives no recourse but either to let him go or to knock him down. They were thus placed in a serious dilemma. They had their duty to do, but in doing it they might have to shed the blood of one of their own countrymen, and of one who was a recognized chief among them. To the shedding of human blood in the interests of an inanimate thing like a flagstaff they were wholly adverse, and, therefore, when it came to a question of letting Heke cut the flagstaff down or cutting Heke down they not unnaturally took the line of least resistance and permitted him to work his will upon the offending pole.*

When making his appeal to Sir George Gipps, Governor FitzRoy had expressed the opinion that the troops he was asking for would not be required for a longer period than three months, by which time he was confident Heke's rebellion could be crushed. In this FitzRoy was perhaps more optimistic than the circumstances warranted. He did not appear to be aware of the real state of the case, for there was in truth a widespread dissatisfaction among the natives, the loyalty of even the best of them being strained by insidious rumours which flew upon the wind, magnifying real and fancied wrongs. Heke had, in fact, a great volume of Nga-Puhi sympathy behind him, and at any hour the whole tide of that sympathy might begin to flow in his favour. He had skilfully succeeded in enticing to his side the great majority of the younger men of almost every Nga-Puhi *hapu*, his success in this respect having a

---

* The British soldier, who has ever been a humorist, even under the most distressing circumstances, was able to supply a reason of his own for Heke's antipathy to the flagstaff. In their rough and ready way the men of the 96th translated his name, John Heke, into Johnny Hickey. Out of this they evolved the theory that he was an Irishman who was opposing the Government in order to avenge the wrongs of his country.

retroactive influence upon the older folks, who, though
not necessarily sympathizing with his aims, " could not,"
to use their own words, " see their children—the hope of
their people—die, though in an unjust cause, without at
least endeavouring to protect them from the wrath of
the stranger."

Even men like Waaka Nene were sorely stressed by
doubt, and for the moment began to wonder whether, after
all, they had not been misled by the missionaries, and
whether they had acted wisely in supporting the Governor.
Here is the position as described by the Rev. Richard Davis
in a letter to the Protector of the Aborigines :—

Since I last wrote I have had communication with the
hostile party. Heke's party is strong—in fact, I do not know,
but it consists of nearly the whole of Nga-Puhi. Heke has
done much mischief by instilling into the minds of the natives
that the *mana* of the Island is invested in the Queen of England,
and that they are thereby made thoroughly poor men and
slaves. This, from the manner in which he has introduced it,
has seriously affected the native mind, and many have been
brought over to his way of thinking, although they do not stand
so prominently forward in the cause. Had it not been for this
feeling, or some of a similar nature, the last flagstaff would not
have been cut down without bloodshed. The quiet removal of
that flagstaff in the face of those who had engaged to protect
it is, or ought to be to us, a sufficient indication as to what
the mind of the natives is, and of the little reliance which can
be placed on them. They (the hostile party) declare that they
have no anger to the Queen of England—to the Governor ; but
seeing that they are a lost people—they and their children—
for ever, they now wish to have undone what they ignorantly
did, or to make an effort to save themselves and their children
from ruin, or perish in the attempt. They say : " It is for
the Governor to save or destroy us. If the flagstaff be again
raised it will be a sufficient indication to us as to what the
Governor's intention is—namely, our destruction. Should he
permit the flagstaff to remain down we are friends again."
But, " Listen ! " said they, " We shall not deal with the flagstaff
as we last did, by going in the night to cut it down, but what
we do will be done in the light of day." Heretofore I have
heard the natives boast, but there was no appearance of anything of the kind—all was solemn.

The Government at this moment stood in a parlous position; the authority of the Queen hung by a slender thread. In this crisis an important meeting of the northern chiefs was begun at Paroa, Bay of Islands, on the 28th January, 1845, which, at the invitation of Waaka Nene, the Rev. Henry Williams attended. In plunging into these political discussions Henry Williams took a great personal and religious risk. He stood in imminent danger of offending the natives by appearing too zealous in the interests of the Crown; he was equally liable to be misunderstood by the white settlers, who might have thought him over-friendly towards the natives. He by no means avoided this dual accusation, but that he escaped being crushed between the upper and the nether stones says much for his sincerity and his diplomacy. This is how he regarded the position of himself and of his fellow-missionaries, as expressed in a letter to the Rev. E. G. Marsh a few days before this meeting :—

Though we are of no party, we also, I presume, shall be involved in the general confusion. I have long seen the anomalous position of the Governor—a man with no power. This served very well for a time, but the natives soon found the weakness of the English, and the consequence is that now they have set the Governor at open defiance. As we stand between the two, I expect we shall have no favour from either.

At the Paroa conference the grievances of the Maoris were discussed with the utmost frankness at *koreros* extending over four days, often lasting long into the night. Much of the discussion naturally turned upon the intentions of the Government, and whether the Treaty of Waitangi was, as Heke said it was, *he mea tinihanga*,* and whether the law of the *pakeha* was indeed the law of *Hura*.† Waaka Nene had been much displeased by Governor Hobson's regulation prohibiting the cutting of kauri timber, and at this meeting openly declared that

---

* "*He mea tinihanga* " = " A trick. The thing (or work) that deceives."

† " *Hura,*" usually rendered " *Hura Ikariote* " = " Judas Iscariot."

if the Governor had been at Hokianga he would have felled a spar in his presence to see what would happen. Both Waaka and Rewa expressed the opinion that they had been overhasty in signing the Treaty of Waitangi, and that from it all their troubles arose. At this stage Henry Williams threw the weight of his influence on to the side of the treaty, for the acceptance of which he, more than any man, was responsible. He denied there was the remotest intention on the part of the Government to deprive the natives of their just rights by means of the treaty, or in any other way. He took the document, read it clause by clause, explained it, and defended it on the ground that there was not a word in it that justified the assumption or assertion that the country had gone, or would go, from the natives without their consent. This allocution at length prevailed. The chiefs expressed their satisfaction with what had been told them, and those who had been so inclined immediately renounced their determination to assist Heke. Thus was the tide of popular feeling diverted from the cause of rebellion, and for this national service Mr. Williams received the grateful thanks of the Governor.

Henry Williams, writing at this juncture to Bishop Selwyn, says :—

I have had a singular battle to fight. I know not what other term to use, and, as a matter of course, have been accused of aiding and abetting these turbulent feelings—wellnigh cut down for having taken the part I did, relative to the treaty, in 1840—the natives having been perpetually told that I had betrayed them in that act. I was compelled, therefore, to fall back upon the treaty, and by explaining and distributing several copies amongst the chiefs maintained my ground and the honour of the Queen, all acknowledging that the terms of the treaty were good and honest. But for the timely distribution of the treaty I hesitate not to say that the native population to a man would have been in arms, and the question of possession might have been settled for a time by the extermination of all the Europeans in this part of the Island, leaving, as in the melancholy affair of Cabul, others at some future day to exact *utu* (payment). Feeling as I did that the terms of the treaty were a sacred compact between the British Government and the chiefs of New Zealand, I was enabled to speak with confidence as to the integrity and honour of England—that it was impossible that the Queen or the Governor could admit of any *tinihanga* (tricky nonsense) towards them.

Since the treaty has been more particularly explained, I am happy to say that a large body of the natives disapprove of Heke's conduct and say they will not join him, though they must not be expected to act against him. The Kawakawa natives have told me they will come to this place on the first indication of mischief. Heke is expected at Wahapu on Monday or Tuesday next by invitation from certain Europeans.* What this may lead to we cannot surmise, but are not without our fears.

* This doubtless refers to the intercourse which was taking place between Heke and the Acting American Consul, who lived at Wahapu. About this time Heke began to carry, with evident pride, an American flag at the stern of his canoe as he moved about the Bay. How he became possessed of this emblem of a rival nation is uncertain, but in all probability it was received from Henry Green Smith, who had become Acting American Consul after the departure of Captain Mayhew. It was known that Heke was on friendly terms with these men, from whom he learned something of the revolt of the American colonists which served to stimulate rather than to stifle his own revolutionary ideas. It was also known that he had been in close conference with Smith within a few days of his last adventure against the flagstaff. The ostentatious manner in which Smith flew the American flag at his store at Wahapu so annoyed Mr. Beckham, the Police Magistrate, that he took steps to have the practice prohibited by the Governor.

CHAPTER III.

THE FALL OF KORORAREKA.

IN answering her recall from Wellington the *Hazard* had an extremely rough passage round the East Cape, during which she had to jettison seven of her eighteen guns, reaching Auckland on the 9th February in a somewhat battered condition. She sailed for the Bay of Islands on the 12th, and on her arrival there active steps were taken to give effect to the Governor's scheme of defence, which, according to his express instructions to Acting-Commander Robertson, was to be of a strictly unprovocative character :—

I wish to impress upon your mind that your present course should be strictly defensive, and that no taunts or provocation, whether from Europeans or natives, should induce you to be drawn into hostilities, except in self-defence.

To Mr. Beckham, the Police Magistrate, he wrote :—

The *Victoria* will convey a sergeant and ten privates of the 96th Regiment to reinforce your small garrison. Prepare a new flagstaff in the town, to be in readiness for placing on the hill in its former situation after the blockhouse is secured and you are still further reinforced. Another ten men will be sent with the blockhouse when ready.

In accordance with these instructions a new and stouter flagstaff was erected, the lower shaft being, at the Governor's suggestion, shod with iron, as proof against Maori axes ; a wide and deep ditch surrounded it, and as

a further protection it was guarded by a blockhouse in
which were stationed twenty soldiers of the 96th, under
a young and, as it proved, inexperienced subaltern,
Ensign Campbell. Lower down the hill a second blockhouse was built,* directly overlooking the house of Mr.
Polack, which had been transformed into a stockade for
the reception of the non-combatants.   In this lower blockhouse was placed a battery of three old guns, which,
under the direction of Mr. Cornthwaite Hector, afterwards
played their part in the defence of the town.

   When it became known that additional soldiers had
arrived at Kororareka and that more were to follow there
was a great stir in Maori circles. "Fear came like a
fog on all Nga-Puhi," says a native account. "No chief
but Heke had any courage left." He called his people
together, saying, "I will fight the soldiers. I will cut
down the flagstaff. I will fulfil the last words of Hongi.
Be not afraid of the soldiers. All men are but *men*.
The soldiers are not gods. Lead will kill them, and if we
are beaten at last we shall be beaten by a brave and
noble people and need not be ashamed."

   Pursuant to this bold decision he sent his war-runners
to all the divisions of the Nga-Puhi people, and his
message was this : "Come, stand at my back. The red
garment is on the shore. Let us fight for our country.
Remember the last words of Hongi Hika : ' *Kia toa,
kia ora ai koutou* ' (' Be brave that you may live ')."

   By this time, however, the chiefs of Nga-Puhi had
become sufficiently impressed with the resources of Great
Britain to be sceptical of their powers to overcome the
soldiers, who if they were men were at least still regarded
as supermen. They accordingly asked Heke's messengers
and advocates this pertinent question : "How long will
the fire of the Maori burn before it is extinguished ? " Not
receiving an answer to their satisfaction, they paid tribute

   * This was the suggestion of a civilian, Mr. J. Watson, J.P., who
also superintended its erection. Lieutenant Barclay, in his report, admits
that it proved the key to the defence of the town.

to caution and said : " We will wait until a battle has been fought, and if he is successful we will join him." His first recruits in these circumstances were mainly from his own *hapu* and numbered about four hundred men. While the military preparations were in progress Heke, at Kaikohe, was vigilant and well informed. In conversation with some of the chiefs he one day referred to the fortified flagstaff, saying he had been told that the snake whose head he had cut off had grown into a monster, and that he was extremely anxious to see the strange sight. He then began to brood upon fresh plans. On Wednesday, the 5th February, the Rev. Henry Williams met him by appointment at Kaikohe to discuss the situation with him. Heke was not disposed to pay much attention to the missionary, and insisted that the Treaty of Waitangi was " all soap." " It is," he said, " very smooth and oily, but treachery is hidden under it " ; and Mr. Williams could make nothing of him. Towards the end of February it became evident further trouble was brewing, as large and small armed parties of natives were daily seen passing through Waimate from Kaikohe to the Bay. Reading these signs as portending a movement of some magnitude, the Rev. Mr. Burrows went to Kaikohe to again urge moderation upon Heke. The interview took place in Heke's house. The chief was civil, but obdurate. He was, he said, in want of some fish, and he was going to the sea with his " net." On the 3rd March he arrived at Waimate with 150 men, who were doubtless the metaphorical " net " of which he had spoken. The news that Heke was again on the march soon spread, and natives from all parts of the district came flocking into Waimate to see him. His explanation to Mr. Burrows of this movement was that he was going to the Bay to satisfy his craving for fish. The missionary, pointing to the guns in the hands of his followers, asked : " Are these necessary for fishing ? " Heke, taking advantage of a native custom which decreed. that it was discourteous to go unarmed into the presence of armed men, quickly

replied : " Is there not a man-of-war in the Bay, and
are there not redcoats at Kororareka ?   We must not go
without our *pu* (musket)."

During the afternoon, when there were about four
hundred natives at the mission station, a meeting was held
at which speeches were delivered.   Heke was warned by
Paratene* and others that if he was responsible for further
mischief at the Bay they would join Waaka Nene and
oppose his return inland ; but Heke still felt constrained
to cast his " net " in the Bay, and next day he had
proceeded as far as Waitangi.   Here he was intercepted
by the Rev. Henry Williams and Mr. Burrows, the latter
of whom had ridden to Paihia on the previous evening to
inform Mr. Williams of what had happened at Waimate
and to consult with him as to the measures to be taken.
Mr. Williams sternly rebuked the chief for the trouble
he was bringing upon every one.   Heke professed to be
anxious to avoid causing inconvenience to the settlers, but
reminded the missionary that the flagstaff had been re-
erected, and the Governor had placed a price upon his head,
an indignity that especially hurt the proud soul of Heke.
He again spoke resentfully of the Treaty of Waitangi, and
upbraided the missionaries for inducing so many chiefs to
sign it, well knowing that by so doing they were signing
away their lands.   Here, however, he met his match.
Giving the chief that peculiar look which he was often
known to give over his spectacles,† Mr. Williams said
emphatically : " Your salvation is in that treaty."   He
then delivered a speech to all present, in which he dwelt
upon the principles underlying the treaty, but for which
he declared the native race would have been submerged in
anarchy and confusion, and would, in all probability, have
become subject to some other and less considerate nation.

This oration made no perceptible impression upon
Heke.   The re-erection of the flagstaff still rankled in his

---

* Frequently referred to as Broughton.
† The natives called Henry Williams *Karu wha* (Four eyes).   William
Williams was always known as *parata* (brother).

mind, and he was anxious to see the " monster " that had reared its head on Maiki Hill. When he did see it the spectacle was not so pleasing, for he then knew he must come to grips with the problem of the flagstaff in a manner that would reduce his past proceedings to child's play. He became restless and anxious, and meeting Henry Williams outside his camp at Wahapu he gave him his gold-laced cap to *tangi* (cry) over in the event of his being killed.

It was in the early days of March that the movement began which resulted in the fusion of the forces of Heke and Kawiti.* Up to this time both men had pursued their own way animated by different motives : Heke to purge the country of the flagstaff ; Kawiti to measure himself in contest with the soldiers. What, then, brought these men with separate purposes together ? The over-tures came first from Kawiti, who regarded as the acme of foolishness the division of a force that might become irresistible if it were but happily united. During their discussions Kawiti told Heke that if he again contemplated cutting down the flagstaff he must first cut off its arms and legs, otherwise he could not hope to succeed, meaning thereby that the Europeans must be got rid of, and that to do this Heke must join him in his war against the soldiers.

Heke listened appreciatively to the suggestion for fusion because he saw that without augmented strength his resolution to destroy the fortified flagstaff could never be accomplished. The missionaries, knowing that the move-ment for fusion was afoot, spent days arguing with Heke in the hope of dissuading him from an alliance which they felt must inevitably bring upon the country a crop of evil. Hitherto they had regarded him as one more to be pitied than blamed ; as one who had been misled by

---

* Kawiti's particular section of the Nga-Puhi tribe was Ngati-Hine. Connected with him were Roroa, Kapotai, Ngarehauata, Ngati-Tu, Para-whau of Whangarei, Ngati-Toki of Mangakahia, and Ngati-Wai of Whanga-ruru. Heke's people were Nga-Puhi proper. The Rawhiti people were *tino* Nga-Puhi—Nga-Puhi of Nga-Puhi.

designing Europeans; as one who was mischievous rather
than criminal. "He is a daring fellow," wrote the Rev.
Mr. Davis, "but does not appear to me to be maliciously
wicked." In association with and under the influence of
Kawiti even this modified approval might not be possible,
and, being fearful of this, Mr. Davis not only strove to avert
the union of the two chiefs, but believed the surest way to
do so was to arrange a conference between the Governor
and Heke. Such a *korero* would, he thought, be regarded
as a compliment by the chief; it would afford an opportunity for much plain talk and for the clearing-away of
misapprehensions. He accordingly sent an urgent message
to the Government suggesting the expediency of a meeting
between the Governor and the chief. Heke acknowledged
to Mr. Davis that his *whakaaro* was *ngoikore haere** in
consequence of the danger he saw the quiet settlers were
in—and would be in—if he persisted in his intention to
again cut down the flagstaff. His *mea whawhai*,† he said,
was the flagstaff, and that alone; but he was afraid it
was not altogether so with many of his followers, some of
whom now had their eyes on the white people and the
spoil that would fall to the victors. The position, he
feared, was passing out of his hands, and therefore he
was anxiously looking for a reply to Mr. Davis's letter
suggesting an interview with the Governor, which might
leave him a way out and an opportunity to compose an
honourable peace.

Either from the habit of official dilatoriness or from
a feeling that such a meeting would be regarded as a
concession granted from fear or weakness, the conference
was never arranged, leaving the way open to negotiations
of a different kind. In the first week in March a deputation came to Heke, at Wahapu, from Kawiti to urge
upon him the wisdom of concerted action. While these
parleys were in progress the missionaries had frequent but
fruitless interviews with Heke, and as a final shot Mr. Davis

---

* His *whakaaro* was *ngoikore haere* = His mind was wavering.
† His *mea whawhai* = The thing he was combating.

told him if he went to Kororareka the soldiers there
would arrest and imprison him. His reply was : " They
may do as they please. I fear not death." The
following Sunday Mr. Kemp spent all day endeavouring
to dissuade him from what was evidently now a set
purpose. On the Monday Mr. Davis made another effort,
and then found him surrounded by Kawiti's deputation.
" I plainly perceived," says Mr. Davis, " that there was a
heavy lowering on his brow, which indicated the darker
movements of his uneasy mind. I requested him not to
go to the Bay, but to return quietly to his home ; but in
respectful tones he gave me to understand that nothing
should deter him."

In a few days the fusion of the forces took place at a
joint camp formed at Te Uruti, near Kororareka. Here
the next attack upon the flagstaff was planned ; for " See,"
said Heke, " the flagstaff does mean a taking possession,
or why else should they persist in re-erecting it.*

Immediately the fusion of the forces was complete
hostilities in a mild form commenced. Native skirmishers
began to appear in the vicinity of Kororareka, and where
it was possible to loot property they did so. To disperse
a number of these raiders a detachment from the *Hazard*,
under Acting Lieutenant Morgan, was sent in an armed
pinnace on the 3rd March, and on this boat the natives
fired, thus committing the first act of war upon Her
Majesty's forces. The following day Lieutenant Phillpotts
and Mr. Parrot, both officers of the *Hazard*, rode out
towards Matauhi Bay to reconnoitre a party of Heke's
men who were observed on the opposite side of the water.
Before they were conscious of the fact they rode straight
into the midst of a band of Kawiti's scouts who unhorsed

* When Heke was agitating the northern natives by his arguments
against the Government he took great pains to show them that the
British flag being hoisted on any territory was a sign that the land
belonged to the Sovereign of Great Britain, and that the people of that
land would become slaves, and that to preserve the freedom of the New-
Zealanders the British flag must not be admitted to their territory."—
Vide *FitzRoy's " Remarks on New Zealand."*

them and made them prisoners. They were taken before Kawiti, who, learning that they had made no resistance, acted generously, merely disarming them, and sending them back to the ship with an injunction to exercise greater care in the future. On Sunday, the 9th March, the Rev. Mr. (afterwards Archdeacon) Brown visited Heke's camp, and preached from the not inappropriate text in the Gospel of James (iv, 1), "From whence come wars and fightings amongst you." After the service Heke walked up to the missionary and remarked to him that he had better preach that sermon to the soldiers, who had more need of it.*

Having now completed his dispositions, Heke determined that his next assault upon the flagstaff would be made at daylight on the morning of Tuesday, the 11th. The attack was to begin simultaneously from three different points, the signal for its commencement being the rising of the star Pleiades—the dawn star—above the horizon. At that moment Kawiti and Pumuka were to march upon the town from Matauhi Bay with a force of two hundred Ngati-Hine men drawn from Kawakawa and its inland districts ; a similar force, consisting mainly of men of the Kapotai tribe, from Waikare, was to attack in the centre from the hills above the town, these movements being in the nature of a diversion to keep the soldiers busy while Heke, with his own people, was to make his effort against his especial *bête noire*—the flagstaff. This composite force did not exceed six hundred men, who for the most part were armed with tomahawks, which some of their owners boasted would flash in the sunlight to some purpose before the day was done.

When the plan of attack was decided upon, the *tohungas* (priests) of the war-party were called in, and threw darts to divine the event. In Heke's case the omens were

---

* A Roman Catholic priest performed a like service for Kawiti's men, who were professing Christians. Kawiti himself was still a heathen. Archdeacon Brown believed the united forces to number about four hundred, though Pumuka and his party had not then arrived. They entered the camp next day.

entirely fair, and they then knew that the soldiers would be defeated, and that the flagstaff would fall. Kawiti, who was something of a *tohunga*, threw a *rakau* (divining-stick) for himself and one for the soldiers. Both rods went straight and fair, but both turned wrong side up. In consequence they knew there would be a stiff fight in which both would lose a number of men. " Our enemy," said Kawiti, " will prove brave and strong ; they will suffer much from us, and we from them. It is good, for this is war, not play."

In accordance with native custom, which was nothing if not chivalrous, Heke made no secret of his intention.* He gave minute particulars of the time, direction, and manner of his attack, and this information was brought to the authorities at Kororareka by Mr. Gilbert Mair, a gentleman of high standing in the community and one thoroughly familiar with native thought and native habit. As usual, this information was treated with derision and contempt by many of the inhabitants, who professed to believe that no natives would dare to attack them, surrounded as they were by so substantial a naval and military force. How substantial the force was may be judged by the fact that, outside the ninety marines and sailors of the *Hazard*, the 96th numbered one lieutenant, one ensign, two sergeants, and fifty rank and file. The civilians under arms mustered 110 all told, these having been formed into what was called the " Civic Guard."†

* Under these circumstances the element of surprise should have played no part in the attack, yet the event found the British strangely unprepared for it, especially in the matter of a co-ordinated command. Acting-Commander Robertson, of the *Hazard*, was the senior officer present, and had he not been wounded he might have instilled some order and cohesion into the defending forces ; but after he fell the whole scheme—if such it could be called—of defence went rapidly from bad to worse in the absence of a controlling mind.

† By the end of February the inhabitants of Kororareka were being drilled privately, and civil and military patrols were established in the town, but there was a shortage of arms. On the 4th March Mr. Beckham wrote : " I am much in want of about fifty muskets and ammunition to complete the arming of the inhabitants ; also shot and cartridges for the 9- and 12-pounder cannons." Forty stand of arms and 1,000 rounds were supplied within the next few days.

Fortunately, Heke's warning was not so lightly regarded by Acting-Commander Robertson, of the *Hazard*, who on being told of the scheme for taking the town, with the true spirit of the British tar—and possibly with something of his picturesque vocabulary—declared : " Then they will have to pass over my body first." Prophetic words these, for in a few hours he was carried from the field full of wounds and honours won in a desperate hand-to-hand conflict against a brave and determined foe.

Monday passed quietly, but in consequence of persistent rumours and universal fears that the natives were about to attack the town Acting-Commander Robertson landed from the *Hazard* a small gun which, with a piquet in charge, he stationed at a narrow pass on the road to Matauhi, the idea being that it was to be fired as a signal of approaching danger, rather than as a serious attempt to check the hostile advance. That evening he brought on shore a detachment of about forty-five sailors and marines, and took up his quarters in the town. Between the hours of 4 and 5 o'clock next morning, while it was still dark, he moved out with his men, intending to throw up some entrenchments on a hill on the right of the road leading to Matauhi and which would command the south-western entrance to Kororareka. The morning was thick and hazy, and as the little force trudged along the road, never dreaming the enemy was afoot, they were startled by the sound of firing at the point where the gun had been stationed. Pushing forward, they were met by the retiring piquet, from whom they learned that the guard had been surprised and the gunner killed while attempting to spike the gun.

Scarcely had they realized the critical nature of the situation and formed into line than there burst through the mist the band of rebels under Kawiti on their way to attack the town. Instantly the fight began, both sides firing almost muzzle to muzzle as rapidly as their im-perfect weapons would permit, and as accurately as the

ADMIRAL ROBERTSON-MACDONALD.
After the picture in the Hocken Collection, Dunedin.

low visibility would allow.* For twenty minutes the battle raged with no apparent advantage to either force, but at the first streak of dawn the sailors got together, charged those in front of them, and before their onslaught the Maoris broke and fled. During this time Acting-Commander Robertson had been stationed at the left of his line, which was protected by the churchyard fence. Cutlass in hand he had laid about him in the mêlée with a will. He is credited with having killed three Maoris in personal combat, and in pursuing a fourth in the darkness he became separated from his men. When close upon his quarry, the chief, who proved to be no less a personage than Pumuka, Kawiti's second in command, turned and fired a double-barrelled pistol directly at him, one shot slightly wounding his right elbow, the other grazing his scalp. This momentarily checked the onward rush of the sailor, but the chief was overtaken and killed by two men who had followed their Commander. Almost immediately one of these men was killed and the other seriously wounded.

Robertson now sought to rejoin his own men, but to his alarm he found his way barred by a number of natives who had practically outflanked his little column, which by this time had moved a considerable distance forward in pursuit of the retreating rebels. In these circumstances discretion became the better part of valour. He therefore concealed himself behind some bushes, hoping for a more favourable opportunity to come up with his command. While lying under the shelter of the friendly shrubs, the natives, unconscious of the strategic advantage they possessed, suddenly came upon the dead body of Pumuka, and, picking it up,† began to file past the prone form

* " The young men did not look for the light of this world. Their only thought was who should kill the first man and so elevate his name. Pumuka gained a name. He killed the first man in the battle, but he had not long to rejoice, for he himself fell a *mataika* for the pakeha."— *Native account.*

† The natives invariably made it a point of honour to carry away their dead and wounded, and therefore it was always difficult to estimate their casualties. It was never known how many they lost in this section of the attack, but it is generally understood that among their leaders, besides Pumuka, Kawiti lost one of his sons. Their killed and wounded were estimated at twenty and fifty respectively.

3—First War.

of the Commander in their retirement. The last to go, however, saw him, and, firing as he went, inflicted a severe wound in his right thigh, shattering the bone and causing a compound fracture. Robertson now lay helpless and in intense pain.

Meantime the main body of the *Hazard's* men had carried on the fight with a success highly flattering to the paucity of their numbers. The natives were beaten off, and finding their Commander missing and the sergeant of marines killed* they decided to retire upon the town. As they went they were fired upon by a small party of natives, who, more courageous than the rest, had not wholly abandoned the field. This fire was returned by the sailors. By a strange irony of fate the British Commander, lying wounded amongst the scrub, came into the direct line of these conflicting fusilades. The bullets whistled over him, and one shot, more surely directed by misfortune than the rest, culminated his sufferings by passing through his hitherto uninjured left leg, rendering him even more helpless than before. As the day was growing lighter, Robertson, knowing that his men were in the vicinity, raised his handkerchief above the bushes in which he now had lain for two hours. Fortunately, his signal was seen ; his men, who believed him dead, came to his assistance and carried him on board his ship,

---

* The *Hazard* lost two marines and four seamen in this fight : Colour-Sergeant J. McCarthy, aged 35 ; Private A. May, 20 ; Seamen W. Lovell, 24 ; W. Love, 20 ; W. Denby, 34 ; and F. G. Minikin, 23. They lie buried in the little cemetery at Russell, and whenever a British warship visits the Bay of Islands their grave is the subject of solicitous care on the part of the officers and crew. In the Mission Church near-by there has been erected to their memory a tablet on which is inscribed—with slight variation—Mrs. Hemans' stirring lines, from " England's Dead " :—

> The warlike of the Isles,
>   The men of field and wave—
> Are not the rocks their funeral pyre,
>   The seas and shore their grave ?
>
> Go, stranger, track the deep,
>   Free, free the white sail spread;
> Wave may not foam, nor wild wind beat,
>   Where rests not England's dead.

where he was to remain for many weeks hovering between life and death.*

While all this had been happening at the Matauhi end of the town, the central attacking force was doing its best to attract the attention of the soldiers in the town itself. Its members, scattered amongst the wooded hills at the back of the settlement, maintained a brisk fire, but had not attempted any general assault. A small detachment of soldiers had been moved up by Lieutenant Barclay behind the houses to reply to this fire, but the greater portion of his force was kept inside the stockade and remained inactive during the whole of the engagement. Such men as he did use were supported by the guns set up on a platform in front of the blockhouse below the flagstaff. These guns, most assiduously worked by Mr. Cornthwaite Hector and two old soldiers, had but little military value, since a native hidden in the scrub was a somewhat intangible target, but their moral effect was perhaps more serviceable to the cause of the defenders, since they made much noise and no little splutter.

With Kawiti routed and Kapotai held in check the defence up to this point appeared to be progressing favourably. There was, however, a different tale to tell at the flagstaff, where the wily Heke had charge of the attack. He had secretly marched his men behind the town, and carefully concealed them amongst the scrub which grew in profusion on the hillside. As they crept through the fern, forming their semi-cordon round the hill,

* David Robertson was the grandson of the Rev. Dr. Robertson, historian of Scotland, and author of "The History of the Reign of Charles V." He was born in 1817. He was appointed first lieutenant of the *Hazard* on the 1st October, 1841, when that vessel was first commissioned. He assumed command of the sloop on the death of Captain Bell. His conduct in defence of Kororareka was the one bright spot in that miserable affair, and for years afterwards the natives spoke with admiration of his prowess. In recognition of his services on that occasion the residents of Auckland subscribed and made him a presentation of a sword. In the House of Commons Sir Robert Peel eulogized his gallant conduct, which he announced would be rewarded with promotion in his profession. He was then made Commander, and subsequently rose to be an Admiral. He afterwards became known as Admiral David Robertson-MacDonald.

3*

they kept in touch with each other in the darkness by imitating the cry of the *ruru*,* the plaintive note of this native owl echoing and re-echoing across the night air with a strange persistency, yet its unusual frequency excited no suspicion in the mind of the sentry on the hill. By the practice of a further device, this time learned from sacred history,† his men were able to steal so close to the block-house and its approaches that they might have stretched out their hands and touched the soldiers as they passed to and fro.

All unconscious that they were surrounded by a hidden and determined enemy the soldiers passed the night in the blockhouse. At about 4 o'clock in the morning Ensign Campbell, the officer in charge, left the fortification, taking five men with him, armed, and carrying spades, their intention being to dig a trench on the heights above Oneroa Beach. They had just turned the first few sods when they heard firing in the direction of Matauhi Bay, the echo of Kawiti's attack. Work was immediately suspended, the Ensign and his men walking back towards the blockhouse. For a moment or two they stood on the brow of the hill overlooking the harbour, listening to the snap · of the guns as the echoes rang through the crisp morning air. At this sound the other soldiers who comprised the guard at the flagstaff turned out, and were busy accoutring themselves in their belts outside the blockhouse when suddenly the cry was raised that the natives were upon them. Heke knew how many men were guarding the staff, and as they emerged he told them off until there were but four left. Then he made his rush. In an instant his men swarmed round the blockhouse and

---

* *Ninox novæ-zealandiæ.*

† This is upon Heke's own authority. He stated that he directed his men to cut down the *kahikatea* bushes, under cover of which they crept out from the ambush. He said that he took the idea of the ambush from the Book of Joshua, at the taking of Ai. He knew more of Joshua than of Macbeth, otherwise he might have remembered how Birnam Wood came up to high Dunsinane Hill. Blame was imputed to the missionaries for having put the Old Testament into the hands of the Maoris.— *Carleton.*

poured through the door in the palisade. The surprised
and unarmed soldiers, many of whom had been straggling
about the hillside endeavouring to see what was going on
below, now aware of their danger,* incontinently plunged
into the scrub and made their way to the blockhouses
below; but the sentry, who was pinned to his position,
fired at the first of the assailants, and was immediately
overpowered and killed. The three soldiers who yet
lingered inside the blockhouse were quickly despatched,
the signalman, Tapper, was wounded, and a half-caste
child accidentally shot.† Those natives who were not so
engaged opened fire on the soldiers outside, and Ensign
Campbell's men sent back a volley in return. Before
they could fire a second, however, they detected another
party of natives coming from the opposite direction, and,
seeing that they must inevitably be cut off unless they
were able to elude these newcomers, the Ensign and his
men beat a precipitate retreat to the blockhouse below
and left the flagstaff to its fate.

What that fate was to be did not long remain in doubt,
for Heke's men applied their axes with a will until the tall
shaft‡ swam giddily in the air, then fell with a thundering
crash to the ground, amidst the frantic shouts of rebellious
Nga-Puhi.

A few of Heke's followers then gave their attention
to the blockhouse below the flagstaff, firing from a distance of not more than seventy yards. Mr. Hector,
finding their fire both annoying and dangerous, appealed
to Lieutenant Barclay for some assistance to drive these
assailants away. In this he was not supported, but
snubbed for his pains. He at length succeeded in getting

* The natives expressed great surprise, and perhaps something of
contempt, for the soldiers in the blockhouse, because they had not a man
among them capable of feeling that "they lay between the open jaws
of war," and were not conscious that defeat and death were so near.
"This," said one of them, "is the only foolishness I see about the *pakeha*,
they are quite ignorant and inexperienced in omens."

† The natives lost no men in this part of the attack.

‡ So substantial was the flagstaff that the natives were working at it
for an hour and a half before they brought it down.

one of his guns directed upon them, and by a lucky shot cleared out the troublesome nest, though not before one of his men had been disabled and another dangerously wounded.* This danger, however, had been got rid of only to be followed by another not less critical. A party of the Kapotai men, some twenty in number, had crept along the hillside, and, taking shelter near the barracks, began a sniping fire upon the gunners. Mr. Hector this time appealed to Lieutenant Phillpotts for some aid from the 150 armed men in the stockade, but with no better success. Angered at these refusals, the valiant civilian, who at this stage was almost fighting the whole battle himself, went down to the stockade and called for volunteers to go out with him and drive the Maoris away. Six men responded, and together they made a rush upon the rebels and succeeded in clearing them out. Mr. Hector left his men to hold the post, but no sooner had he returned to the blockhouse than the natives, rein-forced, charged down upon the unsupported guard and drove them back. Again the gun was brought to play upon the attackers, and a stronger force going out drove them farther up the hill, and this time kept them at bay. But Mr. Hector's troubles were by no means over. His ammunition was running low, and cartridges for the guns had to be improvised. Again he went down to the stockade, and there explaining his difficulties the women gladly tore up portions of their garments to give him material in which to wrap the powder. His gunners sacrificed their shirts in the same good cause, and with his two gallant sons,† who acted as powder-monkeys all day, he worked amidst the heat and grime and smoke with a grim determination which no other leader in the garrison seemed to share.

As the morning wore on there was an evident slacken-ing in the Kapotai attack, and at 10.30 a.m. it ceased.

---

* These men were Private Duross, of the 96th, and Mr. Thomas Tapper, the signalman, who had escaped from the upper blockhouse.

† One of these boys subsequently became Captain Hector, of the P. and O. ship *Carthage*.

Lieutenant Barclay believed he had been called upon to
resist a combined assault upon the town and so reported
to his superior officer.   As a matter of fact, the attack
had been singularly deficient in combination, and really
consisted of three separate offensives, any one of which
might have been repulsed, as Kawiti's was, had there been
an officer in charge with sufficient military initiative to
grasp the waiting opportunity.   Kawiti's men after their
repulse at Matauhi might have re-formed and joined
Kapotai in an effort to penetrate the town at its centre,
for no one made the smallest effort to prevent such a
junction, but they did not do so ; they remained inactive
spectators of the fight for the remainder of the day.

Neither was there any attempt on Heke's part to aid
the men from Waikare, who were left to carry on the
attack single-handed.   After the fall of the flagstaff Heke's
followers for the most part grounded their arms and
complacently watched the battle between the soldiers and
their comrades.*   The reason for this inaction on the part
of the two wings of the Maori force is that the attacks
upon the settlement were not meant to capture the town ;
they were merely in the nature of skilful diversions,
designed to prevent a concentrated resistance to Heke's
interference with the flagstaff.   That object having been
achieved, Heke made no effort to throw the weight of
his numbers into the scale against the troops.   He had
accomplished all that he had hoped to accomplish, and
at that moment had no further designs on hand.   What
subsequently happened, when the town was sacked and
burned, was merely the seizing of an opportunity
gratuitously and unexpectedly presented, which completely
corroborates Heke's later contention that so far as he
was concerned the destruction of the flagstaff, and not
the town, was the object of the attack.

* Shortly before the firing ceased Heke had hoisted a flag of truce
on the flagstaff hill, which was disregarded by the European combatants.
His object was to ensure safe conduct for two women who had been found
in the blockhouse when it was taken.   Finding that the firing continued,
Heke sent the women down under the escort of his own brother, telling
him not to return until he had seen them safe with the *pakeha.*

At noon, then, the attack had practically ceased ; the town was intact, and the stockade at Mr. Polack's house, into which the non-combatants had been gathered, had suffered no damage, nor had it even been threatened. The moment was ripe for some concerted action on the part of the defenders, had the man been there to direct it. When the sailors from the *Hazard* returned from the repulse of Kawiti's men they had not re-embarked, but marched to the stockade, and had not since fired a shot. The greater part of the soldiers had also sheltered there, and had suffered neither from exertion nor casualties. A brave show at this stage might have worked wonders. Instead of that, timidity and indecision took possession of their counsels.*

If the conditions governing the defence of the town were disorganized, those prevailing within the stockade at Polack's were chaotic and not more creditable to the officers than any other section of the resistance. Even the simplest precautions were not taken to guard that vital spot — the magazine — in connection with which the grossest carelessness was exercised, soldiers and sailors being permitted to smoke their pipes in closest proximity to the kegs of powder. In the light of subsequent events and later criticism Lieutenant Phillpotts evidently felt that what had happened there stood in need of some explanation, and in his despatch to the Governor he thus put forward condoning circumstances as they appealed to him :—

There will no doubt appear to Your Excellency's mind that a want of discipline existed in the stockade ; but when you consider that 110 men were enrolled who were entirely ignorant of military discipline till within last week, though only sixty-eight remained after the loss of the blockhouse, and that their wives and families were within a few yards of them, and, of course, constantly requiring their attention, causing confusion and interrupting the discipline which otherwise would have been maintained, I trust you will make every allowance.

* The inaction of the leaders has been justified by them on the ground that the instructions to the military were to act only in self-defence, but such instructions should have been read in the light of subsequent events, which could not have been known to the authorities when the original instructions were issued.

GUN USED IN DEFENCE OF KORORAREKA.

When at one stage of the fight Lieutenant Barclay reached the stockade in search of ammunition for the guns he noted its extremely crowded condition. He thereupon suggested to Acting-Commander Robertson, who was lying there prior to being taken on board his ship, that it would be a wise precaution to remove the women and children to the vessels anchored in the harbour. The wounded officer concurred, and this was done, the natives in the meantime watching the process from the hilltops and chivalrously refraining from in any way hampering the movement. There, however, the matter did not end. A council of war was held on board the *Hazard*, at which it was decided to evacuate the place. Who was responsible for this suggestion is not clear, but it certainly was not Mr. Hector, who stoutly protested against this exhibition of weakness in the face of "a mob of undisciplined savages." He even volunteered, with the aid of forty men, to hold the town at all costs and against all odds. In this resolve he was promptly overruled by Lieutenant Phillpotts, who as senior officer of the *Hazard* now seems to have taken command. While this argument was proceeding, some one — no one ever knew who — settled all arguments by surreptitiously spiking the guns which Hector had so assiduously worked in the town's defence.

The evacuation was accordingly carried out and without mishap, the fugitives being taken on board the *Hazard*, the American man-of-war *St. Louis*, the English whaler *Matilda*, the Government brig *Victoria*, the schooner *Dolphin*, and Bishop Selwyn's little vessel, the *Flying Fish*, in which the Bishop had arrived from Auckland on the previous day. The whaler *Matilda* sailed into the Bay while the fight was on, and Captain Bliss promptly and humanely offered every assistance to the settlers which the limited accommodation of his ship would afford. The *Flying Fish* received on board four mothers and ten children. A place among these was offered to young Nelson Hector, who had been assisting at the lower blockhouse all day, but he promptly replied to the Bishop's invitation, "Thank you, sir, but I would like to stay with my father "; and away he went to continue his labour of carrying ammunition to the guns. At the moment the attack upon the town was opened both Henry Williams and Bishop Selwyn were at the Paihia Mission Station, and as soon as it was light enough the Archdeacon watched the progress of the fight through his glasses. Seeing that matters were becoming serious, the Bishop and he crossed over to Kororareka and immediately set to work to attend to the wounded and perform such offices of help and mercy as lay within their means and power. It was while engaged in these ministrations that the Archdeacon made some pointed references to the conduct of Lieutenant Phillpotts, who later on, encountering the missionary, retaliated by calling him a "traitor" to his face.

When the evacuation had been completed the natives came down from the hills and entered the town, which was given up—not taken. Heke, with his usual penchant for Scriptural* reference, said it was delivered to him by a miracle.

At 1 o'clock the most dramatic incident of the day occurred, when the magazine enclosed within Mr. Polack's house suddenly exploded, scattering the whole pile of buildings and two cottages adjoining. Mr. Polack, together with some other persons, were buried beneath the wreckage, but providentially escaped with their lives. Two unfortunate men, however, met their death in the flames which soon enveloped the ruins, consuming a large amount of money and property belonging to the inhabitants. Whether this culminating misfortune was the result of an accident or was the malignant act of an incendiary was not known

* On this phase of Heke's character Henry Williams has this to say : " It is astonishing to see Heke, how close he keeps to his Testament and Prayer Book. I am disposed to think he considers he is doing good work, as previous to his attack on the flagstaff he asked a blessing on his proceedings, and after he had completed his mischief he returned thanks for having strength for his work."

then, and has not since been determined.* A welter
of riot and plunder now commenced. The hostile natives
came down from the hills and, breaking into the houses
and stores, pilfered what they could, and under the
influence of unlimited grog destroyed much of what they
could not appropriate. Seeing this, Lieutenant Phillpotts
had the guns of the *Hazard* trained on the town, and a
few shots were fired into the settlement, which could have
had no possible effect except to exasperate the natives and
destroy what property they had left.†

In the midst of this bombardment Henry Williams
ascended the flagstaff hill and made his way to the upper
blockhouse. This he did in response to a flag of truce
hoisted by Heke, an intimation that the bodies of the
dead soldiers might be removed for burial. These, together with the body of the half-caste child, were, with
the assistance of some of Heke's own people, brought
down and placed on board the *Hazard*. On this mission
Mr. Williams also secured the sword of Ensign Campbell,
which had been left in the blockhouse, and as he passed
it up out of the boat he naïvely remarked : " Here is
something that one of you gentlemen has left behind."
This gentle jibe brought upon him a storm of abuse from
those on board the ship, and he had to sheer off to
prevent personal injury being done to himself and the
friendly natives who comprised the crew of his boat.

Of these later incidents in the day's happenings Bishop
Selwyn has left the following interesting account :—

Mr. Williams and I went on shore to recover and bury the
bodies of the dead, fearing lest the barbarous customs, now
almost extinct, should have been revived by that portion of

* Henry Williams's account of this affair is as follows : " The
magazine on shore had been put in charge of a person who knew not the
care required in such a charge. The powder was placed in a cellar, where
much of the property of the town had been deposited. This person was
observed to be in the magazine with a pipe, which, falling on the floor,
determined the fate of the day and of this part of the Island—at least
for a long period."

† In this bombardment the little wooden church in the town was hit
oftener than anything else, the holes made by some of the round shot
being visible in the walls for many years.

the native force which was still in an unconverted and heathen state. We found the town in the possession of the natives, who were busily engaged in plundering the houses. Their behaviour to us and to Mr. Philip King, of Te Puna, who accompanied us, was perfectly civil and inoffensive. Several immediately guided us to the spots where the bodies were lying, where we found them with their clothes and accoutrements untouched, no indignity of any kind having been attempted. The corpses of those who fell near the church were laid, as we found them, in the burial-ground at Kororareka, together with the burnt remains which we found in the stockaded house. I buried six in one grave just as the sun went down on this day of sorrow.* . . . The state of the town after the withdrawal of the troops was very characteristic. The natives carried on their work of plunder with perfect composure, neither quarrelling amongst themselves nor resisting any attempt on the part of the English to recover portions of their property. Several of the people of the town landed in the midst of them, and were allowed to carry away such things as were not particularly desired by the spoilers. With sorrow I observed that many of the natives were wheeling off casks of spirits ; but they listened patiently to my remonstrations, and in one instance they allowed me to turn the cock and let the liquor run out on the ground. Another assured me he would drink very little of it.† On ascending the hill to the flagstaff we found the staff lying on the ground, having been chopped through near the ground. A few musket-shots had buried themselves in the walls of the blockhouse, but the building was otherwise uninjured. A large body of natives were resting in the valley below, and other large parties were filing off along the paths over the hills. Altogether there must have been five hundred

---

* The soldiers killed and wounded were all members of the 96th Regiment. Those killed at the taking of the upper blockhouse were Privates Miller, Giddens, Jackson, and Ireson. Those wounded were—at the lower blockhouse, Private Duross, dangerously ; in the town, Privates Welton, Gutteridge, Scott, and Marris. All these latter were wounded severely. The total European casualties were thirteen killed and twenty-three wounded ; the natives' loss was estimated at the time at thirty-four killed and sixty-nine wounded.

† On the 14th March the Rev. Mr. Burrows, of Waimate, paid a hurried visit to Kororareka. Of this visit he says : " On my arrival at the Bay the houses at Kororareka were still being plundered and burnt. I saw and conversed with two or three of those who were at their work of destruction. One was rolling along towards the beach what appeared to be a cask of spirits. I asked him to allow me to knock the head in, but he refused. Another had a bottle of lollies under his arm, which he was deliberately feeding himself with, and invited me to share them with him."

men on the ground. As far as I have been able to ascertain they lost about thirty-four men killed ; the number of wounded I could not learn. By request of the Postmaster I went to his house to ascertain whether he could safely go on shore to recover his papers. The house was being plundered, but when I asked the natives in possession to spare the written papers one immediately replied, "I will save them." The private despatches of the Police Magistrate were brought off by Mr. Williams. When we left the beach a little after sunset many of the inhabitants were engaged in removing their property, and some of our countrymen, I fear, were taking part with the plunderers.

So closed what Mr. Williams has described as "a humiliating day—a day of extreme folly."

Next morning, while Bishop Selwyn was engaged in burying several of the victims in the little cemetery at Paihia,* a number of the Europeans landed on the beach in a final effort to save some of their property and effects. To this the natives offered little objection, and, indeed, in many instances showed a chivalrous spirit. Two of Henry Williams's sons, who had come across from Paihia to render what assistance they could in saving the property of the inhabitants, proceeded to a baker's shop where a party of natives was busily employed carrying off sacks of flour. It was suggested to them by one of the missionary's sons that the settlers would require some of this flour on board the vessels where they were refuging. "Of course," said the natives. "Carry away as much as you can ; there is plenty for all, and it is only right that the women and children should have something to eat on board." At young Mr. Williams's request, Te Haara, a leading chief of Kawiti's party, stood sentry over the door while a boatload of this flour was secured and delivered on board the *Matilda*.

Aided by Henry Williams, his sons, and by some of the more friendly natives the settlers were making excellent progress in the recovery of their goods, when in one

* At this service the Bishop was attended by Archdeacon Brown and the Rev. Mr. Dudley.

of those strange freaks of mind for which he was ever remarkable Lieutenant Phillpotts again ordered the guns of the *Hazard* to be fired into the town—fired upon friend and foe alike—thus destroying what little sense of security the Europeans had, and completely sapping the confidence of the Maoris, many of whom were now maddened by excessive drinking. Salvaging operations were thus abruptly suspended, and the treasure - seekers sullenly returned on board the ships, the last European to leave the beach being Henry Williams.

That evening the town took fire, or was set on fire, and the work of pillage, violence, and dissipation went on all night under the glare and garish light of leaping flames.* On the following morning the beach was lined with boats and canoes filled by the more sober Maoris with the plunder of the sack, but no effort was made to retake the looted property.†

As might be supposed, the ships were unwholesomely crowded and dreadfully confused by the invasion of the affrighted populace. Doctor Veitch, Acting - Surgeon on board the *Hazard*, attended to the sick and wounded with assiduous care, but, fearing that the shortage of water and the congested conditions might induce an epidemic, he represented to Lieutenant Phillpotts that an effort should be made to get the patients to hospital with as little delay as possible. So far as that officer was concerned, there was no apparent alternative : " The flagstaff down, the town sacked and burned, what use to remain. We had nothing left to protect, and therefore I deemed it advisable to sail with all despatch."

---

* Six Europeans were killed that night, and it was generally supposed at the time that this was done as a reprisal for Lieutenant Phillpotts's action in firing upon the town, but it is more probable that the victims were rival raiders whose depredations were resented.

† Heke drew a line across the town south of which no buildings were to be destroyed. By this means the Mission Church and Bishop Pompallier's house were saved. The Roman Catholic Church, which was on the hillside, also escaped destruction. Heke, in a letter to the Governor, stated that a chief named Te Aho was responsible for firing the town.

Early next morning the ships drew out of the Bay and headed for Auckland, leaving the worldly all of the settlers in the hands of the raiders,* whilst their homes stood beneath the shadow of the hills, a line of black and smoking ruins.

The following are the official despatches describing the details of this tragedy, sent to their superior officer by the two officers of the 96th Regiment who were in charge at Kororareka at the time. As the capture of the blockhouse and flagstaff on the hill was the main purpose of the attack, it will perhaps preserve the sequence of events best if we allow Ensign Campbell to first explain how he was outwitted by the wily Heke :—

Auckland, New Zealand,

SIR,— 16th March, 1845.

I have the honour to state for your information that on the morning of the 11th instant, at Kororareka, Bay of Islands, I proceeded about 4 o'clock in the morning with a party of five men from the blockhouse where I was stationed, armed, and carrying spades to dig a trench on the heights over Oneroa Beach. We had just commenced digging when we heard firing at Matavia (Matauhi) Bay. We immediately returned, and I remained with eight or nine men on the hill overlooking the town, about 200 yards distant from the blockhouse at the flagstaff. The remainder of the men had got their arms and were putting on their belts on the outside of the ditch facing the town when suddenly I heard an alarm, and some one called out that the natives were in the palisades, and that there was no one in the blockhouse. (I would here remark that the doorway is enclosed in the palisades.) I immediately turned round and saw a number of natives rushing into the palisades and ditches and opening fire on us. I then immediately opened on them, but before a second round could be fired another party of natives advanced by the Tapeka Road with the intention of cutting us off from the lower blockhouse. I was then obliged, seeing a large body of natives in front and another close to my rear, to retire to the lower blockhouse, which I immediately occupied, and

* Heke subsequently told the Rev. Mr. Burrows that those who sacked and burned Kororareka were no more Kawiti's people than they were his. They were natives from all parts, many of whom had since " backed out " of the war.

checked the further advance of the natives. Four of my men
were killed in the upper blockhouse, and one was wounded in
retiring. I remained at the lower blockhouse till Mr. Polack's
house was blown up and the general retreat to the shipping
took place.

I have, &c.,

J. CAMPBELL,

Lieutenant, 96th Regiment.

Here, then, we have in official language the story of
how, while the Ensign and his men were watching the
fighting in the town below, Heke and his braves slipped
into the undefended blockhouse, killed the soldiers who
were sleeping in it, and once more proceeded to cut
down the flagstaff. Lieutenant Barclay, the senior officer
in charge of the detachment of the regiment on the flat
below, has thus related his experience during those exciting
hours while the attack was in progress :—

Her Majesty's Sloop *Hazard*,

15th March, 1845.

SIR,—

I have the honour to report that between the hours
of 4 and 5 o'clock on the morning of the 11th instant Captain
Robertson, of Her Majesty's sloop *Hazard*, with about forty-five
seamen and marines, proceeded from their quarters on shore
for the night at Kororareka, Bay of Islands, to a hill on the
right of the road leading to Matavia (Matauhi) Bay commanding
the town, for the purpose of throwing up an entrenchment. The
morning was thick and hazy. On their departure I proceeded
to the barracks to turn out the detachment by way of precaution,
not having at the same time any reason to suspect a movement
on the part of the natives towards the town. Captain Robertson
and his party had arrived on the hill when they were suddenly
attacked by about two hundred natives. The detachment, having
slept armed and accoutred, arms loaded, formed immediately
in front of the barracks, when Mr. Mobray and Mr. Spain, R.N.,
came to me and begged me not to fire on the party in front,
which I was about to do, as they had been cut off from their
party, and they knew not which, the seamen or the natives,
were nearest to us. I then immediately commenced firing, in
extended order, on parties of the natives who made their
appearance scattered on the hill to the left of the barracks,
towards the Oneroa Beach, and checked their advance on the

barracks. We were also fired upon from the rising ground behind the barracks. On looking round I was first aware that the natives had possession of the blockhouse on the flagstaff hill. At this time I received a message from Lieutenant Morgan, R.N., informing me that a party of the natives were at the church at the back of the town. I advanced in extended order to dislodge them, firing on our way upon the natives who appeared amongst the houses on our front. I then learnt—I forget from whom— that the seamen had nearly expended their ammunition, and turned back towards the beach to join them, when they appeared at some distance on the beach, as on their way to the stockade (Mr. Polack's house), advancing towards us, having effectually driven back the natives, who I observed retiring down the road to Matavia (Matauhi) Bay. I then moved on to the lower blockhouse, which commands the stockade which the seamen took possession of, and in which were the townspeople and women and children. I found Ensign Campbell and his party in the blockhouse checking the advance of the body of natives who were in possession of flagstaff hill and the gullies between the upper and lower blockhouses. I did not enter the block-house then or afterwards. I remained outside on a platform in front where the seamen from the *Hazard* were working two ship's guns assisted by . . . . Hector, Esq., and two of the townspeople (old soldiers, I believe). My party commenced firing—there was room for no more on the platform; they fired from the sloping ground on each side of the blockhouse towards the rear of the building, also on the natives on the adjoining hill behind Mr. Beckham's house. The hill is deeply covered with brushwood. A very sharp fire was kept up by the natives, and was well returned by us. This continued all the morning. Two or three of the seamen joined us. A party of my detachment also assisted Mr. Campbell in the blockhouse —as many as had room. The remainder were in the stockade with the seamen and townspeople, commanded by Lieutenant Phillpotts, R.N.

After a considerable time I went down to the stockade to get some ammunition for the ship's guns, and left Ensign Campbell in charge. The natives soon after ceased firing, nor was it afterwards renewed; it had lasted for some hours.

Immediately after the first attack on Captain Robertson's party in the morning the natives on that side of the town retired in a body from the town towards Matavia (Matauhi) Bay, carrying off their dead and wounded. The body of the natives who had surprised and taken the blockhouse on flag-staff hill were the assailants of the lower blockhouse held by the military. The stockade (Mr. Polack's house) was at no time attacked or threatened ; the lower blockhouse commanded it and prevented such an attempt. A party of seven or eight of the townspeople from the stockade skirmished with the natives on the hill to the left of the blockhouse. With the exception of this, the force in the stockade was not engaged during the day since the attack in which Captain Robertson was wounded at daybreak. Immediately on my arrival at the stockade to obtain ammunition I suggested to Captain Robertson the urgent necessity of sending the women and children on board the ships in the harbour, seeing Mr. Polack's house and cellars were crowded with them. Shortly after they got on board, the magazine, which was in the same house, blew up, and the building was completely destroyed. None of the soldiers or seamen was injured. Lieutenant Morgan, R.N., received a slight wound in the face from a splinter. Whether the explosion occurred by accident or was the work of an incendiary remains unknown.

A council was held on board Her Majesty's ship *Hazard*, when it was decided to evacuate the town, which was done, the townspeople embarking first. The party of military in the blockhouse were the last to embark. During the embarkation the natives surrounded the hills commanding the town, but without making any hostile movement. Occasionally a random shot was fired. During the evening a few of the townspeople, who were, I believe, most popular with the natives, were employed in bringing off portions of their property. In the afternoon of the following day the natives burnt the town with the exception of the churches and the houses of the missionaries. Information was received that they intended attacking H.M.S. *Hazard* during the night. Every precaution was accordingly made by Lieutenant Phillpotts, commanding. The attack was not made, and next day the *Hazard* sailed for Auckland in company with the United States corvette *St. Louis*, the whaleship *Matilda*, and the *Dolphin*, having on board the inhabitants of the town.

Killed, of the 96th Regiment, at the blockhouse, flagstaff hill :—Four privates—viz., Miller, Giddens, Jackson, and Ireson. Wounded : Private Duross, at the lower blockhouse, dangerously ; Private Welton, in the town, severely ; Private Gutteridge, severely ; Private Scott, severely ; Private Marris, severely.

The conduct of the soldiers of the regiment throughout the affair was in every respect praiseworthy and honourable to themselves and the regiment. It is with feelings of deep regret I have to report that the gallant Commander of Her Majesty's

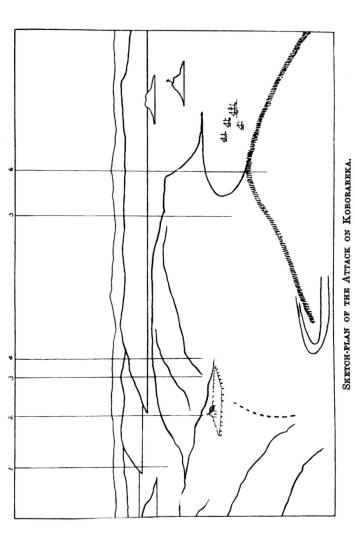

SKETCH-PLAN OF THE ATTACK ON KORORAREKA.

1, Matauhi Bay; 2, Mission Church; 3, British Piquet; 4, Fight with Kawiti; 5, Town of Kororareka; 6, Flagstaff and Upper Blockhouse; – – – – – – Kapotai Attacking Force.

ship *Hazard* fell in the first attack severely wounded. The sergeant of marines and a private were killed, and four seamen. Mr. Tapper, the signalman, was severely wounded, fighting bravely.

I would here notice the very gallant conduct of . . . . Hector, Esq., and the two old soldiers previously mentioned in assisting in working the guns in front of the lower blockhouse ; yet but little execution was done by them in consequence of the natives being so scattered and lying concealed in the brush-wood. Mr. Hector's two boys also behaved most gallantly in bringing up ammunition from the stockade during the heaviest of the firing.

I have, &c.,
E. BARCLAY,
Lieutenant, 96th Regiment, Commanding Detachment.

I am of opinion that had the lower blockhouse, occupied by the military, not been erected the stockade in which the women and children had sought protection must have been evacuated, as it was perfectly commanded by the hill on which the block-house stood. The houses to the left would also have afforded protection to the natives in attacking it. Great credit is due to J. Watson, Esq., J.P., who first suggested the erection of the lower blockhouse and superintended the erection of it. The body of the natives who occupied the chain of hills on which the flagstaff and upper blockhouse stood might have made a general rush, had they been so inclined, on the stockade, but were prevented from doing so by our having possession of the blockhouse.

E. BARCLAY,
Lieutenant, 96th Regiment.

After the destruction of Kororareka, Kawiti retired inland to Waiomio, and Heke to Pakaraka and finally to Puketutu, in the heart of the Mawhe district, there to await developments, and where the latter was to make his next stand.

CHAPTER IV.

IN PURSUIT OF THE REBELS.

THE fall of Kororareka was an event of startling importance. The reality of the disaster, concerning which there had been many rumours, created the wildest excitement in Auckland when the little fleet arrived with the fugitives on the 16th March. As is usual under such circumstances, the tales told by survivors were a strange mixture of fact and fiction, in which the element of fiction seemed more probable than the element of fact. The first official tidings had reached the Governor on the previous day, and Captain FitzRoy, in an effort to calm the public fears, made all haste to summon the Legislative Council, which, being in session, immediately met to debate the grave issues of the moment. At this meeting there were present the Governor, Captain FitzRoy; the Colonial Secretary, Dr. Sinclair; the Attorney-General, Mr. Swainson; the Colonial Treasurer, Mr. Shepherd; Messrs. Frederick Whitaker, William Donnelly, and Theophilus Heale, the unofficial members of the Council. In opening the proceedings the Governor suggested that the consideration of the ordinary business should be postponed, as he was anxious to lay before the members all the information he had received in reference to the events which had so recently occurred at the Bay of Islands. He also wished to have the opportunity of stating his own view upon the measures to be adopted to meet the emergency, after which he would be happy to hear the opinions and suggestions of the members of the Council. The postponement, as suggested, was agreed to. The Governor then read the despatches received from Captain Beckham, R.M., and from Lieutenant Phillpotts, of the *Hazard*. He also stated that there were neither despatches nor returns from the military, but from such information as had come into his possession he proceeded to review the circumstances which had brought about a crisis in his Government. He made it clear that in the attack upon Kororareka there were two separate parties of natives, between whom there was a nominal union, yet their objects were quite different, and upon these differences the tribes had angrily disputed on the night before the attack.

Heke, he said, and his natives avowed their intent was simply against the flagstaff and the soldiers, and that the inhabitants of Kororareka and their property would remain untouched by them. Indeed, Heke had saved the life of the wife of the signalman, who was shot through the back. The natives had captured the blockhouse and signal-station before Heke arrived, and were about to murder the wife of the signal-man when Heke interfered and sent her and her child with the wounded man into the town. The purpose of Kawiti and his people, on the other hand, was nothing but plunder and outrage. The tribes at Kawakawa were heathens, and Kawiti had for a length of time declared his enmity to Europeans. But he (the Governor) believed the other tribes were well disposed ; indeed, they had cautioned Heke that he must abide the consequences that might ensue from any conflict with the Europeans. Mr. Beckham had written stating that some of the tribes had offered their assistance in defending the Europeans against Heke and his companions, but Mr. Beckham had declined the offer, for the reason that it would be very difficult in any action to distinguish friend from foe ; and he considered Mr. Beckham had judged wisely and discreetly. He, for similar reasons, had declined the offer of neighbouring tribes in this district, and he should not resort to such an expedient but at the last extremity. In accepting the assistance of such friends, or professed friends, there was the danger hereafter, when they had discovered our weakness and their own importance, of their wishing and endeavouring, from auxiliaries, to become our masters. He thought, notwithstanding the lamentable event at the Bay of Islands, there was not any real cause for fear or alarm to the neighbourhood of Auckland, and he considered that it would be wise in any measures which the Council might suggest that there should be no display or demonstration which the surrounding natives might construe into symptoms of fear, or of any distrust or suspicion of their intentions. From the time he arrived in Sydney, when he first heard of the Wairau affair, he was persuaded that the best course to pursue, considering the small means of defence or of protection the Executive Government of the colony had at its command, was to avoid every act that should evince our comparative weakness to the natives, and also not to attempt even any measures towards them which we could not fully and practically carry into execution. This had been his view and principle, and they were still the same. When he found himself firmly in a position by sufficient military and naval forces, then he assuredly would be found to be firm and uncompromising. He deemed it most impolitic to add in the least to the present excitement, which most naturally had arisen from this lamentable event, or to create any unnecessary alarm. And most astonished was he that any one could be so inconsiderate as to circulate among the inhabitants such an exciting document as that which he had before him, calling on the public to arm themselves and to form a volunteer corps. He would read the document. [His Excellency then read the placard* which had been posted about the town early in the morning.] How far Mr. John Moore, the printer of this document, was amenable to the law unless he gave up his author would be seen. As to the calumny and falsehood of the concluding sentence, that the Governor had wilfully and wantonly disobeyed the commands of the Queen and Privy Council, he should only observe that Her Majesty, by Her Privy Council, had issued no such instructions whatever. Lord Stanley had instructed him to submit to the consideration of the Legislative Council a Bill for the formation of Militia, which he had done ; but the Council, as was well known, was unanimously opposed to such a measure. But he would ask, had not the Governor feelings in common with the rest of the settlers in adopting precautionary measures to prevent, if possible, tumult, strife, and bloodshed ? Had he no family— no home—no ties—dear to him ? Had he nothing at stake in preserving the peace of the colony ? Was he not deeply responsible in his capacity as Governor ? Every hour he expected troops from Sydney, and he doubted not that ere long there would be considerable reinforcements from England. In

* The author has not been able to find a copy of this document.

every despatch he had written to the Secretary of State he had urged the extreme necessity of the Home Government sending immediate and considerable reinforcements, both naval and military. By the *Nourwahal*, which sailed from this colony in June last and arrived in England in September, he had written to Lord Stanley immediately after the first outrage of John Heke, but to that despatch he had not yet received any reply. It was our great distance from England that rendered it so difficult and which occasioned such a length of time to expire before we could be effectively assisted.

His Excellency then read various extracts from his own despatches to Lord Stanley, all depicting the warlike character of the Maoris, and the extreme inefficiency and weakness of the forces at present in the colony, rendering it perfectly impossible for him either to protect the settlers from aggression or robbery, or to enforce the decrees of justice and obedience to the laws for the maintenance of social order and good government among the native population. Sir Maurice O'Connell, he said, had also strongly represented to the Home Government the expediency of having permanently in New Zealand at least one entire regiment, and Sir George Gipps had likewise urged upon the authorities in England the absolute necessity for similar measures. He therefore hoped that if with the present inadequate means at his disposal he should be able to maintain order and peace undisturbed for a few months there would be by such period arrived sufficient force, both naval and military, as to secure the inhabitants in all the settlements against any further outrage by the native population.*

The Governor then said he should be happy to hear the sentiments of any member of the Council, whereupon Mr. Whitaker rose, and said:—

Although far from wishing to create unnecessary alarm or add to the present great excitement existing, he should avail himself of the permission of His Excellency and plainly state his

* A return compiled by the Chief Protector of the Aborigines and laid before the Legislative Council in 1845 estimated that the native population of New Zealand was 109,550, of whom about seventy thousand were within three hundred miles of Auckland.

opinion on the lamentable crisis which was the subject of their serious consideration. Whatever may have been the cause of the late conflict that led to the disastrous sequel, it was quite clear that the settlement at the Bay of Islands was swept away from the map of New Zealand. To prevent such unfortunate similar consequences here he thought prompt measures should be taken, considering that the best security for peace and safety to their families was to be prepared for any hostile and predatory proceedings on the part of the natives. He considered two steps essentially indispensable : The first was to fix on some place to be fortified and rendered impregnable as possible from sudden assault, to which females and children could be immediately sent in case of any hostile advance by the natives. The other precautionary measure which he would strongly urge on His Excellency and the Council was that the European population be embodied so as to act in unison in defence of the town. Which should be the spot—whether the barracks, the church, or some other—and in what mode the adult population should be assembled so as to act effectively he should not discuss, but leave such details to the Executive Government ; but he trusted not a moment would be lost, for in his opinion it was quite clear that they were at present completely at the mercy of the native population.

After a few observations from all the members, and some discussions as to the embodying of the population, the Attorney-General moved the following resolution, which was agreed to unanimously :—

That the barracks be immediately made impregnable against musketry, and sufficient as a place of refuge for the inhabitants of Auckland, and that the male population of the settlement be sworn in as special constables and efficiently armed ; and that such arrangements and preparations be made that such armed force can be brought into active service at the shortest notice under experienced and efficient leaders.

The Council then adjourned until Tuesday, the 18th March.

The promptitude of the Governor and his Council seemed, in a measure, to subdue the spirit of panic ; nevertheless the public mind was still receptive ground for innumerable alarms, not the least distracting of which was the widely circulated rumour that at the next full moon Heke was coming with a thousand men to attack the town. For weeks the people were kept in a state of ferment by such fears, as groundless as they were persistent. Many, believing that nothing but flight stood between them and annihilation, sold their lands and houses, their goods and chattels, for whatever their speculative neighbours would offer, and then sat down on the beach to wait for a ship to take them to Sydney. Of the social state of Auckland during this trying time perhaps the best picture is that given by W. T. Bainbridge, one of the tutors at St. John's College. This gentleman kept a parchment-bound diary* of daily events, wherein he noted things as he saw them and as they impressed him, sometimes with refreshing frankness :—

Sunday, March 16th.—This morning I saw two ships-of-war and one whaler, besides a great many small craft, anchored in the bay. They were filled with passengers. I went to the landing-place, and the first object that met my eyes was the poor soldiers just returned from the Bay being filed off to the barracks. They appeared disappointed and dejected. They came by the *Hazard* soon after the fight. The other man-of-war was the *St. Louis*, of the United States, commanded by Captain McKeever, who with the officers and company behaved very considerately to the Kororarekans. The *Hazard* had her wounded Captain on board, and the English whaler, the *Matilda*, was crowded with people, for whom provision was made by the Government. Empty houses were engaged for their reception, and orders given upon various grocers, bakers, &c., to supply them with food. I was horror-struck every now and then to hear the ignorant and cruel expressions from various persons as I posted through the town. With varied feelings I attended church, and heard the Bishop preach a sermon appropriate to the present unpleasant situation of this colony. His Lordship appeared downcast, referring in a very delicate manner to the affair at Kororareka, and ended by making a very strong appeal to the benevolence of the Auckland people on behalf of the unfortunate Bay inhabitants. Small settlers have continued to arrive during the day, and, according to the Bishop's sermon, 200 persons are thrown upon the generosity of the public.

* This interesting volume is in the Turnbull Library. Bainbridge was an excellent penman, his diary being written in a copperplate hand, and is freely illustrated with pen-and-ink sketches.

Contributions of either land, money, food, or clothing would
be very acceptable, and he also warned them of being afraid to
crowd or inconvenience their houses.*

Monday, March 17th.—Reports not to be depended upon
still continue to disturb the public, and, amongst the rest,
that Heke had arrived off Kaipara on his way to Auckland.
It is utterly without foundation. I went to the Bishop to offer
assistance in any department His Lordship might think proper.
I was just in time to receive the Bishop's wishes respecting an
address of thanks to Captain McKeever from the passengers
who came from Kororareka on board the American corvette
St. Louis. In the afternoon walked into town and saw preparations were commenced for fortifying the church. The barracks
also are being placed in a state of defence. A trench is being
dug and a breastwork thrown up. A blockhouse is also in a
state of forwardness. It will command the road leading past
the bank from the church. Whilst standing on the beach I
heard Chief Commissioner Spain congratulated on the passing
of the measures in Council for fortifying Auckland and making
various preparations against attack, and that the measures
would be published immediately. At 8 o'clock this morning
the American man-of-war saluted the Governor. It was answered
very irregularly from the barracks. In the afternoon the Governor visited the American, and was saluted on his departure,
which was also answered as in the morning. Everything is in a
state of activity and excitement.

Tuesday, March 18th.—Attended church with my dear wife,
and afterwards strolled round town shopping. One of the shopkeepers, with a very long countenance, assured us that it would
be very advisable to lay in a quantity of provisions, for all kinds
of articles would be, in a week's time, materially raised in price.
I suppose it is on account of its being "war-time." Called at
Mr. G.'s, whose wife we found packing up ready to start if the
aspect of affairs continues as it is. Many others we heard of
have already engaged to sail for Sydney in the *Slains Castle.*
Some young friends who have decided upon immediately leaving
the colony wished to part with their goat at half price, so we
went round to their house and purchased the poor creature and
led it home ourselves very orderly ; so in the midst of confusion
we have added to our cares—a goat. In the afternoon I went
into the church to see the preparations for fortifying it. 'Tis a
sad state of affairs when such measures are obliged to be adopted
—the House of God, in which is read and preached the Gospel

* Governor FitzRoy states that all the most necessitous cases were
placed in comparative comfort before they had been two days in town.

of peace, converted into a standing place of warfare. May the Lord preserve us from beholding such melancholy consequences issuing from the church. The windows are being blocked up with ball-proof boards, and the workmen are requested to do them to-day if possible. Mr. G. told me he was afraid the works would not be finished in time. He thought the natives would be upon us too soon to allow of our making very much preparation. The people seem to be panic-struck, and as the Waikato natives are expected in the bay near our house to wait on the Governor and express their condolence the folk here imagine there is not a sincerely good man amongst the native population. This is quite an error. A great number of them would be greatly improved by living with consistent Europeans, but the example of the Europeans is very evil. Yesterday they were reeling through the town in a state of stupid intoxication. Some of the more respectable inhabitants interfered to prevent the nuisance, but they failed, and, moreover, they were loaded with insult. I am truly sorry our countrymen do not display more care for their character, instead of which they seem to expose themselves to scorn and derision from those to whom we ought to be as patterns of goodness.

The American* sailed this morning on her way, it is reported, to warn the American whalers from the Bay, and from thence to Tahiti to send assistance to us. The Government brig also sails to-morrow morning to Hobart Town for a supply of troops. The mail per Sydney to-day brought the intelligence that in consequence of difficulties concerning obtaining of vessels for conveying troops from Sydney much delay was caused, but 400 men and two field-pieces are on their way, and are daily expected to enter the harbour. Their arrival would cheer the inhabitants very much. The Captain of the *Hazard*, who was shot at the Bay, is better. It is very generally supposed that the Europeans were observed plundering at Kororareka with the natives, and offering for sale various portions of their booty.

Wednesday, March 19th. — That a day should pass now without news is hardly supportable. We have watched the proceedings of some Europeans on the hill at the back of the Government House, and by this evening we see a blockhouse erected. It holds a very commanding position, and will, no doubt, if the Maoris have any evil intentions towards our magnificent city, prove a very annoying neighbour to them. The Volunteers were also drilled to-day for the first time—no doubt a rag-tag and bobtail assemblage. I suppose in due time they will be measured off in regular tallenettes and assume

* The corvette *St. Louis.*

the appearance of a regiment of the "regulars." I wonder how they behaved themselves. One man—I heard it from the best authority—was trudging off to the drilling-ground with a musket on his shoulder, which for the sake of brilliancy was set off with a coat or two of black paint.

The Bishop leaves for Wellington to-morrow. Why, is a mystery. There are now two blockhouses erected in the barracks.

Thursday, March 20th.—This morning I attended on the Bishop, who is up to his eyes in business preparing to depart for Wellington, which His Lordship promised to visit by the end of this month. Nothing seems to change the proposals of His Lordship. He seems to consider the present state of things as affecting colonists only, and not religious operations.

As it is thought that all parties will be compelled to take up arms I mentioned the subject. His Lordship gave me to understand that if the path of duty appeared clear the best way would be to follow it and by no means to shrink from it. Whilst there I heard further unfortunate intelligence from the Bay of Islands. It appears that since the *Hazard* left the Bay plundering had continued, and that Europeans have been massacred. Reports state that nine have perished. It is most probable that either they were intoxicated or otherwise exposing themselves to the revenge of the natives. Some of the bodies were buried by Archdeacon Williams ; some are supposed to have been burnt in the houses. The news arrived by the *Russell,* which left the Bay on Sunday night. She was chartered by the Roman Catholic Bishop, immediately before the late melancholy affray, to bring his most valued goods down to Auckland. The goods have arrived, but the Bishop has returned to Kororareka. His house and the Rev. W. C. Dudley's, with one or two other buildings of no importance, are still standing, as is also the church. This evening the Bishop went on board the Government brig, which is to sail in the night.

Friday, March 21st.—I cannot tell what will be the result if the troops do not arrive very shortly. Many intend to go out of the country, and some may possibly go out of their minds. Inquiries are continually being made, such as : "How far are the Maoris on their way to Auckland ? " "Do you think the fortifications will be sufficiently manned ? " "Is it known whether troops have started from Sydney or not ? " &c.—all indications of fear almost as extensive as their minds will allow. As many as can "raise the wind " appear to be decided upon the "necessity of leaving the country." The colony will certainly be reduced to great necessity if this opinion continues to spread, and it is to be feared that some will take advantage of the

times for eluding their bills. I do not wish to be uncharitable,
but I cannot help hearing.

Saturday, March 22nd.—This afternoon the *Neptune* arrived
and brought the rest of the folks from Waimate connected with
the Bishop's establishment. Happily, the natives are quarrelling
amongst themselves. Tamati Waaka, with a large force, is at
the Waimate for its protection. Heke, whilst on his way to
Kaikohe, was met by Waaka and fired upon. He thought proper
to flee. Whether the differences existing amongst themselves
will benefit the Europeans further than giving them time to
make their escape is very unlikely. All the property plundered
will be destroyed, nor will Europeans for a long time venture
to settle in that district. This evening I went on board the
Slains Castle, which is crammed with persons terrified at the
state of affairs. A man in his eagerness to obtain a passage to
Sydney sold his three houses for £15 ; and another, having a
better knowledge of the value of property, sold a very good house
for his passage-money—namely, £10. I should think they were
both mad. I myself bought a beautiful goat, within a few days
of kidding, for 7s. 6d., about one-third of its value, so determined
are the folks to be off. This morning the Militia were passed,
and all connected with the college and medical men are exempted.

Sunday, March 23rd.—Early this morning or late last night
the *North Star* arrived in the harbour with troops on board—
about 150. They have not been landed yet. I dare say
many of the Auckland folks will attend upon their various
duties with more courage and cheerfulness now that the soldiers
are come. I can only deplore the lack of religious tendency
on the part of the Auckland people, and think the idea of the
church being used for purposes of war repulsive.

Monday, March 24th. — This morning, soon after 6.30,
soldiers were landed from the *North Star*. A schooner also
came in with 60 or 70 troops on board. They were formed
into line on the beach and marched into town. 'Tis rumoured
that Waaka is determined to kill John Heke for the mischief
he has caused. It is certain all the natives in the Bay district
are quarrelling amongst themselves, but it will end in no benefit
to the Europeans.

Tuesday, March 25th.—Strange to say, no news. Reports
are rife concerning a conflict between the Europeans and natives
at Nelson.

Wednesday, March 26th.—The town is beginning to wear a
warlike appearance. I suppose it is intended to make but
moderate demonstrations at present ; by and by it seems they
are going to make a stand at the barracks. They are advancing
very rapidly with the trench round it, and if none else are safe

in case of an attack by the Maoris, those who are enclosed within the trench will be certainly safe. The trench is the same dimension as that at Torres Vedras, in Spain, with which Wellington opposed Soult.*

Sunday, March 30th.—The public is distracted about fighting, and all the conversation during the week is about fighting the natives. Let the Europeans preserve a straightforward line of conduct and they will have nothing to fear from the natives of this district.

Tuesday, April 1st.—The people were thrown into a state of alarm by the firing of guns in the neighbourhood of Auckland. The Militia turned out, but it proved to be nothing worse than some natives paying their last respects to a dead tribesman. It had the effect of causing many people to remember the 1st April, 1845.

Thursday, April 3rd.—Another false alarm. Captain Lewington received a note in the dead of night : " Bring your wife and family into town ; *the natives have surrounded the town.*" I hear the man who raised this false alarm has been imprisoned.

Friday, April 4th.—The day passed without any fresh news to harass the poor people of Auckland, who harass themselves more than reason warrants. The natives of the district are peaceably inclined, and as to Heke's coming here it is all fancy of their poor distracted brains. He has a vast amount of arrangement to make before he can repeat his impudence. However, military preparations are by no means on a small scale among the Europeans. If they continue much longer I think the barracks will be entirely excluded from the public gaze. However lightly some may think of the present state of affairs, the majority appears as if their death - warrant was sealed and fully persuaded they are to be victims of native treachery.

Tuesday, April 8th.—The *North Star* returned this morning from the Bay with 70 or 80 passengers, including some of the missionaries' families. The natives are fighting amongst themselves. Waaka is making war against Heke. There has been a skirmish, with very little loss of life.

Wednesday, April 9th.—I begin to think better of the Auckland people. They appear to become wiser as time advances. The fortifications have been carried on very rapidly. Fears are diminishing, and, indeed, folks are bold enough to say that John Heke is not likely to come yet at any rate. This is a change from what it was a short time ago.

* It was Masséna, not Soult, to whom Wellington was opposed at Torres Vedras.

The missionaries, too, were greatly alarmed and deeply disheartened. Their schools were emptied, their Church services almost deserted, and the minds of their adherents were sadly confused by the conflicting rumours that flew from *pa* to *pa*. No work was being done, because there was no security for the fruits of labour; no crops were being planted, because the sower could never be sure who the reaper would be. The Rev. Mr. Davis, writing from his station at Kaikohe to Mr. George Clarke, said : " The state of the country is truly deplorable. Only the presence of Christ will support us now." Even the Rev. Henry Williams, a man of wonderful moral courage, temporarily gave way under the strain of uncertainty, and to a friend a few days later he wrote :—

It may be said it is only Kororareka that is gone ; but Kororareka was the right arm, and it is my opinion that in three months there will not be an Englishman outside Auckland. Mark my words, New Zealand is overturned from end to end ! Of this I have no doubt, for I feel persuaded that an adequate force will not be sent. How many are ruined by this fatal stroke ? I am sorry, sorry, sorry, and wellnigh overdone.

The peacefully disposed natives were not less deeply affected. How they felt upon the matter may be judged from a letter that was sent to the Governor shortly after the event and published in the *Maori Gazette*. In the following poetic terms the native writer drew a picture of stagnation and despair :—

The wind is from the north. At the head of the canoe the current is rapid, and we can make no progress. Our beautiful island is not yet restored to or to be seen in its former state. Darkness is the covering of the Bay of Islands. The sun shines on that place with a faint light. The *tui* is silently perched on the blossoms of the *kowhai*. The fruit of the *koroi** is concealed by the wings of the pigeon. The warbling birds of the morning are sitting silently among the branches of the trees. The waters of the marshes of Ohaeawai are rising, but are unheeded ;

* The native name for the female species of the *kahikatea* tree (white-pine), which bears berries and on to which in the fruiting season the native pigeons were wont to flock.

their owners are in the dust. The water-springs of Mawhe are bubbling forth, but no one will drink; they are defiled with blood. Alas, what sorrow fills me on account of the haunt of my friends being overrun with blood. "The day succeeds the night; neither day nor night a ray of comfort yields. My tears incessant flow."

These gloomy sentiments were not altogether shared by Governor FitzRoy, who, after the first effects of the shock had passed, settled down to a somewhat philosophical view of the matter. He looked upon the destruction of Kororareka as something in the nature of a blessing — as a visitation of Divine Providence, which had "removed the most blighting house of corruption in the colony." Still, a position so pregnant with lawlessness and fraught with so much social disorder could not be permitted to go by default, though his first inclination was to proceed no further than to pass a sentence of outlawry upon Heke and Kawiti, and to push on with the defences of Auckland. So far as punitive measures were concerned, he was disposed to let matters rest until adequate reinforcements had arrived. But there presently arose in the local Press an unrestrained cry for the immediate punishment of the rebels. The Governor was violently assailed by writers in the papers and by "other thoughtless persons, burning for vengeance and blind to all risk from its hasty indulgence." To this popular clamour the Governor weakly yielded, and, sorely against his own judgment and expressed opinion, he subsequently gave directions for the organization of an expedition, which he placed under the command of Lieut.-Colonel Hulme. He also waived his objections to the enrolment of a Militia. The redoubts and fortified places in the town were strengthened, and a general air of military ardour permeated the place* until the arrival of the *North Star* with the anxiously expected reinforcements. Late in the previous January FitzRoy had written to Sir George Gipps making a further appeal for military aid, stating that "a strong permanent

* As already indicated by Bainbridge.

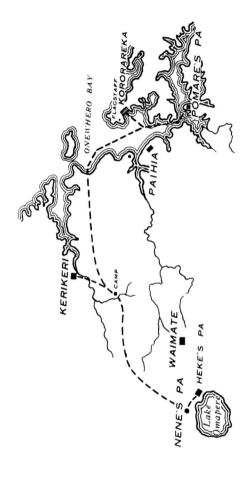

LIEUT.-COLONEL HULME'S ROUTES.

reinforcement of the military in this colony had now become absolutely indispensable to prevent plunder and massacre." This was clear and definite enough, but an unfortunate expression in his letter led Gipps to suppose there was no urgency about the matter. On the 12th February the New South Wales Executive agreed that reinforcements should be sent, but the Governor dallied for a month or more bargaining with shipowners about the cost of transport. In the meantime Kororareka fell, and at a public meeting held in Sydney to sympathize with the former inhabitants of that town the Rev. Dr. Dunmore Lang described this bargaining as " contemptible higgling on the part of the Executive over a few pounds, shillings, and pence." The meeting passed a vigorously worded resolution, and decided to send a strong deputation to Sir George to urge upon him the need for the immediate despatch of troops to New Zealand. Within a few days H.M.S. *North Star** and her accompanying ships sailed, arriving in Auckland on the 23rd March. On the following day the transport schooner *Velocity*, with the heavy baggage, stores, ordnance, and 280 officers and men of the 58th Regiment, under Captain Grant, arrived ; on the 22nd April the *Slains Castle*† came in with a further 215 officers and men of the 58th, under Major Cyprian Bridge.

Though now possessed of a force of some six hundred men the Governor's difficulties were by no means at an end. He had practically no military equipment, and the

* The *North Star*, a frigate of twenty-eight guns, and the *Hazard*, a corvette of eighteen guns, were both on the China Station before being ordered to Australian waters. The *North Star* was sent from Sydney to assist in the installation of Governor FitzRoy and to take him south to inquire into the circumstances surrounding the affair at the Wairau. Shortly after her return to Sydney the native troubles began to loom large in New Zealand, and she and the *Hazard* were ordered to Auckland in response to a request from FitzRoy for some naval support.

† The *Slains Castle* (Captain Dawson) was a barque, and was employed as a transport and hospital ship throughout the war. She was chartered at Sydney to bring over troops, and was continued in the service at the rate of £1 per month per ton. She was a comfortable, roomy ship, and answered very well all the demands made upon her. Prior to this she had been carrying emigrants for the New Zealand Company, and in this service she first arrived in Port Nicholson, 23rd January, 1841.

4—First War.

position of the colony was such that on any day he might have to divide his little army and send portion of it to the south, where there was every indication of an imminent native rising. He also discovered that he stood in gravest danger of losing the services of the *North Star*, upon the co-operation of which he had confidently relied. On the 22nd April FitzRoy wrote to her Captain, Sir Everard Home, requesting him to convey about one hundred and twenty men of the 96th and 58th Regiments to the Bay of Islands, as they could not be accommodated on board the *Slains Castle* with the main body of the forces, those men being necessary to " carry into execution imme- diate measures against the rebellious natives while there is a large party of friendly natives in arms desirous of supporting British authority and while the season is favourable for military operations."

Sir Everard Home replied on the same day, pointing out that on the 12th January last he had received an order from his Commander-in-Chief to proceed to Hong Kong as soon as he had seen the *Hazard*. This order was dated the 24th August, 1844. In direct opposition to this instruction he had proceeded to New Zealand at the urgent request of Sir George Gipps, carrying troops for the protection of the colony. Hearing that Auckland was likely to be attacked by the rebellious natives, he had remained in New Zealand waters until the garrison had been so far reinforced as to render the position safe. Those reinforcements having arrived that morning, he con- sidered the presence of the *North Star* for the protection of the inhabitants no longer necessary. He would, however, most readily comply with the request to convey the men to the Bay of Islands, and give every assistance in landing them ; " but from the nature of the orders I have received I should not be justified were I to continue longer to disobey them by remaining in New Zealand to assist in carrying on hostilities against the enemy."

On the following day FitzRoy acknowledged this letter. He recognized the force of the position taken up by

Captain Home, and did not presume to influence him against immediate compliance with his orders. He, however, felt with the departure of the *North Star* he would not yet be strong enough to take the field, and intimated that as " he did not consider the troops at his disposal sufficient for the measures at the Bay of Islands without the continued presence and active co-operation of more naval force than H.M.S. *Hazard*, it was not his intention to undertake active operations until further reinforced." The presence of the troops at Auckland and Wellington was, in his opinion, sufficient to secure the present safety of those settlements.

The difficulties of the situation were discussed at several council meetings, at which naval and military officers assisted the Governor. In view of Sir Everard Home's imperative orders, it at one moment looked as if the expedition must be delayed, if not entirely abandoned, when the whole aspect of events was changed by the arrival in Auckland of the chief Paratene, who had been sent by Tamati Waaka Nene with an urgent message asking for the immediate assistance of the troops to check the depredations of Heke. Sir Everard Home then decided that the conditions were such as would warrant him indefinitely delaying his departure; and at 6 o'clock on the morning of the 27th April a hurriedly assembled and ill-equipped force of 470 officers and men, including fifty Volunteers under Mr. Hector, set sail for the Bay of Islands.

After the sacking of Kororareka, Heke returned inland, establishing himself first at Pakaraka and then at Te Ahuahu, where he had a small *pa*, and where his successes brought important accessions to his ranks. Still, there were doubters — men who said : " Now tens of thousands of soldiers will come to fight with Heke, and he will be utterly destroyed." This feeling served as a healthy antidote to Heke's preaching and his propaganda.

4*

Against Heke the first native chief to take up arms was Tamati Waaka Nene.* He had heard of the fate of Kororareka, which he regarded as a flagrant breach of the bond for Heke's good behaviour into which he and the other chiefs had entered with the Governor in the previous September. The offender must therefore be swiftly and sharply chastised. To that end he called out his Nga-Puhi fighting-men, and coming from his home at Hokianga at the head of 250 of his warriors he strode into Waimate on the 19th March.† He immediately proceeded to the house of the Rev. Mr. Burrows, the resident missionary, and to him he made a declaration which, in justice to Waaka, should be stated, because it puts in precise terms his attitude towards Heke.‡ This was that he desired neither revenge nor plunder, as has been so often stated, but that his sole purpose was to preserve order and to chastise one whom he regarded " as an intruder and an upstart — a mutineer who flouted venerable leaders and mocked at constitutional authority with a mixture of aristocratic insolence and democratic brutality."§

* Waaka Nene had received a letter from Tamati Pukututu, written from Paihia, calling upon him to come and see *te matenga o te Wiremu* (the death of Mr. Williams) at the hands of Kawiti and Heke. This was regarded by Waaka as an appeal to come to the help of the Europeans.

† To Waaka's aid came also the tribe of Ngati-Pou, who had been driven from their country and almost exterminated by Hongi. They were able to send only forty men, so great had been the decimation of their forces; but they fought bravely throughout the war, for deep was their hatred of Hongi. The first man killed in the war on Heke's side was killed by a Ngati-Pou; and the first man lost by Waaka was a Ngati-Pou. It was by this tribe that Hongi was wounded, of which wound he died a few years afterwards.

‡ In the division of the native people into rebels and loyalists that now took place the wars of Hongi played a prominent part. Owing to his close relationship with Hongi, those tribes who had been most intimately associated with the great conqueror naturally followed Heke, while those who had suffered at Hongi's hands arrayed themselves on the side of the Government. Thus Waaka Nene was constantly accused of fighting to avenge the death of his elder relation, Te Tihi, who had been killed at Hokianga by Hongi, who had there swallowed Te Tihi's eyes. Taonui was also an enemy of Hongi.

§ These words describe the light in which the leaders of the Conservative party regarded Lord Randolph Churchill when he first entered British politics. They are just as applicable to the view taken of Hone Heke at this period by the elder chiefs of Nga-Puhi.

After exchanging salutations with Mr. Burrows he said to the missionary :—

I know you will preach peace, as Mr. Hobbs has done, but I am determined to put a stop to the doings of this *hikaka* (rash) fellow, and you know that in the step I am taking I am only fulfilling the promise I made to the Governor on this spot. That man (meaning Heke) has turned a deaf ear to your warnings as missionaries, and to ours as chiefs of Nga-Puhi. Who is John Heke that he should despise our counsels, who are older than he ? Who is he, or what is he, that he should thus trample under foot the advice of his fathers ? Does he pride himself upon being the son-in-law of the dead Hongi ? We also are related to Hongi. He was a friend of the *pakeha*. Moreover, I have pledged myself to uphold the law established among us, and I mean to do it.

Mr. Burrows endeavoured to persuade Waaka that delay was desirable. He had not yet received a reply to his letter to the Governor, and it would be discreet to await His Excellency's wishes.* To this Waaka replied : " Let Heke stay at the Bay of Islands, where he has done his mischief, and I will wait ; but if he returns inland with his plunder I will oppose him, and he will have to fight his way to Kaikohe."

This, then, was Waaka Nene's attitude of mind when he reached Waimate, and it was not varied by a meeting at which speeches were made, and in which he was strongly urged by Heke's friends to leave Heke in the hands of the Governor, who would administer such punishment as a vindication of the law might demand. A second letter was written to the Governor, telling him of Waaka's arrival at Waimate, and of his willingness, and of that of the other Nga-Puhi chiefs, to keep the pledge that they had given him. From that moment there was no wavering on the part of Waaka Nene and his native allies.

During these early days Heke was deeply concerned at the prospect of Waaka Nene becoming an active ally of the Government, and warmly resented what he called his

* Waaka had already written to the Governor stating that he intended to range himself on the side of the Crown.

interference in the quarrel. Doubting his ability to drive
Waaka from the field, he endeavoured to make peace with
him, but his proud soul would not permit him to accept
Waaka's terms, which were that he should disperse his
force and himself withdraw from the district. Heke sought
to impose the initial concession upon Waaka by stipulating
that Waaka should first remove to his home at Hokianga.
He even sent his wife to Waaka's camp at Waimate to
proffer the olive-branch and to plead his cause. Waaka,
however, was not to be so easily moved. He resisted the
blandishments of Hariata, and in a speech full of simu-
lated anger he denounced Heke's outrages at Kororareka,
declared he would redeem his pledge to the Governor, and
treat Heke as an outcast, and prevent him returning to his
own home. "I am on my own land," he said, "and here
I will remain until I hear from the Governor, unless Heke
first removes from Mawhe." As neither chief would yield
the point to the other the peace negotiations fell through.

Since his arrival at Waimate on the 19th Waaka Nene
had been camped near the mission station, a fact which
was gravely exercising the mind of Mr. Burrows, who feared
that if hostilities broke out between the native forces the
mission station would become involved and might even be
destroyed. Indeed, he had been told as much by Heke,
who frankly advised the missionary that he regarded Waaka's
presence there as a violation of the station's sacred character,
which he had hitherto respected, and that if Waaka did not
remove he would not be responsible for the consequences.
Acceding to the missionary's persuasions, Waaka removed
from Waimate with his whole force on the 25th, and proceeding to Okaihau he there built a new *pa*, from which
he could closely watch the movements of the ambitious
rebel, with whose conduct he was bitterly disappointed and
deeply angered. In this attitude he had in the most
intimate alliance with him the Te Popoto chief, Taonui
Makoare,* and of Mohi Tawhai, of Mahurehure.

* Taonui Makoare—frequently referred to as "Macquarie."

Sallying out from their respective *pas*, Heke at Te
Ahuahu and Waaka Nene at Okaihau, plundering and
fighting went on between the friendly and rebel forces
every day, and although the skirmishes were not serious
Waaka Nene lost some intimate relations and important
men, but Heke lost more, being worsted in every engagement.   Irritated at this, he sent a message to Waaka,
saying : " If you go on this way, when the soldiers return
there will be no one to fight them.   Who will there be
to fight with you, and who to fight the red garment ? "
To this half question, half appeal, Waaka's uncomprising
answer was, " I will fight on till I arrive at the end."*

Much of this native fighting had its humorous as well
as its serious side, the skirmishes often being conducted
in the most accommodating manner.   Two contending
parties, having taken up positions on opposite sides of a
road, were on one occasion blazing away at each other
with tremendous ardour, when, suddenly, a small body
of horsemen was seen approaching.   The call was immediately raised to clear the road for the travellers, which
was at once done, both parties ceasing fire until the
strangers had passed, when hostilities were immediately
resumed.   On another occasion, after being out fighting
for some considerable time without partaking of any
refreshment, one of the combatants suggested a cessation
of hostilities until they had obtained something to eat.
" Quite right," replied the others ; " how can we fight on
empty stomachs."   Both parties then retired and partook
of their food, advancing again to renew the fight at the
conclusion of their meal.

Up to this time no communication had been held with
Auckland.   Waaka's proceedings had been quite unautho-
rized, and were just as illegal as Heke's.   So also was that
of at least two European settlers, Maning and Webster,
who had supplied Waaka with arms and ammunition and

* Though Waaka would not consent to slacken his attacks on Heke,
there was a mutual arrangement by which there were to be no ambushes
and no fighting by night.

not a little military advice, in the full confidence that ultimately his and their conduct would meet with official approval. When the Government at length did take cognizance of what was happening, ample supplies of powder, blankets, flour, and tobacco were sent to aid Waaka in upholding the law, together with a letter of approval which, though well meant, came near to wrecking the whole campaign. The Governor, while recognizing Waaka Nene and Taonui as fighting in the same cause, evidently did not regard them as separate entities. He accordingly wrote only to Waaka Nene. This greatly offended Taonui, who in a fit of chagrin threatened to withdraw his men and leave the Governor and Waaka to fight Heke themselves. His injured pride was, however, soothed by the diplomatic Waaka, who realized the value of his assistance, since at that juncture Taonui had more men in the field than Waaka had. With this temporary irritation removed the two chiefs remained companions in arms until the end of the war.

Communication with Auckland was now regular and frequent, and it was not long before the chiefs were cheered with the intelligence that the native forces would be supported by an expedition of soldiers. This news also reached Heke, who thereupon decided to abandon his position at Te Ahuahu, and commenced building a strong fighting *pa* on the clear ground at Puketutu, not far from Lake Omapere, for, he said, he would fight the soldiers on the spot where the last words of Hongi Hika had been spoken.

When it was finished the *pa* was blessed by the most celebrated *tohunga* at the service of all Nga-Puhi. That worthy gave Heke an assurance of success against the soldiers if he would but observe all the sacred rights and customs of his ancestors. " Fight and pray " was to be the watchword of the *pa*. " Fear not the shot. I will turn them aside, and they will do you no harm," was the encouraging promise the warriors received, the priestly homily concluding with this piece of practical advice, almost

Cromwellian in its mixture of spiritual and worldly sagacity :
" Touch not the spoils of the slain ; abstain from human
flesh lest the European God should be angry ; and be
careful not to offend the Maori gods. It is good to have
more than one God to trust to. Be brave ; be strong ; be
patient."

On the 28th April Lieut.-Colonel Hulme landed a portion
of his little army on the beach at Kororareka, where the
Union Jack was hoisted, the Proclamation of martial law
was read, the guns of the *North Star* thundered forth the
Royal salute, and amidst it all the band of the 58th played
the National Anthem. Fortified by this patriotic demonstration, the troops were re-embarked, and the ships set
sail for Kawakawa, where the chief Pomare, suspected of
disloyalty, was taken prisoner and his *pa* destroyed.

What justification there was for this act of aggression
has never been made quite clear, for the proceeding of the
authorities seems to have been founded on nothing better
than suspicion. In the early part of 1845 some letters
addressed to Te Wherowhero, of Waikato, and supposed
to be written by Pomare, were brought to the notice of
the Governor. These letters being inimical to the public
weal as tending to incite Te Wherowhero to oppose the
Government, it was deemed proper to take immediate
measures against Pomare and secure his person. Accordingly Lieut.-Colonel Hulme was instructed by the Governor
to carry this decision into effect as soon as possible after
arrival at the Bay of Islands.

That night at the officers' dinner-table on board the
North Star " it was arranged to sail at break of day to
Pomare's *pa* at Otuihu, and knock it about his ears and
raze it to the ground."

Both wind and tide proved unfavourable to this enterprise, and, though the men in the boats towed laboriously
all day, it was not until after midnight that the laggard
ships reached the anchorage in front of the threatened *pa*.
At daylight Lieut.-Colonel Hulme was much surprised to
see a white flag flying from the flagstaff in the *pa*, but as

the Governor's Proclamation only authorized loyal natives
to display this colour he decided that he could not recognize it as an emblem of peace from a supposed rebel.
He therefore ordered the disembarkation of the troops
to commence, and when they were landed he sent two
interpreters with a message into the *pa*, desiring Pomare
to come to him immediately. Pomare's haughty answer
to this summons was : " The Colonel must go to me."
He sent a similar answer to a second message and
appeared to have settled down into an obdurate mood.
To ease the situation, one of the interpreters now
offered to remain in the *pa* as a hostage, but Hulme
would not hear of such a concession, and sent his final
message in peremptory terms, that if the chief did not
surrender himself within five minutes his *pa* would be
attacked.

This threat induced Pomare to alter his mind, and
slowly and sullenly he came down to the beach supported
by a few of his people carrying a white flag. Hulme then
had it explained to the recalcitrant chief that the Governor
regarded his conduct as exceedingly reprehensible, that he
must go on board the *North Star*, and that he must
proceed to Auckland, there to clear his name as best he
could from the suspicion which rested upon him.

Lieut.-Colonel Hulme, in proffering to Pomare the
opportunity to surrender before attacking his *pa*, acted
with characteristic discretion. Although the chief was a
somewhat demoralized person as the result of his contact
with dissolute Europeans, the soldier was wise in taking
cognizance of the fact that he was closely connected with
almost every powerful chief in the north, and that his
death at the hands of the military might have converted
all the neutral tribes into enemies of the Government.
It was also an open question with Hulme whether an
attack upon Pomare would not have shaken the loyalty
of Tamati Waaka Nene and brought many of the tribes
in the south to the aid of Heke. Hulme was therefore
anxious to secure the person of Pomare peacefully rather

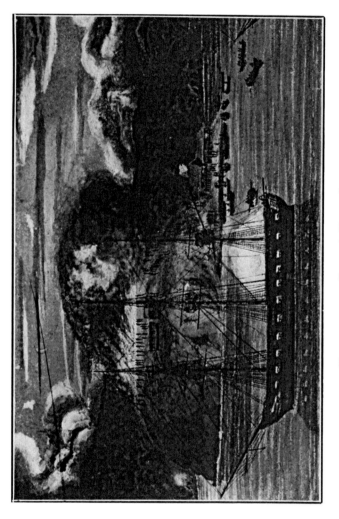

DESTRUCTION OF POMARE'S PA AT OTUIHU.

After the drawing by Sergeant Williams, in the Hocken Collection, Dunedin.

than forcefully, but in the execution of his orders there
was neither the trickery nor the treachery which has so
often been attributed to him in connection with this incident.   As a matter of fact, Pomare did not evince much
reluctance to go on board the *North Star*, and during his
semi-captivity he and his family were treated with much
kindness by Sir Everard Home.

At 2 o'clock in the afternoon an order was sent to the
inhabitants of the *pa* that they must "lay down their arms
and deliver them up within two hours." As an alternative,
the *pa* was to be destroyed; but no precautions were
taken to prevent the natives escaping with their arms to
the bush.   Of this opportunity they freely availed themselves, and at the expiration of the ultimatum three stand
of arms only had been surrendered, the remainder, together
with all the ammunition, being carried away to the
interior.   The order to destroy the *pa* was then given.
The men were, however, first allowed to take what they
found to be of use to them, and looting on a vigorous
scale commenced.   Major Bridge describes as "a most
laughable scene" the spectacle of officers and men running
after pigs, ducks, goats, &c., some shooting them, and
some cutting off their heads with swords.   He likewise declares that the men of his own regiment behaved
splendidly; but he says, "The men of the 96th, on the
contrary, commenced plundering before the fire began or
before any orders were received on shore relative to the
pa being destroyed, and the 58th had to place sentries to
prevent their depredations." At 5 o'clock the match was
applied to the *pa*, which was soon a sheet of seething
flame, throwing its garish light across the Bay and against
the hills as the shadows of the night fell.

Pomare was taken to Auckland, and when Waaka Nene
heard of his fate he sent a strong deputation of chiefs to
the capital to intercede on behalf of their countryman.
As a result of their representations the Governor was convinced that Pomare was not the author of the offending

letters, and that, although they issued from his own *pa*, he knew nothing of them. For the rest it was agreed between the Governor and the deputation that Pomare had not displayed that zeal in the interests of the Crown which was expected of him, but upon receiving from the friendly chiefs an assurance that his future conduct would be unexceptional the Governor agreed to overlook the past. Pomare was accordingly released and returned to his home, which he found a deserted heap of ashes.

For the part he had played in his capture, and in the precipitate destruction of his *pa*, Pomare never forgave Lieut.-Colonel Hulme.

It had been Hulme's intention, after Pomare's *pa* had been destroyed, not to attack Heke, but to follow Kawiti to Waiomio, and for the purpose of this "forward movement" the men had already been provided with two days' cooked provisions. Fortunately, upon the merits of this project a council of war was at the last moment held on board the *North Star*, to which the Rev. Henry Williams was invited. To him, with his intimate knowledge of the country—rugged and wooded in every mile—the scheme presented no prospect but one of failure. He strongly protested against the foolhardiness of advancing between the forces of Kawiti on the one hand and those of Pomare* on the other, through a roadless region, unaided by experienced guides. To his argument that the country was roadless the military men had a ready reply, for they pointed to a sketch some natives had drawn upon the deck of the *North Star*, delineating what they (the military men) believed to be roads, or at least passable tracks. Williams, closely scrutinizing these chalk-marks, at once changed the whole complexion of the situation by pronouncing them to be not roads but rivers, at the same time remarking to Lieut.-Colonel Hulme, "You may go

---

* Those of Pomare's men who had escaped from his *pa* had remained in the neighbourhood after the arrest of their chief and were believed to be ready to take sides with Kawiti.

to Waiomio, but you will never get back." Sir Everard
Home, Captain of the *North Star*, then interposed : " Colonel,
you are going you know not where ; you had better
re-embark the men." Hulme at once saw the force
of the suggestion, and was too good a soldier and too
sensible a man to permit any false pride to warp his
judgment. He accordingly gave the order to re-embark,
and the men were meekly taken back to Kororareka.
Here they met Waaka Nene, who had come down to the
Bay to meet the soldiers. With him a conference was
held and a fresh plan of compaign agreed upon.* The
objective this time was to be not Kawiti, but Heke, whose
new fighting *pa* at Puketutu was reported by Waaka to be
well advanced.

This decision involved the landing of the force at
Onewhero Beach, on the opposite side of the Bay,
a movement which was accomplished at daybreak on
Saturday, the 3rd May, and then commenced what has
been described as " the first march of what was surely
the most ill-conceived and badly executed campaign in
which British soldier was ever concerned."

Hearing that the soldiers had actually arrived at the
Bay, the Rev. Mr. Burrows visited Heke at his new *pa* on
the 30th April for the purpose of ascertaining whether this
new circumstance had in any way changed his opinions or
induced him to modify his attitude. The chief was civil,
but unconcerned. He merely said he would await the
result. He had heard that Waaka, with a portion of his
force, had gone to the Bay to welcome the troops and
to show them the way inland ; he would therefore
closely watch their movements, but he would not desert
his *pa*.

It was one of the official calculations that the distance
to Okaihau—some eighteen miles—would be traversed in
two days at most. It soon became evident, however, owing

* A native *haka* was also danced, for which Waaka Nene's wife acted
as *kai takitaki*, or time-beater.

to the difficulties of the road selected* and the imperfect
nature of the transport arrangements, that this could not
be. No proper provision had been made for carrying either
food or ammunition. Consequently the men had to burden
themselves with five days' provisions, consisting of meat
and biscuits, in addition to thirty rounds of ball cartridge.
There were no tents, no cooking-utensils, no camp equipage,
no artillery, only a few 3 lb. rockets from the stores of
the *Hazard*—a paucity of equipment which told only too
plainly how fatally the British officer underrated the fighting-
qualities of the Maori.   The first day's march — only a
nine-mile one—was greatly impeded by the difficulty which
arose in carrying the rocket gear. The track, rough and
ill-formed, passed over hills, down into deep gullies, over
swampy hollows, marshy flats, and scoria hillocks. Travel
was thus rendered slow, laborious, and even dangerous, and
it was not until late in the afternoon that they reached
a pretty valley with a stream running through it, where it
was decided to pitch camp for the night.

Here the bivouac-fires were lighted, at which the natives
cooked their *kumara*†; the soldiers ate their tasteless meal,
and sought to enliven the cheerless hour by telling stories
and singing comic songs. One who was present and who
witnessed the evening's festivity has left it on record that
" it presented such a scene as possibly had never been
witnessed before. An encampment of British soldiers and
natives sitting in perfect amity around their camp-fires
singing songs alternately."   A man of the 58th—John Smith,
no less—astonished and delighted the company with a song

---

* Some attempt has been made to censure Lieut. Colonel Hulme for
adopting this unsatisfactory route, and equally to blame the missionaries
for inducing him to do so, in preference to taking the dray-road to
Waimate. Although it was true Mr. Burrows was most anxious that
the soldiers should not come to Waimate, and thereby destroy its *tapu*,
there is no evidence that he interfered in any way to prevent them doing
so.   The probability is that the choice of route rested entirely with Waaka
Nene, into whose hands Lieut.-Colonel Hulme had unreservedly to commit
himself on a matter of which he was quite ignorant ; and Waaka, no
doubt, was influenced in his choice by the knowledge that Mr. Burrows
was desirous not to have the mission-station compromised by the presence
of the troops.

† *Kumara* = a species of sweet potato.

called " The Irish Policeman," into which the Irish whoop, the play of the shillelagh, and the Irish jig were introduced. The natives sat round with staring eyes and gaping mouths, and when the song was concluded they gave their warmest approval to this new rival of their own animated *haka*. Intermingled with all this joviality was yet another note which the same observer says produced a most beautiful effect. This was the singing by Waaka Nene and the more sedate natives of the Evening Hymn, and again, as the day dawned, the Morning Hymn.*

At midnight, when all but the sentries were sleeping, it commenced to rain, which for some hours continued to fall in torrential showers. By morning the slender shelters under which the men had crept were destroyed, three-fourths of their food was soaked and sodden, the greater part of the ammunition was rendered useless, and the men rose at bugle-call from their dripping beds, drenched, cold,

* MAORI MORNING HYMN.

Maranga ki te whakapai
Mahara ki te atawhai
A toku Wairua.
Mahara ki nga tino pai
Nga oha kua riro mai
No toku Atua.

The idea underlying these lines may be said to be as follows : Arise and give praise. Meditate upon the abundance of (God's) goodness, O my soul. Think of the many blessings and the heritage we have received from my God.

EVENING HYMN.

Ano te pai e mea ma
O ta Ihowa mahinga.
He tini ana hanga pai
He hui tona atawhai.

How great, O friends, are the acts of Jehovah. His good works are many, His kindness is great.

For these hymns I am indebted to the Rev. T. G. Hammond, who informs me that the Morning Hymn was the joint composition of the Wesleyan missionaries, Messrs. Hobbs and Turner. The Evening Hymn was the work of Mr. Hobbs alone. For the translation I am indebted to Mr. Elsdon Best.—*Author.*

and dispirited. Major Bridge vowed that a more miserable
night he had never spent.*

When the march was resumed a detour of four miles
was made to reach Kerikeri Mission Station, where it was
proposed to give the troops a chance to recuperate. Here
they remained for two days in incessant rain, and on the
6th, the weather having moderated, the final stage of the
march was begun at daylight.† The same wretched roads
and trackless spaces were experienced on this section of
the march, only, if anything, they had been rendered still
more difficult by the rains which had fallen during the
preceding days. Towards evening the force came to a
dense wood through which the Pioneers had to cut a
track before they could pass on. Indeed, the story of
that march was one of incessant and increasing travail ;
but after the men had dragged their heavy loads through
mud and mire all day the worn-out party reached their
final camping-ground at Okaihau, two miles from Heke's
pa, at sunset.

Here some attempt at providing shelter had been made
by Waaka Nene's men, who had erected a few huts,
constructed from leaves of the fern and *nikau* palm, but
their efforts — well meant, no doubt — were slender and
insufficient. A band of Nga-Puhi men and women met and
welcomed the soldiers with their native songs ; blazing
fires were lighted, and the tired redcoats were treated to
a satisfying feast of pork and potatoes.

* Acting-Commander Johnson, of the *Hazard*, who was in charge of
the Naval Brigade, gives the following account of the night's experiences :
" After a long day's march we halted and lit fires. We only carried two
days' grub with us, expecting to make short work of John Heke. We
made our beds of fern, and had an hour's sleep when down came the rain
in torrents. The river overflowed its banks, and we were soon knee-
deep in water. The heavy rain extinguished the fires, and the whole
brigade had to stand upright with only the blanket over the shoulders
till break of day." Lieutenant Johnson was made Acting-Commander
of the *Hazard* after Acting-Commander Robertson had been incapacitated
by wounds at the sacking of Kororareka. He was subsequently superseded
by the arrival of Commander Egerton, when he took up his old post as
Lieutenant of the *North Star*.

† In the meantime fresh supplies of ammunition had been procured
from the shipping.

It is clear from the insufficient force sent out, and more especially from the indifferent nature of its equipment, that the official view of a native *pa* was that it consisted of no more than a rude structure of reeds and poles, which would fall before the first onslaught of British troops. A reconnaissance made by Lieut.-Colonel Hulme on the morning following his arrival at the camp soon undeceived him if he shared these contemptuous opinions. The *pa* was built on a slight eminence, was square of shape, but zigzagged at the corners in order to bring a cross-fire to bear upon its assailants. It had three rows of tree-trunk palisades, 15 ft. in height, sunk for several feet in the ground, each tree-trunk being 5 in. or 6 in. in diameter, set close together. A mass of stone rubble collected from the volcanic debris strewn about further strengthened the foundations of the *pekerangi*.* The palisading was carefully caulked with green flax to prevent enemy bullets penetrating the apertures. Loopholes were everywhere prepared to facilitate the defence, and to render its storming still more difficult a deep trench was dug between each of the wooden walls.

While the troops were marching on Okaihau the Rev. Mr. Burrows again visited Heke at Puketutu to ascertain whether he could be the bearer of any terms or proposal to Lieut.-Colonel Hulme or to Waaka Nene. Heke received the request with quietness and civility, stating by way of reply that he would not begin hostilities, but was content to await the attack of the soldiers. This reluctance to take the initiative arose from a superstitious belief, common among the Maori, that the firing of the first shot sometimes tempted misfortune, and it was precisely this fear that induced the rebels to remain passive while the soldiers were on the march and where they might have handled them roughly had their tactics been governed by ideas less primitive than they were.

---

* The *pekerangi* was the outer fence of the *pa*, of not quite such stout construction as the inner fences, acting more as a screen than a main line of defence.

Though Heke would not yield to the missionary's counsels of peace at this interview, he promised to think over what had been said to him, and invited Mr. Burrows to return next morning to hear his final decision. This the missionary did. Riding over to the *pa* in the early morning he found the rebel camp a scene of energy and activity, every man being under arms; the women doing much of the manual work—as, indeed, they and the men had been labouring all through the night—to complete the defences. In this they achieved a degree of success at which Mr. Burrows could not fail to marvel, and thought almost incredible.

To the missionary's question whether he had anything to communicate to the leader of the British force Heke replied: " I suppose nothing short of surrender will satisfy him, and I am not prepared for that. No; let him come and attack us." That was finality so far as Heke was concerned, and the missionary left him to join the neutral natives and to watch from an adjoining hill the movements of the troops, who were now appearing before the *pa*.

At 7 o'clock on the morning of the 8th, after another night of soaking rain, the bugle had sounded the advance. Wet and cheerless as the night had been, the morning was not less miserable. There was no food, and the troops started out on their two-mile journey hungry, dispirited, and dejected. By 8 o'clock the men were on the ground. A hurried reconnaissance of the position was made by Lieut.-Colonel Hulme and Major Bridge from a neighbouring height, and as they searched the *pa* through their glasses they could distinctly see the natives still carrying in huge bundles of flax with which the faces of the *pa* were being protected. Here a plan of attack was decided upon. It was agreed to concentrate the main force on the face of the *pa* nearest to Okaihau; to push a strong storming-party between the end of the *pa* and the edge of the lake; these men to take up a position on elevated ground behind the *pa*, from which they could rush down when the favourable moment arrived. The left face of the *pa* was to be watched by Waaka Nene and his natives, who were posted between the *pa* and the fringe of the neighbouring bush. The right face was considered to be sufficiently protected by its contiguity to the shores of the lake. The rocket party with its novel apparatus,* which was counted upon more than anything else to terrify the natives, was posted, under Lieutenant Egerton of the *North Star*, on a slight elevation in front of the *pa* about 150 yards away, a position obviously too close, for most of the rockets flew over instead of into the structure.

These dispositions indicate that it was Lieut.-Colonel Hulme's intention first to practically surround the *pa*, reduce the defenders to a state of panic by means of his rockets, and then capture the position by an irresistible rush upon the affrighted garrison. Indeed, so simple did the whole operation appear that some of the soldiers assured their native allies they would take the *pa* in a few minutes and be home to breakfast. The natives had not as yet had much experience of the soldiers' methods of fighting, and while allowing they might be able to do things the Maori could not hope to achieve, they early in the day became distinctly sceptical of their success against Heke. Their suspicions were aroused not so much by the military defects of the expedition — about which they knew very little—as by their superstitious dislike to certain features of its equipment. They commented, not unjustly, upon the manner in which the soldiers were overloaded on the march   but the thing to which they took the gravest objection was the fact that the soldiers brought with them litters on which to carry the killed and wounded. This, they said, was a tempting of Providence indeed— it was coaxing death—and when the soldiers laughingly refused to leave the litters behind the natives said : " This is not a war-party ; it is a funeral procession."

---

* The Maori interest in the rocket was aroused by the rumour which had gained currency that it was a species of consuming monster which would go into the *pa*, where it would twist and turn about in pursuit of the people until it had killed every one.

They then declined to be further associated with it, and with the exception of about forty who would not desert Waaka Nene they proceeded in a body and sat on the side of Taumata Kakaramu Hill to watch what they believed would be the sure and certain defeat of the soldiers.

It was one of Hulme's dictums that "the chances of war are many and uncertain," and perhaps his dependence upon these chances had been better founded had his rocket-fire been better directed. To watch to greater advantage the opening of the attack Heke daringly came out of the *pa* and stood leaning against one of the gates murmuring a Maori prayer the while, and when the first and the second rockets flew wide and high* he sneeringly remarked : " What prize can be won by such a gun ? " † Inside the *pa* the people said : " Thshee ! is that all ? " as they saw the new and wondrous " gun " disappear in a stream of flame into the bush behind the *pa*. The third rocket, by a more lucky direction, cut through the palisade and exploded inside the inner wall, causing considerable consternation. The dogs barked, and some few of the natives rushed outside, but Heke put his people in good heart by sarcastically dubbing the rockets *mata taurekareka* — the bullets of slaves — an appellation that amused them greatly, and the main body of the defenders remained firm and grim.

Slight as the commotion was, Lieut.-Colonel Hulme deemed it prudent to take advantage of it, and sent the storming-party to seize the hill from which they would make their final charge. This party consisted of the Light Company of the 58th, under Captain Denny and Lieutenant Elliott ; the 96th detachment and the marines, under Lieutenant McLerie and Ensign Campbell ; and a party of

* The natives believed that in accordance with his promise the *tohunga* had blown with his breath upon the rockets and turned them away.

† This has since become a saying among the Nga-Puhi people, who, whenever they hear a man boasting of what he can do, smile and say : " What prize can be won by such a gun ? "

ATTACK ON PUKETUTU PA.

After the drawing by Sergeant Williams, in the Hocken Collection, Dunedin.

sailors, under Acting-Commander Johnson, of the *Hazard*. At the double they advanced under a galling fire* opened on them from the walls of the *pa*. All seemed to be going well with them, but just as they appeared to have achieved their object they came suddenly upon a body of Kawiti's men who had been marching all night to relieve Heke, and who, unknown to the British, had arrived on the scene only a few minutes before. Anticipating Hulme's stroke, they had reached the high ground first. Here a desperate struggle of the "hugger - mugger" type took place, the issue of which was for some time doubtful; but slowly the natives were driven back, fighting every inch of the way. Having compelled the retirement of Kawiti, the stormers lay down on their newly won ground, taking shelter under an old Maori *parepare* (breastwork) to avoid being hit by stray rockets and to await events.

An hour of inaction passed, by which time the nine rockets — their whole stock — had been expended without producing the expected panic. Lieut.-Colonel Hulme then decided to storm. With this in view the advance party was protected by flanking supports as they stealthily moved down the hill. As they came down, Heke, addressing the defenders, said : " Now let every man defend the spot on which he stands, and think of no other. I on my side will look after the great fish (main body) that lies extended on our front."

When the soldiers were about to make their decisive rush a friendly native, Hone Hopiha,† called out in loud and excited tones, " Kawiti ! " " Kawiti ! " On looking round, Hulme, who was in charge of one of the flanking parties, saw the rebel chief with three hundred of his followers scarcely 50 yards in the rear. Quietly these daring warriors had collected in the bush after their

* Major Bridge says : " This was the first time I had ever heard a shot fired in earnest. It has a sharp, discordant sort of sound when whistling close to your ear, but after a little one gets accustomed to it and does not heed it."

† Hone Hopiha—anglicized, John Hobbs; no doubt so named after the Wesleyan missionary at Hokianga.

repulse on the hill, and in their renewed strength had again sprung to the attack.

Taking in the situation at a glance, the Lieutenant-Colonel ordered his men, a company of the 58th, to "Right about," "Fix bayonets," and "Charge." This they did to such purpose that Kawiti's force was soon again dispersed, many of his best warriors biting the dust. How this bayonet charge, the first in the history of the Maori wars, presented itself to the native mind has been thus quaintly told by a native chronicler who was present and knew something of its exciting moments:—

A number of the red tribe who had not joined in the attack on our *pa* came at our people with a rush with their bayonets fixed on their muskets, yelling horribly, grinding their teeth, and cursing.* Down went Kawiti's choicest warriors; the ground was strewn with them. Alas, it was a fatal mistake. We never tried that move again. Once was quite enough. But it was wrong of the red tribe to curse us. We were doing no harm; we were merely fighting them.

Signalling by means of flags now took place between Heke within the *pa* and Kawiti without, whereupon about two hundred of Heke's men, led by Tupori,† rushed out of the fortification and made for the few British soldiers who remained on the hill. The storming-party then rushed to succour their comrades, they in turn being pursued by Kawiti's regathering force. The contending parties met on the brow of the hill, and a fierce hand-to-hand struggle commenced. The insurgents sought to drive the soldiers down into the Omapere Lake below; the soldiers strove

---

* "Our armies swore terribly in Flanders." From the above they appear to have done much the same in New Zealand.

† Tupori, having observed that Kawiti had twice been engaged in hand-to-hand conflicts with the soldiers and had thereby elevated his name as a warrior, was anxious to emulate his example. He therefore called for volunteers to make this sortie, and so intrepid was their charge that they reached the breastwork behind which the British were sheltering. When being driven back Tupori was wounded, but managed to get safely into the *pa*. "Great is the courage of Tupori," says an admirer. "He has made his name heard as that of a *toa*."

to maintain their higher ground—redcoats, marines, brown skins, and sailors mingling in a desperate, swaying, clashing mass.

Gradually the British were able to get together in more solid formation, and then, taking to the bayonet again, they, with a cheer, made a supreme effort and succeeded in forcing the enemy down the sloping ground. With still another cheer they got them on the run, the chase and the slaughter continuing until the foot of the hill was reached. Here the fight waxed hot again, and here the greater part of the British casualties were sustained, for as the soldiers pressed upon Kawiti they came under a withering fire from the *pa*, and their dead and wounded fell before the relentless hail of lead and could not be removed. Fortunately, the conflict was not long maintained, the novel experience of the bayonet cooling the ardour of the Maori for the mêlée, and they gradually withdrew, leaving Kawiti—unknown to the British—among the wounded on the field. An eye-witness* has said of this encounter :—

Kawiti's people were gallantly charged by the "regulars," and a terrible slaughter took place. I was standing near a group of friendly natives at the time, and they all allowed that our men engaged in that charge acted most gallantly. From all I can gather of the opinions of the natives in the engagement I am persuaded they feel the complete and utter superiority of our countrymen. Of the soldiers and sailors especially they speak in the highest terms of praise. The consequence of this engagement, in the opinion of the natives, is this : that Kawiti is broken and dispersed ; or, to use his own language, he is "like a canoe bottom upwards."

The *pa*, however, was still untaken, and the incidents of the last hour had made it impossible to surprise it. The storming-party therefore returned to the hill, hoping that some fortuitous circumstance would give them their chance, but that chance never came. For four hours they

* James Merrett, the interpreter.

waited while the main body kept up a fruitless fire upon the *pa*, which was sharply returned. All parties were now firing. "Lead whistled through the air in all directions; the whole country seemed on fire, and brave men worked their work." When it became evident that the attack had failed, those who formed the storming - party were faced with the problem of regaining the position from which they had marched earlier in the day. In effecting this movement they had to recross the open ground on the margin of the lake, this time hampered not only by a biting fire from the *pa*, but their difficulties were increased by the duty of carrying their wounded, and the operation could not be effected until they had received the assistance of a supporting party under Captain Grant.

The main body reached, the abortive attempt to take Puketutu *pa* ended. The rebels remained masters of the situation at the end of a strenuous day, and Lieut.-Colonel Hulme, with something added to his experience as a soldier, was compelled to march his men back to the camp. Here the prospect was rendered still more discouraging by the discovery that the commissariat had failed. The weary, hungry men had therefore no recourse but to lie down supperless on their beds of fern. Rain, mingled with driving sleet, then began to fall, and the troops lay all night drenched to the skin and chilled to the bone. Not till they had undergone a fast of thirty hours did they get anything to eat. Then a wandering bullock was caught and slaughtered —*sans* leave—*sans* ceremony.

The roll-call showed that thirteen of the British had been killed and thirty-nine wounded,* of which the 96th's share was five killed and thirteen wounded. The native losses were not ascertained, but their killed were certainly much greater, probably from twenty to thirty, one of their

---

* One soldier who was wounded was left beside the lake. Next morning two slaves found him and, pretending to be friends, persuaded him to give up his gun; then seizing him held his head under the water until he was dead.—*Native account.*

number being Kawiti's son,* the second he had lost in the war.

Heke behaved with the utmost propriety towards the dead, which perforce had been left where they fell. He forebade his people to strip them of their clothing, and, summoning the Rev. Mr. Burrows, he saw that they received a Christian burial, even if their grave was the very ditch from which a few hours before they had leaped to storm. A day's rest at the camp and the troops were marched back to the mission station at Kerikeri,† where the hale were fed and the wounded cared for. Thence they proceeded down the river in boats, and re-embarked on board the *Hazard*, the *North Star* and *Slains Castle* not having arrived from Paihia.

Governor FitzRoy has been severely blamed for this ill-thought-out and ill-organized expedition. Whether the blame justly rested with him may well be a matter of doubt, but certainly some one laid themselves open to censure, for the equipment of the force — especially the absence of artillery—showed unpardonable ignorance of the strength of a Maori *pa*, to say nothing of an equally unpardonable contempt for the Maori as a fighter. Once the expedition was on its way it would appear that Lieut.-Colonel Hulme made the best of his indifferent circumstances, and it is incontestably clear that his officers and men — wet, cold, and hungry as they were — showed fine qualities of endurance and unflinching courage under the exacting conditions into which the hurried despatch of the expedition suddenly precipitated them.

* Taura was the name of Kawiti's son who was killed at Puketutu. He had not been very keen for the fight at Kororareka, and his father had not seen him where he expected to find him, in the front ranks of the combatants. When, however, the town was being sacked Taura was well to the fore in sampling the grog, and his father bitterly reproached him for being so ready to drink when he was so loath to fight. The reproof cut the young man to the quick, and when the clash came at Puketutu he rushed into the thick of the fight and fell among the slain.

† On Saturday, the 10th, a grenadier of the 96th was buried at the camp, and a sailor belonging to the *Hazard*, who died during the night, was buried on the Sunday morning, before the force commenced their march back to Kerikeri.

On Monday, the 12th May, the *North Star* moved to
Auckland with Lieut.-Colonel Hulme, who was carrying
despatches to the Governor, and the *Hazard*, *Velocity*, and
Slains Castle came to anchor off Kororareka. The troops
remaining at the Bay were left under the command of
Major Bridge, who previous to parting with Lieut.-Colonel
Hulme had been told that he might exercise his own
discretion as to whether or not he attacked a *pa* of
the Kapotai tribe situated on the Waikare River, the
inhabitants of which were known to be in possession of
much of the plunder taken from Kororareka. The Major
could not resist the temptation to have a little war of his
own, and decided that he would make the attack. The next
few days were spent in perfecting his arrangements. He
obtained a description of the river from Mr. Clendon, the
Police Magistrate ; he sent a man named Cook to reconnoitre the *pa*, and collected a flotilla of small boats in
which to convey the troops to the scene of action. The
final touches were put to his arrangements on board the
Hazard on Thursday, the 15th, when he held a consultation
with the ship's officers, Mr. Clendon, and Repa, a Nga-
Puhi chief. It was then arranged to embark the troops
that night at 11 o'clock in order to take advantage of the
tide, reach the *pa* before daylight, surround it, and by the
element of surprise prevent the escape of the inhabitants.
For this purpose Acting-Commander Johnson, of the *Hazard*,
lent a 12-pounder carronade, and men under a midshipman
to work it. An armed seaman was put in each boat to
steer, the intention being that these men should also act
as a guard over the boats when the troops had been
disembarked. In this expedition Major Bridge employed no
men of the 96th, for whom he appears to have had no
love, but took the sergeants and 192 of the rank and
file of his own regiment, eight Maoris, and four Volunteers
to act as guides. This comprised the European section of
the force, which was to be accompanied in their canoes
by 100 native allies under Repa and Mohi Tawhai, two of
Waaka Nene's most trusted lieutenants. The seamen were

placed under Lieutenant Phillpotts, who also had charge
of the flotilla, which quietly left the ship's side at midnight amidst sharp showers of rain and the watery beams
of a waning moon. All went well while the boats were in
the open Bay or following the main course of the river,
but when an attempt was made to navigate the narrow
creeks the flotilla was quickly thrown into the greatest
confusion. Some of the boats, by wild steering, were run
aground on the mud-flats ; others for lack of competent
guides went off in a wrong direction, thereby dangerously
dispersing the force. As they went they startled the wild
ducks nesting in the river. These, flying screaming over
the *pa*, alarmed the inhabitants, destroying the element
of surprise so essential to such a venture. At this point
Major Bridge had to confess that the whole business was
" most infamously managed."

    " The consequence was," he says, " that when I reached
the shore where the main body was to land I had only about
twenty men there. Thirty more shortly afterwards came up
in another boat, and with these few men I found myself close
under the stronghold, and could hear the natives talking and
directing each of them to be firm and stick to their *pa* and
fight to the last. I had directed a party of fifty, under Captain
Grant and a subaltern, to go up a creek to the left of my
position and proceed towards the right of the *pa*, my intention
being to surround the left of it and to wait on the inland side
and cut off the enemy's retreat ; but I could not tell whether
the boats containing his party had reached their proper destination or not. I had therefore to send the friendly natives,
under Repa and Rivers (Rewa), round to the left of the *pa* to
flank it, while I drew up my small band on its front under
cover of a low bank and some scrub. This was just at dawn of
day, and I sent Pine* and another person down to the creek to
endeavour to get up other boats, or bring up men out of those
boats that were aground on the mud-flats. Some men landed
lower down and marched through the swamp and undergroves
and joined me shortly after daylight. At this time the inhabitants of the *pa* were at prayers, or had about finished. They
had fired a few shots, too, while Repa and his men were creeping
round under cover. In about half an hour we had a few more

* Doctor Pine, of the 58th Regiment.

shots at intervals, and then a shout, and down rushed the Maoris towards the *pa*, crying out that the enemy was running away, and before we could follow and get into it they had already set a hut on fire and proceeded through the *pa* in pursuit of the flying Waikares. They kept up their fire all the while, and this sort of fighting continued for some hours between the natives while we were plundering and burning the *pa*. There was little of any value found in it. The chief things of use to the men were pigs, potatoes, and onions. We had scarcely finished the destruction of the *pa* when one of the Maoris (Moses) came in and said that his men were being beaten back by the enemy and wanted ammunition and support from me. I gave them ammunition, and sent the Grenadier Company back with him. At the same time I disposed of the rest of my men so as to prevent our being surprised and attacked on our flanks. Went down to the boats to see that all was right there, and ascertain when the tide would serve to embark the men again and return to the ship. I found it would be an hour or two before it would be high enough. Found the gun mounted on the bank, and Pine there attending to the wounded Maoris. Saw him cut a ball out of the breast of poor Jack Robinson, the fellow who behaved so well at Heke's *pa* and saved all our chaps from being cut off by Kawiti.* He bore it most manfully. On returning to the *pa* found that Captain Grant had brought his company back, as he could not act in the war so high up, and his men were exposed for nothing. The fight seemed still to continue pretty hotly between the natives. I therefore went forward and directed Captain Thompson, who was in advance, to send a line of skirmishers up to the edge of the hill, when the Maoris were to keep up a fire with them on the enemy, and this soon had the desired effect of reducing their fire and driving them off. I then began to conduct our retreat, as the tide was sufficiently high, and was fortunate enough to bring all my men off into the boats and get them safely down the river and on board the ships by half past three o'clock. We had no men killed. Our Maoris had two killed and six or seven wounded. We were all in a pretty dirty state, having had to wade through the muddy swamp to and from the boats, and were heartily glad to get on board ship again."

The old Nga-Puhi chief who narrated the story of " The War in the North " to F. E. Maning gives a vivid account of the native fighting in this attack which is not

---

* The author has not been able to trace any other reference to this incident, either in the Major's diary or elsewhere.

mentioned in any of the European reports. In order to make this history of the war as complete as possible it is here incorporated in full :—

After the Kapotai *pa* had been plundered and burnt, Waaka and his men went in pursuit of the Kapotai, who had retreated into the forest, but the soldiers remained behind on the clear ground near the *pa*. Waaka, Mohi, and Repa went into the woods with three hundred men, followed the Kapotai, and overtook them. When Kapotai perceived they were followed their anger was very great, so they turned and fought with fine courage against Waaka. Waaka was not able to beat them, so they remained a long time fighting in the forest. But Hauraki,* the young Hikutu chief, had, with his thirteen men, taken another path, and he met the young chief of the Kapotai, who had with him sixty men, and they were both young men and fighting for a name, so a desperate fight commenced. Hauraki and his thirteen men thought not of the light of the sun or the number of the enemy ; their only thought was of war and to elevate their names. It was a close fight, and whenever the rifle of Hauraki was heard a man fell, and soon he had killed and wounded several of the Kapotai, who began to fall back. Then Hauraki called out to the retreating Kapotai : " Fly away on the wings of the wood-pigeon, and feed on the berries of the wood, for I have taken your land." Then a certain slave of Kapotai said : " That is Hauraki, a very noble-born man. He is a chief of Te Hikutu, and of Te Rarawa, and of Ngati-Kuri."

Now, when Hari, the young Kapotai chief, heard this he cried aloud to Hauraki, saying, " Swim away on the backs of the fish of the sea, there is no land for you here." Then these two young warriors drew nearer to each other. Hauraki had just loaded his rifle, but the caps which he had were too small, and he was a long time trying to put on a cap. While he was doing this Hari fired at him, and the ball struck him on the breast and passed out at his back ; but so great was his strength and courage that he did not fall, but took another cap and fixed it, and then fired at the Kapotai chief, and the ball struck him on the side under the armpit and went out at the other armpit. So Hari staggered and fell dead. When Hauraki saw this he said, " I die not unavenged," and then sank gently to the ground. His people seeing this, two of them led him

* Hauraki and thirteen of his men had accompanied the British force down to the Bay to assist in carrying the wounded, the balance of his force remaining at Okaihau, as it was not expected there would be any more fighting for some days.

away towards the rear. The Kapotai also carried away their chief, and then, enraged at his death, rushed upon Hikutu, who were only eight in number, the rest having been killed or wounded. These eight were *tino tangata* (practised warriors), but were too few in number, and had lost their chief ; so when the Kapotai rushed upon them they lost heart and fled, and the Kapotai chased them, and soon the foremost of the flying Hikutu overtook Hauraki and the two men who were leading him off. Then Hauraki said : " Do not remain with me to die, but hide me in the fern and escape yourselves, and go to my relation Waaka and tell him to muster all his people and come and carry me off." So they all pressed their noses to the nose of Hauraki, one after another, and tears fell fast, and the balls from the guns of Kapotai whistled round their heads ; so while some returned the fire of the enemy, others hid Hauraki in the long fern. When this was done they all fled, and escaped with great difficulty ; for while they were hiding Hauraki the Kapotai had surrounded them, and they would never have escaped at all but for the great courage of Kaipo and Te Pake, Hauraki's cousins, who broke through the Kapotai and opened a way for the rest.

Now, when Hauraki's eight men got on the clear ground they found that the soldiers were getting into the boats to go away, and Waaka, Mohi, and Repa had just come out of the forest from fighting with the Kapotai. Hauraki's cousins ran to Waaka and said : " Our friend is left behind wounded in the forest, and likely to be taken by the Kapotai." Waaka was very much dismayed when he heard this, and he and Mohi ran to the chiefs of the soldiers and desired them to remain for a while till they could rescue Hauraki ; but the soldiers could not understand what Waaka meant, for the speaker of Maori (the interpreter to the force) had already gone away in one of the boats, and there was great confusion, every one trying to get away, and Waaka's men were also getting into their canoes and going away ; boats and canoes were running foul of each other, and the creek was choked with them. Then came the Kapotai in great force with their allies out of the forest and commenced firing on the departing *taua* from a distance of about two hundred fathoms, so that the soldiers and Waaka got away and returned to Kororareka, and left Hauraki lying alone in the forest, for their bellies were full of fighting. So he lay there till midnight, and the night was wet and cold, and he kept continually thinking what a disgrace it would be to his family if he should be taken alive. And as he lay thus he saw the spirit of the greatest warrior of all his ancestors, who said

to him : " Arise ! Shall my descendant be taken alive ? " Then
Hauraki said : " I am a mere man ; not like unto my ancestors,
half god and half man." Then the spirit said : " In the mind
is the strength of the body. Arise!" So Hauraki arose and
travelled a long way in the night till he found a small canoe by
the river-side ; then he pulled down the river towards the Bay
of Islands till the canoe upset ; then he swam ashore, and when
he got there he was almost dead; but near to where he landed
was the house of a *pakeha*, and the mother of this *pakeha* was
Hauraki's cousin, so that the *pakeha* took him and concealed
him in the house, and took care of him, and before the middle
of the day a party of Waaka's men arrived there in search of
him. So they took him to the Bay of Islands, and the doctors
and the soldiers did what they could to cure him, but without
success. So his tribe, who had arrived at Okaihau, carried him
home to his own place at Hokianga, where he died.*

When Hauraki died and his body lay at Whirinaki, to be
seen for the last time by his relations, there was a great
gathering of the Rarawa and Nga-Puhi to fulfil the last rites
due to a chief. And when the *pihe*† had been sung, then the
chiefs rose one after another to speak in praise of the dead.
This was the speech of Te Anu, he who is known as having been
in his youth the best spearsman of all the Nga-Puhi tribes.
Bounding to and fro before the corpse, with his famous spear
in his hand, he spoke as follows : " Farewell, Hauraki ! Go,
taking with you your kindness and hospitality, your generosity
and valour, and leave none behind you who can take your
place. Your death was noble ; you revenged yourself with
your own hand ; you saved yourself without the help of any
man. Your life was short ; but so it is with heroes. Farewell,
O Hauraki, farewell.‡

After reading Lieut.-Colonel Hulme's despatches and
considering the various reports upon the campaign which
subsequently reached him, Governor FitzRoy was disposed

---

* Hauraki was the brother-in-law of the late Judge Maning. His
death was a great grief to Maning.

† The *pihe* was a song sung over the bodies of the slain. Many of
the words and allusions were no longer understood, and doubtless formed
part of an old hieratic long forgotten.

‡ Hauraki was taken to Te Ramaroa, a cave in the mountains behind
Whirinaki, where his ancestors are buried. When Heke heard of the death
of Hauraki he said : " Now, if I am slain in this war it matters not, for
there is no greater Nga-Puhi chief than Hauraki." What Heke said was
true, but he said it to please Te Hikutu, for Heke is a man of many
thoughts.—*Native account.*

to take a highly optimistic view of the situation. He believed Heke and Kawiti had "fled to the woods "; that their followers were "beaten and dispersed," and he warmly congratulated the Commanding Officer on his supposed success, the beneficial effects of which, he was inclined to think, would be greater and more lasting than might at first be considered probable.

"I have," he wrote to Lieut.-Colonel Hulme, "no hesitation in asserting that mutual good feeling between the two races has been much increased by these proceedings; that each holds the other in greater respect, and a more kindly intercourse will be the consequence. . . . I do not for a moment lose sight of the difficulties and extreme risks which you encountered in such bad weather, without means of transport, without tents, without guns, and by no means certain how far the natives said to be friendly would act up to their professions. On behalf of the colonists, the officers of the Government, and myself, I now beg to offer you, and with yourself Major Bridge and the officers and men under your command, my very cordial and earnest thanks for the public service rendered so willingly and with so much zeal at the most critical period that has yet occurred in the existence of the colony."

No praise which the Governor could lavish on the troops could overlaud the bravery, grit, and devotion with which they had executed his orders, and no thanks he could convey to them on his own or on the colonists' behalf would have been undeserved, but if his deductions from what he had heard of the proceedings at Puketutu led him to conclude that either Heke or Kawiti were fugitives or were in the least chastened in spirit by their encounters with the soldiers he was but paving the way for another official miscalculation, the error of which was soon to be rudely exposed.

With the departure of the soldiers Heke abandoned his untaken *pa* at Puketutu and returned to his old fort at Te Ahuahu to be near his cultivations. The loyal chief who remained to watch him was Taonui, who, hearing that the greater part of Heke's followers had gone to Ohaeawai to kill cattle for food, took sixty men with him

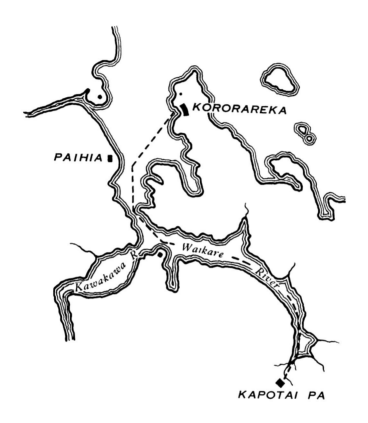

MAJOR BRIDGE'S ROUTE TO KAPOTAI PA.

and on a dark and rainy night captured Te Ahuahu *pa* by surprise, the people in it firing a few shots only and then retreating. With this *pa* the friendlies secured large stores of provisions, as well as a strategical position which opened the road to Okaihau. Waaka Nene then came over and joined Taonui in the captured *pa*, it being decided that they should remain there until the soldiers returned from Auckland.

On Sunday, the 18th May, Major Bridge received a letter from Waaka Nene, telling him that Heke had deserted his *pa* at Puketutu on the day that the troops had marched away ; that he had since returned and burned it down, and was now busy building another fortified *pa* seven miles farther inland. Waaka begged the Major to bring the soldiers back to attack Heke before this new fortification was rendered impregnable, urging that he himself was not in a position to do so, since so many of his men and two of his principal chiefs were still at the Bay. Major Bridge had no instructions to resume operations against Heke on a large scale, and before he could communicate with his superior officer, the *North Star*, *en route* to Sydney, arrived with orders that he should immediately return with his men to Auckland. This he was proceeding to do on the 22nd, when, as the *Velocity* and her consort, a whaler, were beating out, Henry Williams came on board with information that Heke had been to see him, and that he thought the rebel was disposed to make peace. He (Mr. Williams) had ventured to make certain proposals to him which Heke was considering, and he asked the Major to remain for the purpose of receiving the chief's final answer for conveyance to His Excellency the Governor. To this arrangement the Major consented, and ordering the *Velocity* and the whaler to proceed to Auckland with the troops he returned on shore with the missionary. Here he found that what Mr. Williams had suggested as some recompense for the upheaval Heke had caused was that certain places were to be vacated by the natives and ceded to the Crown ; horses, boats, and other property

5—First War.

belonging to the Europeans were to be restored; the
flagstaff to be paid for, "staff for staff"; the rebel
leader himself to retire to Whangaroa for two years, after
which, if he remained quiet, the Governor would receive
him.

On the following day the *Velocity* and the whaler put
back owing to stress of weather, and in attempting to
reach port the former ran ashore, but was floated off
without serious damage.   Close upon the heels of the
Velocity came the French frigate *Le Rhin*, commanded by
Captain Bérard, then the officer in charge of the French
station at Akaroa.   Six weeks after the fall of Kororareka had the tidings of that disaster filtered through to
the South, so slowly did news travel in those days, and
on the 12th May Captain Bérard, after strengthening his
local defences, sailed for the North for the purpose of
tendering such aid to Bishop Pompallier and his French
priests as it might then be within his power to give.
Fortunately, he found that neither they nor their property
had been molested, and that the mission, though necessarily
disturbed, was far from being destroyed.   Immediately
upon *Le Rhin's* arrival the Bishop went on board, dined
with the Captain, and naturally had much of interest to
relate, to which the Captain was not less interested to
listen.   Later that day he landed, and in company with
the Bishop walked through the devasted town, of which
he has thus left his impressions :—

Along with Mgr. Pompallier I visited the ruins of the town
and the surrounding heights. It was a sad sight. Of all these
habitations which formed the most ancient European settlement
in New Zealand there remained only the brick chimneys, most
of which were entire, but some half tumbled down. While
walking through the midst of the general destruction one met
remains of all sorts of utensils, heaps of broken glass, and
pieces of earthenware and of iron used in the structure of
houses, and a large quantity of cask-hoops. The natives were
still searching for nails. They had taken care before the sack
to remove all the lead from the roofs, in order to make bullets
with it. Of the barracks nothing remained but the cellars where

the ammunition had been stored. It has never been explained how this ammunition caught fire. The Maoris say it was not done by them. Some of the inhabitants say it was done of necessity, since there was no other means of determining the embarkation of all the civil population and the troops.

Scarcely had *Le Rhin* anchored than an officer from the *North Star* boarded her to offer the services of her Commander, and shortly afterwards the frigate made the stranger a salute of nine guns, to which the Frenchman replied, gun for gun. Captain Bérard then sent an officer on board the British vessel to thank Sir Everard Home and to offer him his services " whether on the spot or in the distant archipelagos through which *Le Rhin* was soon to pass on her way to France." Sir Everard himself went on board *Le Rhin* that evening and informed Captain Berard that on the next day, the 24th, he was to adorn his vessel with flags and fire a salute in honour of the birthday of Her Majesty the Queen of England.

" I told him," says Captain Bérard, " that I desired to associate myself with them in this display. In fact, I put out flags, as the two corvettes did, and at midday I fired a salute of twenty-one guns. The soldiers of the 58th Regiment, who were passengers on board the two merchant vessels, replied with cheers, and their band played the ' Marseillaise ' and the ' Parisienne.' "

The day was beautifully fine, and the Bay was made bright with every rag of bunting that ships and shore could provide. Major Bridge had a visit from the local chief Hopena (Hobson), who wished to know if it would be a correct proceeding on the part of the natives to hoist the British flag on shore. The chief was told that it would be so regarded, and the Major made the suggestion that it would not do less honour to the occasion if he were to take the flag to the top of the Maiki Hill and hoist it where the flagstaff formerly stood. The Maoris were also told that after the ships had saluted they, too, might fire a salute with small arms, suggestions which

5*

pleased them greatly, and which they carried out with tremendous zest.

In the meantime the Rev. Henry Williams and the missionaries associated with him had been resultlessly engaged in endeavouring to induce Heke to sue for peace. All that happened was that Heke suggested to Kawiti the building of another and a stronger *pa* at Ohaeawai, and became more arrogant than ever. He had now attained the position at which he had doubtless long been aiming. He was *de facto* king of the northern districts. The natives generally, perhaps unconsciously, paid him the greatest deference, and even among those who were not actively following him his *mana* was great. As answer to the missionary representations his reply was : " I am not to be caught like an unfledged *tui*. I thoroughly understand the game the Governor is playing. His cards are great guns and muskets. His words are soft as down, but they mean cannon-balls, soldiers, sailors, and leaden bullets."

On the 20th May the Rev. Mr. Burrows had a further conversation with Heke at Ohaeawai on the subject of peace. The chief was sick with a sore throat, though in no way repentant. As in all previous conversations, he tried to justify himself and cast the blame on the Government. Still the missionary persevered, but in the end made little impression. At the close of the conversation Heke asked, " On what terms do you think the Governor would make peace ? " Mr. Burrows replied, " I cannot tell ; you had better write and ask him." " One condition," said Heke, " must be that he does not erect another flagstaff." Mr. Burrows smiled and asked, " And what compensation have you to make for cutting down the last flagstaff, and for all the plunder and bloodshed that has followed ? " " What ! " Heke said. " Have we not paid enough in the loss we have had in men, houses, food, and canoes ? " This led to a further discussion during which the missionary told Heke, as he had often been told before, that he had commenced the mischief which had resulted in the war and all its disastrous consequences, and therefore it was for him and not for the Governor to sue for peace. These arguments apparently had no effect upon Heke, for on the succeeding day he wrote to the Governor a letter, more remarkable for its display of independence than for its spirit of submission :—

FRIEND THE GOVERNOR,—   May 21st, 1845.

I have no opinion to offer in this affair, because a death's door has been opened. . . . Where is the correctness of the protection offered by the treaty ?* Where is the correctness of the good will of England ? Is it in her great guns ? Is it in her Congreve rockets ? Is the good will of England shown in the curses of Englishmen and in their adulteries ? Is it shown in their calling us slaves ? Or is it shown in their regard for our sacred places ? . . . The Europeans taunt us. They say, "Look at Port Jackson, look at China, and all the islands ; they are but a precedent for this country. That flag of England which takes your country is the commencement." After this the French, and after them the Americans, told us the same. Well, I assented to these speeches . . . and in the fifth year (of these speeches) we interfered with the flagstaff for the first time. We cut it down and it fell. It was re-erected ; and then we said, " All this we have heard is true, because they persist in having the flagstaff up." And we said, " We will die for our country that God has given us." . . .

If you demand our land, where are we to go to ? To Port Jackson ? To England ? If you will consider about giving us a vessel it will be very good. Many people [here he enumerates tribes] took part in the plunder of Kororareka. There were but 200 at the fight, but there were 1,000 at the plundering of the town. Walker's† fighting is nothing at all. He is coaxing you, his friend, for property that you may say that he is faithful. I shall not act so. He did not consider that some of his people were at the plunder of the town . . . It was through me alone that the missionaries and other Europeans were not molested. Were anything to happen to me, all would be confusion. The natives would not consider the harmless Europeans, but would kill in all directions. It is I alone who

* The Treaty of Waitangi.
† Tamati Waaka Nene, who was baptized under the name of Thomas Walker.

restrain them . . . If you say we are to fight, I am agreeable; if you say you will make peace with your enemy, I am equally agreeable. I am on my own land. I now say to you, leave Walker and myself to fight. We are both Maoris. You turn and fight with your own colour. It was Walker who called the soldiers to Okaihau, and therefore they were killed. That is all. Peace must be determined by you, the Governor.

From me,
JOHN WILLIAM POKAI (HEKE).

On the evening of the 24th May this letter was entrusted to Major Bridge* for delivery to the Governor, and that officer, after consultation with Sir Everard Home, decided to sail with his troops for Auckland next day. Before leaving he had an interview with the friendly chiefs, and he wrote to Tamati Waaka Nene, telling him of his departure, and that he hoped soon to return with all the requisites necessary for successfully resuming the war against Heke. The troops reached Auckland on Wednesday, the 28th, and on the following morning Major Bridge delivered Heke's letter to the Governor. As may be supposed, this was by no means the penitent document the Governor had expected to receive, and as it stood it was felt that it offered no basis for peace. FitzRoy therefore decided that he could not relax his efforts to punish Heke, whose truculent tone was as offensive as it was exasperating. The Governor called to his counsel both Lieut.-Colonel Hulme and Major Bridge, who were consulted as to the practicability and expediency of immediately resuming hostilities against Heke, by sending back three hundred men and artillery to Waimate, at which point it was considered they would be near enough to Heke's new *pa* to take advantage of every favourable day.

---

* Heke's letter has just arrived for the Governor. It is not satisfactory. He expresses his willingness either for peace or war, as the Governor may desire. This same letter I forward to your care. In writing to Waaka it may be advisable to mention the names of other chiefs with him, to prevent jealousy. They are Taonui, Mohi Tawhai, Otene, Repa, &c. I hope, also, that an epistle will be forwarded to Heke, giving him to understand what he may expect.—Vide *Henry Williams to Major Bridge.*

These officers gave it as their opinion that there was nothing to prevent the Governor's suggestion being given effect to ; but they stressed the advisability of giving the troops time to recover from their late fatigues, and " to be put into an effectual state before they went back." It was then determined to send a small force of one hundred men and their officers to at once take up a position at Kororareka until the main body could arrive, which would be in about ten days' time. The whole force was then to proceed into the interior and seek satisfaction from Heke.

During the next two days it rained so incessantly and blew so hard that it was impossible to move the troops, and before any steps could be taken to organize the new campaign on the lines so recently agreed upon the *Lady Lee* arrived from Sydney with the news that Colonel Despard and two flank companies of the 99th Regiment were on their way, and that the Colonel was to take command of such augmented forces as were now to be at the Governor's disposal. " This," Major Bridge naïvely remarks, " will alter all the arrangements made by Colonel Hulme, who had decided on remaining in Auckland and sending me in command of the troops to the Bay of Islands, and will completely put his nose out of joint."

CHAPTER V.

OHAEAWAI.

WITHIN the next few days the *British Sovereign* arrived in Auckland Harbour, bringing from Sydney 200 officers and men of the 99th Regiment, under Lieut.-Colonel Henry Despard, an officer of considerable Indian experience, who had been commissioned by Sir Maurice O'Connell "to assume command of all troops in New Zealand, with the temporary rank of Colonel on the staff." All was bustle when he arrived. New hope seemed to animate the soldiers, who, in response to Lieut.-Colonel Hulme's recently formed conviction that nothing could be done against a Maori *pa* without adequate artillery, were busy furbishing up everything in the shape of ordnance the settlement could provide. Of the few guns in Auckland most of them were on carriages so worn and decayed as to render them utterly unfit to take the field, and of necessity the wheels of the four selected had to be removed to prevent their collapse. The guns were therefore being placed on new tumbrels for their better transport, and with this accession to their armament it was confidently felt that a *pa* even more formidable than that which had successfully resisted both rockets and rifles must succumb to the rain of shells that would fall from these four ancient guns on their modern tumbrels. Meantime Heke went on with his *pa* building, and while so engaged he relieved the tedium by indulging in several skirmishes with Waaka Nene's men, in the most serious of which, at Pukenui, on the 12th June, he suffered humiliating defeat. He had sallied out in the morning confident that he would soon overwhelm Nene's smaller force, but before evening he found his attack not only successfully resisted, but his own supporters driven back and completely repulsed.

The purpose of this attack was, if possible, to annihilate Waaka before the soldiers could return from Auckland, and the project had been in course of development for some time. Daily fresh additions to Heke's force had been arriving in response to the appeal of messengers sent to all parts of the country where Heke had friends. With the rank and file came many of the old chiefs who had fought with Hongi, anxious to aid his young relative and to show how the fields of former days had been won. Among these was old Te Kahakaha, of Kaikohe, a leader of great experience in war. He had been the chosen friend of Hongi, and had seen more battles than any chief then alive. Within a week a war-party numbering 450 men had placed themselves under Heke's command, and after resting for a few days at Ohaeawai* they commenced their attack on the Te Ahuahu *pa* in the early hours of the morning.

In the grey of the dawn an old slave woman who was outside Waaka's *pa* gathering sticks for firewood suddenly saw a long dark line emerge from a bank of fog which hung close to the ground. Realizing in a moment what it meant she gave the shrill cry of alarm: " *Te whakaariki e! te whakaariki e!* " (" The enemy! the enemy! ") Instantly the people in the *pa* sprang from their beds and, seizing their weapons, ran to defend its gates. " Remain here and keep our *pa* and I will go out and fight," was Waaka Nene's command to Taonui ; and forthwith Waaka and his followers issued from their fortress and, spreading out into open order, went forward to meet Heke's advancing line. While this movement was in progress another section of the enemy appeared on the opposite side of the *pa*, under the command of Te Kahakaha. Taonui, always sound of judgment, quickly came to the conclusion that this represented the summation

* Ohaeawai signifies " The action of thermal waters."

of the attack. " Now," he said, " we have the enemy in full view ; there are no more in concealment ; we will meet them in the open." Throwing wide the gate on his front of the *pa* he called to his people to advance, but to be wary in the use of their powder. Simultaneously, then, the fight blazed out on both sides of the *pa*, and was soon to develop into the most important native engagement of the war. The best men in the rebel and the loyal camps were present, and each had a motive which spurred him on to victory. Heke was anxious to crush Waaka before the soldiers could arrive ; while Waaka was keen to demonstrate that, though fewer in numbers, he was a match for Heke without the aid of the soldiers. So Waaka charged upon Heke, and Heke's lead came raining down upon Waaka's extended line. Karere Horo, known as the mad priest, was killed, and Taketu and Te Turi and Hangarau, besides nine other men of note. Tinotiu, Waaka Nene's brother, had both his eyes shot out while bravely leading his section of the line.* Wi Repa and his brother, and Hakaraia, chief of the Ngati-Pou, were in those first few minutes among the wounded whose bodies dotted the field where they fell amongst the fern. While his force had been suffering these casualties Waaka had grimly reserved his fire, but now he was close upon the enemy, who appeared in more solid formation than his own. Upon these closed ranks he opened fire with deadly effect, his volleys taking heavy toll, shaking them from end to end. Under this galling fire Heke's men began to retire, and took possession of a low hillside, Waaka following, keeping up a brisk fire the while. " We pressed them hard," says a native account. " Not one of us remembered the light of this world, nor thought of life." To Waaka's advance Heke's reply was a charge which drove him back ; but this time Waaka's skirmishers took shelter behind a low stone wall which once surrounded a *kumara* field, where they maintained an irritating fire, yet almost immune from hurt themselves. Heke's men were now marshalled along the slopes of the

---

* As compensation he was, on the recommendation of Governor Grey, granted a pension by the Imperial Government of £10 per annum.

hillside, firing steadily, but unable to dislodge the enemy from behind their rampart of scoria. With men freely dropping around him Heke realized the superiority of Waaka's tactics, and resolved by one grand charge to clear him out. Calling to his men he ordered them forward, and as they came down the hillside and across the intervening plain " the sound of their feet was like the rush of a waterfall." Being greatly outnumbered, few of those with Waaka expected to survive this onrush, but the chief, cool and brave as ever, called out : " Stand firm ; let them come close ; waste no powder." Not till the breath of the charging enemy was hot upon them did Waaka release his fire. Then a smashing volley went over the stone fence, staggering the advancing wave and stopping it within a few yards of its goal. Here it met with fresh disaster, for amidst the smoke and fumes of powder a number of Waaka's braves, throwing away their empty guns and catching up their tomahawks and clubs, leaped over the wall and began an old-time attack upon the shattered enemy, who, dazed and stunned by the devastating fire, had little relish for a hand-to-hand conflict, and broke and fled, leaving their dead and wounded behind them. Thus what a few minutes before had in it all the elements of an irresistible rush was as quickly turned into a disorderly rout.

While Waaka and Heke were at grips, Taonui and Te Kahakaha were not idle. Their fight had been conducted with varying fortunes, but Te Kahakaha knew by the receding sound of the firing on the other front that Heke had permanently lost ground, and that he must manœuvre to keep in touch with him. He was therefore falling back slowly in order to bring his right division into contact with Heke's left, then to resume the attack. In this operation he was being closely pressed by Taonui, whose little band was fighting with great spirit and with the practical advantage of superior ammunition from the Government stores. Under this pressure and the impression that Heke had been beaten, Te Kahakaha's men began to lose heart, and were imminently inclined to break away. To infuse new courage into his people Te Kahakaha then changed his tactics, turning his retreat into an advance. Taking a light spear in his hand, he called out to his wavering followers : " *Whakahokia, whakahokia.*"* Stepping out lightly, as a young man looking for an opponent for his spear, he encouraged his men to follow. Seeing one of the Ngati-Pou warriors no great distance off, he rushed to encounter him, but before he reached within striking distance he was hit by two shots in quick succession and sank to the ground a dying man, yet with strength enough to say to those about him : " Fight bravely, oh my family and my friends, for this is my last battle."

The fall of Te Kahakaha might well have meant the end of the engagement on his side of the *pa*, for he had been the life and soul of the attack, but his comrade in arms, Wharepapa, chief of the Ihutai tribe and another of the veterans of Hongi's wars, rallied his men and held up Taonui's advance until Te Kahakaha could be removed from the field.

Meantime a boy had carried the news to Heke, as he stood opposed to Waaka on the extreme right of his line. " The old man has fallen " was the message he brought. " What old man ? " asked Heke. " Te Kahakaha," answered the lad. " Is he quite dead ? " anxiously inquired the chief. " Yes, quite dead, and the people are falling back, and his body will be taken by the enemy," was the alarming answer he received. So violently agitated did Heke become at this piece of intelligence that we are told " his heart rolled about in the hollow of his breast." Throwing away his cloak and gun so that his progress might not be impeded, he ran naked and unarmed along the front of the battle until he came to the spot where the dying man was lying. Kneeling down and saluting him he tenderly asked : " Father, are you slain ? " and the old man replied with failing breath : " Son, I am slain, but in whose battle should I die if not in yours. It is good that I should die thus."

* *Whakahokia* = return it—*i.e.*, counter attack.

Heke, rising from the ground, then ran to a number of the warriors and ordered them to assist Wharepapa in holding up Taonui while he saw to the removal of the chief. This the men of Ihutai did right gallantly ; but for the rest they were more bent on getting out of harm's way and were rapidly retreating in all directions. Heke therefore experienced some difficulty in securing bearers. While looking here and there for help he saw Te Atua Wera, the *tohunga*, some distance away with about twenty men around him, whose flight from the field the priest had stopped. To these Heke called : " Advance at once and carry off the old man while it can be done." The *tohunga* asked for a gun and some cartridges, he having nothing but a club, a weapon ill suited to such a fight. Heke, almost beside himself with anger and excitement, told him to take a gun from one of the people standing about, and then commenced to buckle round his waist a cartridge-box which he had plucked from the body of a dead man. Unluckily, this accoutrement was smeared with the blood of its former owner, and when Te Atua Wera saw this he started back and demanded to know where Heke had procured it. " Where should I get it ? " answered Heke. " Is this not war ? " The *tohunga* then saw that Heke, the chief of the war, had himself been the first to transgress the sacred rules and touched the bloody spoils of the slain. He therefore reproached Heke and chided him for his thoughtlessness : " The Maori *atua* are arrayed against us ; the spirits of the dead are now angry ; we are lost, and you are no longer invulnerable. Go not to the front or you will meet with misfortune. Leave the old man where he is ; it cannot now be helped."

Heke's reply was an angry defiance of gods and men. " What care I for men or spirits," he exclaimed. " I fear not. Let the fellow in heaven look to it. Have I not prayed to Him for years. It is for Him to look to me to-day. I will carry the old man off alone." Dashing off in the direction in which Te Kahakaha lay, he was about to be as good as his word, when ten of those who were

with Te Atua Wera, feeling ashamed that the chief should
perform this service alone, followed him to aid in this work
of mercy. With them Te Atua Wera refused to go, but
sat down on a stone beside the path, doubtless to reflect
on the waning influence of his gods and the increasing
recklessness of his leader. All this had occupied but a
few minutes, " for in battle when men's eyes shine there
is no listlessness," but those few minutes had made a
perceptible difference in the fight. Heke's men on the right
were now fairly routed by Waaka Nene, and were beating
a hasty retreat, Waaka following slowly to avoid ambus-
cades, for the ground was covered with brushwood, rocks,
and high fern, and the enemy was still numerous. With
the defeat of Heke's men the battle swung in the direction
where the *tohunga* was anxiously awaiting the return of
Heke. The sound of firing drew nearer, and presently
great numbers of men came running by, among them
those who had gone with Heke, carrying the dead body
of Te Kahakaha. Of these Te Atua Wera inquired the
whereabouts of Heke, and was told he was following
behind. The priest waited fearfully, for he had a presenti-
ment of evil. Still no Heke came, while as the minutes
wore on Taonui's fire grew nearer and nearer as he drove
his opponents back, and his bullets were cutting down the
fern on the right and left. To go himself and search for
Heke was the resolution of the priest ; but just at that
moment Hoao, a noted Nga-Puhi warrior, came jumping
over the fern and seeing Te Atua Wera called out : " Turn,
face the enemy, for Heke has fallen, and unless quickly
rescued will be taken." To inquire where Heke was and
be told was but the work of a moment : " Here in the
hollow, where I have hid him in the high fern, but could
not carry him myself." Closer and closer Taonui's men
were pressing upon them, and Te Atua Wera saw that the
time had arrived when he must do his part. " Come,
follow me, to die for Pokai,"* was his cry, and three

* One of Heke's surnames.

men* started off with him in obedience to his call. By
this time a number of the loyal forces had actually advanced
beyond the line where Heke lay with a shattered thigh,
received while he watched the contest between Wharepapa
and Taonui. The wounded chief was secured, though in
carrying him off his friends were more than once in danger
of being surrounded. They, however, managed to get away
with their burden unperceived, thanks to the density of the
brushwood and the height of the fern, aided perhaps by
the *karakia* (prayers) of the priest, which, as they believed,
rendered them invisible to the enemy.

" So Heke," says the native account, " lost in this battle
many of his best old war-chiefs. He was himself badly wounded,
defeated, and escaped with difficulty to the fort at Ohaeawai,
to which place he was chased by Waaka and Taonui. These
misfortunes could not have happened had Heke not been so
thoughtless as to handle the bloody spoils of the dead before
the proper ceremonies had rendered them common. But there
is nothing in this world so deaf to reason, or so disobedient,
as a warrior when he is enraged. He listens only to his own
courage, and being led away by it—dies."

Waaka Nene buried Heke's dead who had been left
on the field, and there was deep lamentation in both
forts, for the number of killed on both sides was great.
Foremost among those of Heke's friends to die was Te
Kahakaha, whose son was killed shortly after him. So
also was an old chief from Ohaeawai. Wi Pohe, of
Whangarei, was mortally wounded, and several other men
of note were among the lesser casualties. Te Haratua,
Heke's second in command, was wounded in the lungs,
and Patai was severely wounded in the head and taken
prisoner. He was sent by Waaka Nene to Mr. Burrows,
with a request that his wounds might be dressed, and that
he might then be returned to his friends. This was done.
" I dressed the wound," says Mr. Burrows, " and gave the
man shelter for the night. In the morning he took his
departure for Heke's camp "; whereupon Waaka sent a

* Te Pure, Hoao, and Te Ngawe, all noted warriors from Hokianga.

message to Te Haratua : "Remember Patai, and do not
molest the drays." Te Haratua sent back word : "I will
remember." And he did. The British transport was never
molested during all the time the troops were laying siege to
Ohaeawai *pa*, though Colonel Despard probably never knew
the reason why.

Heke's wounds proved to be severe. Though, fortunately, no bones were broken, he suffered considerably
from the crudity of the native surgery during attempts
made to extract the bullet, and he lay upon his bed, a
sick man, for many weeks. During this time he was
visited by Henry Williams and Mr. Burrows at Ohaeawai.
They found him in great pain, due to the laceration of his
flesh. Of them he inquired : "How long is this work to
last ? " They gave him what measure of consolation they
could, but reminded him the future was as much with
him as with any one, to which he replied, "Soon all
will pass." This was the first indication given that he
was undergoing a mental change. As he lay upon his
sick-bed he had ample opportunity to reflect on what was
passing round about him, and on the principle that "The
devil a saint would be " he began to waver in his determination to carry on the war. He accordingly sent for
Kawiti and suggested they should make peace. Kawiti
was extremely angry at this cooling-off on the part of his
ally, and said : "I thought you were ready to dive for
the deepest fish of the sea, but when the water is only up
to your knees you cry for peace."*

To make peace was, however, soon beyond the power of
Heke. So critical did his condition become that his life
was despaired of, and in this crisis he was removed from
Ohaeawai and taken to his own place at Tautoro, fourteen
miles distant, where Te Atua Wera, the *tohunga*, and sixty
men remained with him. Heke was therefore not present
when Colonel Despard attacked Ohaeawai *pa*, the defence
of which became the responsibility of Kawiti and Pene

* Meaning that he understood Heke was prepared to go to the last
extreme, but the moment he met with a reverse he wished to cry off.

Taui, the latter claiming precedence since the *pa* was on his land.

Hearing of Heke's condition, Colonel Despard determined to push on to the front* and assume the offensive before the master brain of the insurgents could personally direct the defence of the new fortress. With him he took the following general instructions from the Governor :—

Government House,
Auckland, 6th June, 1845.

In accordance with the regulations of Her Majesty's colonial service, I have the honour of requesting that you will be pleased to execute the military services for the safety and welfare of the colony which are pointed out in the following instructions.

It is necessary that you should proceed to the Bay of Islands with as large a force as you can assemble, leaving about 100 men at the seat of Government.

Martial law is in force throughout the disturbed districts near the Bay of Islands, and the senior naval officer is required to co-operate with you according to your directions ; but he will not interfere with the transports, or their boats, unless by your desire.

At least one month's supplies should now be taken. Any additional quantity may be forwarded to you from Auckland by the colonial vessels or one of your transports.

The principal object of your expedition is the capture or destruction of the rebel chief Heke and his principal supporters.

No terms of peace can be admitted which do not secure the persons of the chief Heke and his adherents ; but if they give themselves up as prisoners, or should be taken alive, they will not be put to death.

Those chiefs who have become most notorious as supporters and advisers of Heke are Kawiti, Hira te Pure, Hori Kingi, Te Haratua, who, with their followers, should share the fate which their destruction of the settlement of Russell (Kororareka) has rendered inevitable.

I am desirous that you should assure the natives generally that the land forfeited by the rebellious will be divided among the loyal natives, and that no land will be taken by the Government.

* Before Colonel Despard left Sydney he was reported by some of the papers to have said that he would take Heke dead or alive, or die in the attempt ; but this was probably an exaggeration, as there was no love lost between the Colonel and the Sydney Press.

Painful—deeply painful—as it is even to contemplate, much more to authorize, severe measures, although now become imperatively necessary, my duty to our Sovereign, our country, and to the well-disposed tribes of New Zealand requires that I should demand an exemplary chastisement of the rebellious natives who took part in the destruction of Russell (Kororareka).

A British officer will, of course, spare and protect the old, the helpless, the women, the children, and the unresisting.

Were it not that a false and most injurious report has been circulated that our troops give no quarter I should not allude to the necessity of issuing public orders that quarter shall be given. However loyal and well disposed the majority of the natives of New Zealand may be, much caution will, of course, be always necessary in dealing with so sensitive and warlike a people.

The difficulty of distinguishing friend from foe is one which I contemplate with great anxiety. A band round the head or body will be necessary.

That you will not tolerate any injury or insult to a loyal native or prisoner I am well assured ; and I am equally certain that the religious feelings of those who have profited by the zealous efforts of the missionaries will be fully respected.

That the conduct of so difficult and important an expedition, affecting so vitally the welfare of New Zealand and the authority of Her Majesty's Government in the colony, should be entrusted to yourself is most satisfactory.

I rely on your arrangements and decisions with the utmost confidence.

The rendezvous at the Bay of Islands was safely reached on the 10th June, but before the troops could be landed disaster overtook the expedition. The *British Sovereign*, with Colonel Despard on board, ran upon the Brampton Reef* during thick weather, suffering no material injury, but causing a delay of two days in the process of disembarkation. The guns and baggage were taken in boats as far as the Kerikeri Mission Station, the next serious business being how to get them over the same old bad roads, swamps, and rough creek-beds that had harassed their predecessors. Here again the means of

---

* Brampton Reef takes its name from the ship *Brampton*, in which the Rev. Samuel Marsden brought the Rev. Henry Williams and his family to New Zealand in 1823. She struck the reef, was abandoned, and went to pieces there.

transport were found to be woefully deficient. Three bullock-drays and two carts drawn by horses commandeered from the settlers and the missionaries were all that could be procured for the march inland which began at 1 p.m. on the 16th.*

"One of my greatest difficulties," says Colonel Despard, "was the carriage of my four guns, which was effected by attaching them to the tail of a bullock-dray. Scarcely a rivulet was passed that some of the guns did not upset and were sometimes lost sight of in mud and water . . . In crossing the second rivulet, the bottom being unsound, the shaft of a horse-cart broke, and as there was no possibility of repairing it I was obliged to leave a Captain and fifty men to protect it, as it was loaded with ammunition. Two miles farther on two more of our carriages broke down. It was then quite dark and raining in torrents. I made a general halt until the moon rose, and about midnight passed through the wood, 100 men remaining to protect the drays. We arrived at Waimate at 2.30 a.m., having taken thirteen hours to travel twelve miles. The fifty men with the first broken-down cart arrived at 2 p.m., having unloaded the cart and brought the things by hand."

Endless hindrances of this kind hampered the march, during which time the force might have been severely handled by the natives had they chosen to adopt guerrilla tactics. But that was not the Maori way. "Where," said Heke, "would be the use of our taking the food and powder of the soldiers? How could they fight us if we did that?" This was indeed chivalrous, but it was not war, and in the end cost the rebels dearly.

The first section of the British column to reach Waimate was a detachment of marines and sailors from the *Hazard*. They informed Mr. Burrows that the remainder of the force was on its way, but was only making slow progress because the Colonel would not permit the men to march faster than the drays carrying supplies and ammunition

* The Governor gave the settlers notice to bring in their drays to provide transport for the force going against Heke. This the settlers were reluctant to agree to, because it looked like taking sides against the Maoris ; but it was finally agreed, after a deputation had waited on the Governor, that he (the Governor) should commandeer the drays, so taking the responsibility off the settlers, particularly off the Rev. Mr. Davis, one of the missionaries.—*Bainbridge*.

could travel. It was early morning before the Colonel with
the great body of the men reached the mission station,
and when they came they were weary and desperately
hungry, having had nothing to eat on the way beyond a
few biscuits served out to them before starting. The drays
bringing the food had broken down, and the men coiled
up in their blankets more hungry than sleepy. As soon
as it was daylight the soldiers were moving about looking
for food in all directions, inquiring, in their ignorance of
the kind of place they had come to, if there were no
stores where they could purchase bread. Waaka Nene, on
the day before, had sent in a ton of potatoes as a present
for the Colonel. These were pointed out to the men, and
in an incredibly brief time they were lighting fires and
commandeering every utensil in which a potato could be
cooked to provide them with a welcome breakfast.

Mr. Burrows was the happy possessor of a considerable
number of fowls which had been accustomed to wander
all over the station. These were not presented to the
soldiers, but it was no marvel that they disappeared and
found their way into the pots, which fact was made obvious
by their tell-tale legs protruding above the tops of the
utensils in which they were being cooked. A fair-sized
tame pig which had roamed at will was heard to squeak
for the last time, and the division of the carcase became
the matter of dispute among the claimants, but a very
brief wrangle sufficed to settle the argument, as the whole
soon disappeared.

At 2 p.m. on the 17th the loaded drays and the troops
which had been left to guard them came straggling into
the station. The men, who had had no rest all night, were
thoroughly knocked up, but by nightfall the whole force
was fairly well distributed amongst the various buildings
of which Waimate was able to boast. Colonel Despard
expressed surprise at finding such comfortable quarters, and
sweet sleep soon dispelled the hardships of the road.

Much of his tribulation by the way Colonel Despard
subsequently attributed to the failure of those who might

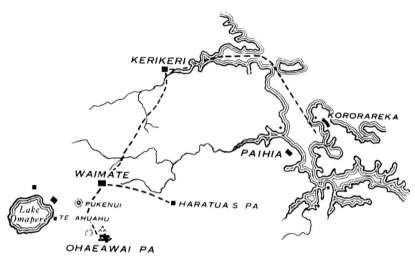

KERIKERI

KORORAREKA

PAIHIA

WAIMATE

Lake
Omapere

PUKENUI

TE AHUAHU

HARATUA S PA

OHAEAWAI PA

KAIKOHE

TAUTORO

COLONEL DESPARD'S ROUTE TO OHAEAWAI PA.

have done so to supply him with reliable information. In a petulant letter to Henry Williams, written on the 15th July, he complained that he had never received any information that was of any sort of use whatsoever. That given to him at Auckland regarding the roads was, he said, decidedly wrong. He had been told there was a good dray-road to Waimate ; he found it execrable. No one could ever tell him where Heke's *pa* was, its internal form, what its defences were, nor the number of its defenders. " There appeared to be," he said, " a general wish to conceal the difficulties, without considering the possible waste of European blood that might take place in consequence."

In this campaign, as in that led by Lieut.-Colonel Hulme, the British soldier on the march was an unfailing source of wonder to the Maori. Accustomed as they were to the freedom of the wilderness, the soldier's equipment appeared to them so cumbersome, so irksome, that their general comment was : " If we Maoris were loaded up in that way we would neither be able to fight nor to run away." They saw him, " all tied up with belts," cheerfully carrying his bundle of clothes, his haversack, his heavy cartridge-box, his water-bottle, his musket, and his bayonet ; and as they watched him march along the muddy roads, erect and " straight as a flight of curlew in the sky," they marvelled and exclaimed : " Great is the patience of the soldier."

In this goodliest of virtues the example of the soldiers was not emulated by their commander. Colonel Despard proved to be a man of hot and hasty temper, and the exasperating experiences of the march from Kerikeri to Waimate are said to have given him ample provocation for displaying his somewhat vivid vocabulary. On reaching Waimate, wet and weary, the Colonel was in no enviable mood ; and when next day he there met Waaka Nene, who offered his services, he answered him harshly, saying that when he wanted the assistance of savages he would ask for it. Colonel Despard had many after-opportunities for recalling these bitter words, which, fortunately, were not understood by Nene, and no one was foolish enough to translate them to him.

Five days were spent at Waimate, and during this time Colonel Despard saw a good deal of his native allies. Although it was known at the time that he entertained the most supreme contempt for the Maori and all his ways, he lived to mellow this harsh opinion, and he has left it on record that generally they showed great shrewdness in their remarks upon the war and modes of carrying it on. "Upon the whole," he says, "I was much pleased with these interviews, as they gave me greater confidence in their fidelity than I was previously possessed of." Of the allied chiefs he was most impressed by Tamati Waaka Nene, whom he found to be quick and penetrating, fortified with a large proportion of common-sense. His loyalty he thought to be unquestionable, though he is uncharitable enough to say that it arose from a selfish interest rather than a belief that his alliance with the British would benefit his race. In this opinion Colonel Despard was entirely mistaken.

During one of these conversations between the Colonel and Waaka Nene the latter propounded the following question to the British officer : "Suppose you take Heke's *pa* and any of the men throw down their arms and give themselves up, what will you do with them ? " "When I told him," says the Colonel, "that it was not the custom of the English to injure any defenceless people, though they might be enemies, and that if the chief himself surrendered to us he would not be injured," he considered for some time and then said : "You are more merciful than we are, and what you say is good and right."

While the troops were waiting at Waimate Colonel Despard was one day surprised to see approaching the settlement a straggling body of natives carrying at their head a large British ensign, a fact that gave him some assurance that they were coming with friendly intent. When their chief reached the Colonel he presented a letter

written by Captain Milne,* of the *British Sovereign,* and
announced that he was Pomare, the chief of Kawakawa,
come to join in the impending attack upon Heke. He
had with him about two hundred followers, all of whom
were well armed, though of doubtful discipline. These were
dismissed by the chief after the usual salutations had been
passed, and then he entered into familiar conversation with
the Colonel and the officers about him. His first request
was for a glass of rum, which having been supplied
he turned upon Lieut.-Colonel Hulme, who was standing
in the group, and with the flash of anger in his eye and
the tone of wrath in his voice he said, with ever-increasing
accents : "You made me prisoner and carried me to Auckland. You burned my *pa* and drove my people out."
While saying this he raised his quivering hands and shook
them in Hulme's face, " with," as an observer remarks, " all
the expression on his countenance of meditated revenge
should an opportunity offer."

Pomare moved up to Ohaeawai with the forces, but
he did not long remain with them. He early discovered
that rum was not so plentiful in the camp as he had
believed and hoped, and soon he became *pouri* (dejected) and
begged the Colonel to excuse him on the ground of his
health, a favour with which Despard was very willing to
comply. In the Colonel's estimation the libatious Pomare
was no sort of use whatever ; and, with his constitutional
distrust of natives, he believed it only required some slight
reverse in his fortunes to induce the supposedly friendly
chief of Kawakawa to transfer his favours to the ranks of
the enemy.

The missionaries were naturally much concerned when
they realized that the military authorities proposed to
make a base of Waimate. Their desire was to preserve
their neutrality intact — to avoid even the semblance of

---

* Captain Milne stated that Pomare had rendered him every assistance in overhauling his vessel (after she struck on the Brampton Reef),
and that he had left twenty to thirty of his men to protect him. He also
stated that his vessel had not sustained much damage as the result of
her misadventure.

favour to one side more than to the other, but to render
to each such assistance as came within the duties of their
sacred calling.   The constitution of Waimate as a military
camp would, they felt, be misunderstood by the rebels, and
might bring down upon them any one of the calamities
inseparable from war.   Heke told Mr. Burrows that he
was not insensible to the advantage the troops would
derive from having such a place as Waimate to come to,
and that it was only his reluctance to put his hand on
any mission property which prevented him from destroying it.   He, however, intimated that once it had been
" sat upon " by the soldiers it would soon become *noa,**
and that should the need arise and the opportunity offer
to destroy it he might not be able to restrain the zeal of
his followers.   He also told the missionary that a proposal
had been made by some of his people to destroy the
bridge over the Waitangi Stream, near Waimate, but he
had overruled them, because he knew that if " his friends
the redjackets " were determined to come to Waimate the
want of a bridge would not prevent them.   They would
simply be put to a little more trouble to slope down the
banks of the river, while the natives and settlers would
be permanent sufferers by the loss of the structure.

Mr. Burrows was therefore somewhat relieved when at
5 o'clock on the morning of the 23rd June the whole
British and allied forces began their march against the
new *pa* at Ohaeawai, seven miles away.   Colonel Despard's
total strength was then as follows :—

Colonel Despard, 99th Regiment, commanding.
58th Regiment, Major Bridge ..	270
99th Regiment, Major MacPherson ..	180
96th Regiment, Lieut.-Colonel Hulme ..	70
Marines, H.M.S. *Hazard*, Acting-Commander Johnson and Lieutenant Phillpotts ..	30
Auckland Volunteers, Lieutenant Figg ..	80
Natives allies, Tamati Waaka Nene ..	250
	880

* *Noa* = common, or secular.

The guns were four in number, two 6-pounders and two 12-pounder carronades, in charge of Captain Marlow and Lieutenant Wilmot of the Engineers.

Although the distance to be travelled was but seven miles, so bad was the road, so difficult the streams to negotiate, that the *pa* was not reached until sunset. When within a mile of the stronghold the sound of musketry was heard in front. Colonel Despard moved rapidly forward with the advance guard, under Major Bridge, to ascertain the cause; but before they had reached the ground the firing had ceased, and Waaka Nene met them just as they came within sight of the *pa*. His information at once reassured the Colonel, for he told him the firing had been caused by his people driving in one of the enemy outposts, and that he had taken up his station on an eminence on the right, which he called "the key to the position." "If," says the Colonel, "he had been brought up under the great Duke himself he could not have made a more correct observation. It was indeed the key to the position, and one which I was afterwards obliged to retain with the utmost care during the whole period of the attack." This point was subsequently known as "Waaka's Hill," and was the scene of more than one stirring episode during the siege.

And what of the *pa* they had come to storm? Built upon the land of Pene Taui, chief of the Ohaeawai district, it had been commenced by that warrior—once loyal, now rebel*—immediately after the fighting at Kororareka. As he had designed it only for his own purpose, it was a structure modest in size though stout in construction. When, however, it was chosen by Heke and Kawiti for their larger operations they doubled its capacity, though they did not increase its strength, pressure of time precluding that solidity of workmanship being devoted to

---

* Pene Taui's disaffection is said to have been caused by an innocent pleasantry made at his expense by Tamati Waaka Nene, which only serves to prove how true it is that many a first-class friend has been lost by a second-class joke.

the second portion which had been bestowed upon the leisurely erection of the first.

When finished, the *pa* and its garrison, whose numbers varied from day to day, were made sacred by the priests, who on the authority of their omens declared it would be a fortunate fortress. The Rev. Mr. Burrows, who saw it in course of erection, thus describes its situation :—

It is on a piece of clear rising ground, 500 yards square, sloping rather suddenly to the south, a small ravine to the westward, a general decline to eastward, and a very easy rise to the northward.

Then Mr. Burrows goes on to remark :—

It does not require the practised eye of a military engineer to see that they are making one fatal mistake in placing the stockade within long rifle range of a conical hill situated to the west and bordering on a small forest. The lines of the new *pa* show that it is to be much larger than the last.

The *pa* was 90 yards long by 50 yards wide. Every wall was broken by an angle or projection, so that no part of its length could be approached without the risk of meeting an enfilading fire. For the scientific nature of these lines the genius of Kawiti was largely responsible, as Mr. Burrows tells us he saw him actively engaged in the work of laying them out ; he even assisted in dragging the logs into position, so energetic was he in the construction of the *pa*. The walls were built of young *puriri* trees cut from the neighbouring forest, some of them being from 30 in. to 50 in. in circumference. They were sunk 6 ft. in the ground, and stood 10 ft. above it. The poles were bound together by stout vines, and round the base there was placed a thick curtain of green flax, which practically rendered that section bullet-proof. Within the outer wall there were two other walls of much the same proportions. The outer wall was 2 ft. from the second, the second 4 ft. from the third. Between the inner and middle walls there was dug in places a ditch 5 ft. deep, with traverses, in which the defenders stood with comparative safety and fired through loopholes in the outer palisade. In other places the ditch was dug inside the inner wall, possibly as a second line of defence in the event of the outer palisade being demolished. Communication with the passages between the palisades was maintained by means of other passages beneath the wall of timber. Within the enclosed area were built a number of *whares* and rough houses, but the interior feature of the *pa* was its shell-proof shelters, 5 ft. and 6 ft. deep—the forerunner of the modern " dug-out " of Flanders and of France—into which the defenders retired when the cannonading became dangerous, and where, in contrast to the soldiers, they could always be warm and dry.

Of these operations Mr. Burrows was one day a spectator, but as he looked on at the progress of the work the observant Pene Taui approached him and politely suggested that perhaps he had better not know too much of the construction of their fortification. Mr. Burrows took the hint and discreetly retired.

What number of men were actually employed upon the work is uncertain, but they must have been both numerous and energetic, for the whole enterprise was completed within some three weeks. When completed, the garrison —said to number 250 strong—filled the storehouse with an abundance of food such as a Maori in war-time could thrive upon. Owing to its proximity to the neighbouring bush the defenders of the *pa* were at liberty to come and go much as they pleased, the attacking force being considered too small to effect its complete investment. Under this liberty the garrison's supplies of food and powder were renewed as required, with little risk or even inconvenience.

In the gathering shadows of the evening the camp of the attacking force was pitched some 400 yards from the *pa*,* amongst the native gardens, which were found to be well stocked with potatoes and other vegetables. Whether from lack of time or lack of care, the initial arrangement

* Those natives who did not accompany Waaka Nene to the hill squatted behind the European camp.

of the camp proved to be both inadequate and inconvenient. It consisted of no more than twelve small rent and leaky bell-tents and such huts as the soldiers and Maoris were able to improvise with the aid of native scrub. This accommodation was never sufficient for the comfortable housing of the men, who for three weeks had to live and sleep in their clothes, surrounded by every circumstance which could contribute to their discomfort, except hunger and sickness. At first the tents were erected with so little regard to plan or system that no space was left between them where the men could muster when called out, with the result that the greatest confusion invariably prevailed when night alarms were given — alarms which fortunately proved always to be false. Further, the tents being pitched on cultivated ground, the tracks between them were soon in a deplorable condition. The almost continuous rain and the unceasing traffic speedily reduced them to a state of liquid mud, which under the most favourable conditions rose well above the boot-tops as the men ploughed through it passing to and from their sodden quarters. These mistakes were subsequently remedied and the inconveniences somewhat reduced by shifting and re-arranging the camp; but the accommodation was never increased, and the men, wearied by incessant duties and harried by frequent alarms, never had anything better on which to lie than beds of damp fern.

When tents were up and sentries posted the stillness of that first night before the *pa* was frequently broken by the stentorian challenge of the rebel sentinels: " Come on, soldiers, and avenge your dead who are lying stiff on Taumata Tutu. *Whai mai ; whai mai* " (" Come on ; come on "). To this defiant cry flung into the frosty night Waaka Nene's men made reply : " We Nga-Puhi have killed you in heaps, and we will kill you again. *Whai mai ; whai mai.*"

Next morning the men were busy erecting, under the direction of Captain Marlow and Lieutenant Wilmot, a platform of stone and earth on which to mount the four guns, and firing was commenced early in the day, but with sadly disappointing results. Such shots as struck the *pa* embedded themselves in the heavy timbers of the palisade, which was scarcely shaken by the impact. The mortars were no more effective, the natives quietly sheltering in their shell-proof holes to evade their fire. Even this precaution was not always necessary, for most of the shells refused to burst, it being afterwards discovered that many of the fuses had been made as far back as 1807 and were perished with their years of hoary age. From these unexploded shells the defenders of the *pa* dug out quantities of valuable powder and bullets, which they in due course returned to the British with anything but friendly intent.

Firing went on in this unprofitable manner for several hours, and then, in hopes of better success, the battery was shifted a little nearer. Three times that day was this expedient resorted to, but with no appreciable result, for every time the guns were shifted a new target was selected. Consequently what little damage was done was almost as quickly repaired by the industrious and intrepid defenders. Here, however, we may profitably turn to Major Bridge's first-hand account of these early days of the attack :—

24th, Tuesday.—The action commenced this morning on our side. The four-gun battery opened its fire on the *pa*, but did no execution, and the enemy never returned a shot for some time. About 10 a.m. they commenced and musket-shots were exchanged, but all their balls passed over our heads. One Volunteer in the battery was hit, and one on the hill whilst assisting in taking up one of the carronades to the hill on the right. One of our Light Company men was shot through the left wrist, more by accident. A native on the hill was also wounded. A constant fire was kept up by the guns, of shell, ball, and grape till dark. Many hit and burst in the *pa*, and I fancy they must have lost many men. All quiet during the night, and although our Pioneers and working-parties were throwing up a breastwork and battery for the guns in another position more to the right and nearer to the *pa* the natives never molested them.

25th, Wednesday. — The guns being brought into the new battery within 200 yards of the *pa*, great hopes were entertained that a breach would soon be made. The natives fired the first shot from the *pa* this morning, and the guns commenced about 8 a.m. and made some very good practice, both from the hill and the new battery. Many shells burst in the ditches and in the *pa*, but owing to the elasticity and tenacity of the flax, which closes up as the ball goes through, it was impossible to see what extent of damage was done to the fence. No practicable breach was made, owing, I think, to the shot not being directed all to one point and to the fire not being kept up, half an hour elapsing between each shot by Colonel Despard's directions. I lost one of my grenadiers to-day. He was shot a little to the right of the battery, where I had posted fifteen good marksmen, with instructions to fire at every one who showed himself within the *pa*. The shot came thick enough about us in the battery, but the mantle of flax protected us. Some balls came in through the portholes through which the guns fire, and, strange, they hit no one   Poor Doherty was the only man hit to-day. The Colonel, finding it impracticable to breach the *pa*, determined on storming it by night, and ordered ladders, &c., to be ready by 2 o'clock in the morning — the forlorn hope — and two attacking parties, one of which I was to command, were told off, with their supports. I lay down to sleep with no pleasurable sensations as to the occupation of the morning, doubting the successful issue of the night attack. Although British valour generally carries everything before it, still there must be a frightful sacrifice of life. It rained heavily after midnight, and at 1 o'clock, when the piquets were called in to form the storming-parties, it was raining so hard that the attack was countermanded, much to my satisfaction. Hope some less hazardous method of attacking the *pa* may be fixed on.

26th, Thursday.—Very wet morning. The guns kept up a fire on the *pa* all day, every half-hour. The Colonel and engineer and artillery officers were reconnoitring the ground for a new battery. They fixed on one close to the right flank of the *pa*, and a battery was to be constructed during the night. Some smart firing on our battery and advanced piquets, but without doing any injury.

27th, Friday.—Visited my piquets early this morning, which were extended as far as the place where they were erecting the new battery, and so close to the *pa* that I was surprised the enemy did not make an attack on them. Reinforced the guard over working-party before daylight. The battery was completed by 8 a.m. and opened fire. So did the other batteries, for they had divided the guns—a very bad plan, I think. This brought on a very hot fire on the new battery, which was so close that many of our men were wounded, and one sailor was shot dead at the gun. The storming-parties were all brought down and formed in rear of this battery, under cover of a wall on the crest of the hill, to await a favourable opportunity of making a rush on the *pa*, as it was believed the guns would soon make a breach. The bullets were flying over us all the time, and we could not move without a shot being fired at us. We lay there for two or three hours, and at length, at about 3 p.m., received an order to return to camp. No breach was made, and the storming was again given up. About 5 or 6 p.m. the enemy made a sortie from the *pa* to endeavour to cut off the guns and party in the battery whilst the guns were being withdrawn, but were repulsed. Two more of our men were wounded, and one Volunteer. Three of the enemy were seen to fall. The whole of the troops were under arms, as they expected a general rally from the *pa ;* but their fire gradually ceased towards dark, and after that Tamati Waaka and the chiefs informed us that they had got information of an intended attack on the camp by night. Every necessary precaution was taken to guard against surprise, and we passed rather an anxious night. Had they done so there must have been terrific slaughter, for we had no breastwork round us to defend.* Our tents were pitched in a hurry without any order—were so crowded up with the huts that the men could not find room to form up and would not have been able to act. The Colonel determined on altering the position of the camp next day.

28th, Saturday.—All passed off quietly during the night, except that one of the sentries of the piquets was fired at. Another gun was taken up the hill, and there kept up a fire through the day, whilst the troops were occupied in striking and re-pitching their tents, forming a street between them for the men to fall in. The day was fine except for a few showers towards evening. Went up the hill and reconnoitred the *pa*. There appeared a good deal of damage done to it, although no breach was observable. A few men and women were seen moving about. Very few shots were fired from the *pa* to-day. Our guns did good execution ; nearly every shot told. A very wet stormy night, with thunder and lightning.

29th, Sunday.—About 2 a.m. two shots of shell were fired into the *pa* from the hill, which must have astonished the weak minds of the natives. About 8 a.m. an alarm was given that the enemy was making a sortie. After a short time it proved to be a false alarm ; only a small body of natives were going out to get potatoes and firewood, and who, when fired on, returned to the *pa* . . . The enemy did not fire a shot at us to-day,

---

* As the siege progressed, the rumoured attacks and the night alarms became so frequent that a breastwork of scoria was thrown up round the camp as an additional means of defence.

but we heard their bell ringing. These savages showed more respect for the Sabbath Day than did our soldiery. Ascended the hill in the afternoon and saw a few cannon-shots thrown into the *pa* with great precision ; but for the elasticity of the flax, which closed up as the shot passed through it, the extent of the damage done to the palisades could not be seen.*

30th, Monday.—The enemy sallied out this morning and attacked our piquets right and left. Some very sharp skirmishing on the right, and a party of friendly natives, under Moses (Mohi) Tawhai, went round through the wood and attacked them in flank, which soon drove them back. After this a very sharp action took place between Moses's party and the defenders in the rear of the *pa*, which I had the satisfaction of witnessing from the top of the hill—a pretty specimen of native skirmishing, at which they are very efficient. Whilst a hot fire was kept up on Moses's party from the rear face of the *pa*, many of the enemy were seen to steal out at the left rear angle of it, and under cover of a low hill covered with scrub they advanced on and attacked Moses in flank, on which he retired in very good skirmishing order to the wood from which he had made his approach, and returned to his *pa*. He had two or three men wounded, but none killed. A hot fire was kept up on us all day from every face and angle of the *pa*, as if to make amends for yesterday's silence. One grenadier of the 99th was killed, and one native was shot through the back whilst standing near the hospital tent.

Colonel Despard was at his wit's end. He had met something new in his experience of fortification ; his guns could make no impression, and his ammunition was running out. In his desperation he had already decided to send for one of the 32-pounders from the decks of the *Hazard*.† That surely would breach the wooden wall

* Much to the annoyance of Colonel Despard, one of the missionaries protested to him against this firing of the guns on Sunday. The Colonel justified it on military grounds.

† Colonel Despard says : " I resolved on applying to Acting-Commander Johnson, of H.M.S. *Hazard*, to send me up one of his 32-pounders. This officer, without a moment's delay, complied with my request, as he had always done with every one which I had made to him."

Lieutenant George Johnson attained the rank of Admiral in 1885 and died in 1903, at the age of ninety-four, his life covering the whole of the nineteenth century. Of him an intimate acquaintance has said : " For all but a very short time of this period he was singularly active, energetic, alert, taking his part in affairs great and small with unceasing interest and devotion to duty and with a keen outlook around him. That, I think, was the first thing every one who knew him would notice about him—his extraordinary alertness and keenness. He was never slack, never dull. Whatever his hand found to do he did it with all his might."

Rev. Robert Burrows, C.M.S.

which had at first excited the soldiers' contempt, but now commanded their silent admiration.

Pending the arrival of the gun the soldiers had little to do, and had the weather been warmer and drier the campaign might have been regarded as something in the nature of a pleasant outing, for the commissariat was now ample and regular. But if the privates were content, Colonel Despard was furious at the delay and at the incessant rain. He fretted and fumed at the inaction imposed upon him, and at the discomfort of the wet tents, for there was scarcely a day on which wintry showers did not fall. At last he cast patience to the winds, and on Sunday afternoon decided he would not wait for the *Hazard's* gun, but would storm the *pa* before daylight the following morning. As officer of the day this decision was conveyed to Major Bridge, who consulted his fellow-officers concerning its wisdom and practicability. Against such a proceeding all the corps commanders immediately protested. Lieut.-Colonel Hulme, who now knew something of what storming a Maori *pa* meant, was emphatic in his resistance of the folly ; Major MacPherson was convinced there was no reason to suppose an assault was other than premature ; Captain Marlow declared the position to be impregnable against assault ; Lieutenant Wilmot called it a "mad act" ; Lieutenant Phillpotts expressed the opinion that success by that road was impossible ; and Waaka Nene* remarked in his quiet decisive way that the Colonel might try to storm the *pa* himself, but for his part he would sacrifice none of his men in the attempt.†

* Waaka Nene became popularly known among the soldiers as "General Walker." The following is the estimate Henry Williams formed of him : "Waaka with his allies were not only the preservation of the country as a British colony, but also the preservation of the troops, preceding them through the woods, by well scouring them to see that the enemy were not in possession. In every instance this has been the case. I see Waaka frequently, and always find him the same—a sober, sensible, quiet, unassuming, well-conducted statesman and soldier, admitted by all the military to be an able field officer.

† Waaka Nene told one of his fellow-chiefs that he felt sick in the stomach when Colonel Despard talked of storming the *pa*, so great a waste of good lives did it seem to him.

6—First War.

While this conference was proceeding, the news was brought into the camp that the naval gun had arrived at Waimate and would reach Ohaeawai that evening or early next morning. In view of this intelligence the officers were more than ever convinced that the assault should be delayed until at least the effect of the gun had been tested. This being the unanimous opinion, Major Bridge was deputed to submit it to the Colonel. Bridge agreed to make the experiment, and with the discretion of one who had learned something of the ways of his superior he pointed out to Colonel Despard that it was the general opinion of the officers that since the naval gun was so near at hand it would be a pity that the attack upon the *pa* should be made before it arrived, as by its heavier calibre it might open a breach for them, and, while ensuring success, be the means of saving many lives. This proposal the Colonel heard, not without objection, but finally he fell in with the views of his officers, and the assault was again countermanded.

The storming project was thus fortuitously shelved by the timely arrival of the *Hazard's* gun, which, considering its size and weight—1½ tons—must have had some surprising adventures by the way. It was brought up under an escort of twenty-five men from the *Hazard*, commanded by Lieutenant Morgan, and so great was the curiosity aroused by its arrival in camp that a body of idle soldiers immediately crowded round to examine it and to gossip with its escort upon their wayside experiences. The rebels in the *pa*, observing so favourable an opportunity, instantly poured in a hot fire upon the group, succeeding in killing a grenadier and wounding a friendly native. That evening the drays, with as many wounded as could be moved, were sent back to Waimate under escort of the *Hazard's* sailors, and at night the piquets were increased, a man to every tent being kept on sentry duty, one of the rumoured attacks from the *pa* being anticipated.

The whole of the day and the greater part of that night were occupied in getting the gun into position, and before a second shot could be fired the defenders, by a successful sortie, all but captured it.   This was on the morning of the 1st July, one of the few days on which the sun had shone and no rain had fallen.   Great things were expected of the new engine of attack.   No one now doubted that a breach would be made, and every one was on the watch for the expected result.   Colonel Despard had walked up "Waaka's Hill" to the point where the 12-pounder was being fired at fitful intervals to keep the defenders occupied and was closely watching through his glasses the effect of the naval gun's first shell.   Suddenly he heard a loud outcry at the summit of the hill, and, looking in that direction, to his amazement he saw the native followers of Waaka Nene pouring over the top and down the sides of the hill in a state of wildest confusion, closely followed by a piquet of the 58th Regiment, consisting of a sergeant and two men, who had been placed there for the protection of the 6-pounder, which a few days before had been taken up to Waaka's camp.   One glance was sufficient to show the Colonel that the enemy had surprised and carried the hill, and that not a moment was to be lost in recovering it.   Turning to a bugler who usually accompanied him, he gave a sharp command, the alarm was sounded, and the troops in camp, not more than 300 yards away, were quickly under arms.   As soon as he could get near enough to make his voice heard—for all his signals for the men to advance had been misunderstood — he ordered part of the 58th Regiment to move rapidly up the hill, making a slight detour to the right so as to bring them to the rear of the enemy, and then charge them with the bayonet.   Under a cross-fire from the defenders in the *pa* and the enemy on the hill this movement, led by Major Bridge, was executed in a manner most gallant; but the delay in bringing the men up had enabled the assailants to commence their retreat into the bush, which was effected with trifling loss.   Into the dense thicket of

6*

the forest it was neither wise nor possible to pursue them.*

Ill as he could afford to divide his force, Colonel Despard then placed Captain Thompson and sixty men of the 58th to defend the post against the further stealth and enterprise of the enemy. Upon order being restored Colonel Despard found that the sentry at the gun had been shot in the first attack, and that Mr. Henry Clarke, his interpreter, was severely wounded. This gentleman had been standing with the Colonel at the lower gun, but as a few stray shots from the *pa* were flying about he deemed he would be safer, as well as able to obtain a better view of the gun-fire, if he ascended the hill. He had not been there more than a few minutes when the attack was made, and in the first flush of the onslaught he received a gun-shot in the thigh which completely shattered the bone and left him helpless upon the ground. Of such are the fortunes of war.

The boldness with which the enemy had executed this sortie left Colonel Despard guessing what next they would attempt. He at once became obsessed with the idea that they were gaining in confidence as the result of the inefficiency of the British gun-fire, and as a result of that confidence they would sooner or later steal out by night and cut off his supplies of food and ammunition, which were laboriously brought up from the rear every two or three days. The danger of this had for some time pressed heavily upon him. From the smallness of the force at his command he believed himself unable to detach any portion of it to guard the drays on the road between Kerikeri and the camp, a distance of from eighteen to

* According to Major Bridge, this attack, led by a chief named Mokaraka, was made for the express purpose of either securing or killing Waaka Nene, whose loyalty to the British especially angered the followers of Heke. They made a close and exhaustive search for him amongst the huts, but, fortunately, the object of their solicitude had gone out into the bush early that morning in an endeavour to cut off some of the enemy foragers who had shot and taken prisoner a man of the Light Company of the 99th Regiment who had ventured too far beyond the British lines in a search for potatoes.

twenty miles. Along this exposed route his inadequate transport was entirely at the mercy of a hostile raid, and should the enemy succeed in destroying his few drays and killing his overworked cattle he would be compelled instantly to retire and leave everything behind him. In this respect Colonel Despard harassed himself unnecessarily, as is shown by the following authenticated incident : A gentleman well known in the north was at this period of the siege proceeding from Waimate to Kerikeri. When near a wood through which the road passed he met a dray laden with commissariat stores for the troops, attended by only the driver and two soldiers. When the traveller entered the wood, ten armed men, whom he recognized as followers of Heke, advanced into the road and shaking hands with him asked him if he had met the dray. " Yes," replied the gentleman, " I passed one just now." " Well," said the natives, " upon that dray is a cask of spirits and probably ammunition as well, but, whatever the load may be, it could easily have been ours had we chosen to take it, being ten to three and well armed. Having, therefore, allowed it to pass unmolested you must feel convinced that plunder is not our motive, and you can tell the Colonel that what has been said about *riri awatea* (fair fighting) is not idle talk but a reality, proof of which we have now given."

There, too, preyed upon the Colonel's mind the fear — equally groundless — that unless he could achieve some immediate and striking success he would not be able to hold his native allies. The danger was, he thought, imminent that if he could not either take the *pa* or so cripple the enemy as to compel him to sue for peace the bulk of the Maoris who were fighting with him, as well as the large section of neutrals, would make terms with Heke and join him in his attacks upon the European settlements. These considerations whirled through the Colonel's agitated mind as he stood upon the hillside that morning, and were rapidly forcing him to the conclusion that before many days he must play the desperate hazard of storming the *pa*, when an incident occurred which cast the fateful die. Above Waaka Nene's camp at the moment of the rebel attack upon it there had been flying a Union Jack. When the enemy was driven away it was discovered that the flag was missing, and to Colonel Despard's horror and indignation it was seen in an incredibly short space of time floating from the staff within the *pa*, but underneath the native flag. A touch of malicious irony was added to the insult by hoisting the Jack at half-mast and upside down. Colonel Despard, whose temper had already been severely tried by the events of the morning, now burst into a storm of passion. His fury knew no bounds, and without further question he determined to storm the *pa* and rescue the captured flag.

The force for this purpose was ordered to parade at 3 o'clock, when the following plan of attack was issued by Lieutenant R. B. Deering, of the 99th, the Acting Brigade-Major :—

The principal attack will be made on or near the right angle on the front face (that face being considered the front one that is opposite the camp), and the whole column for this attack will be formed as follows : 2 sergeants and 20 volunteers from the three corps will form the advance and proceed with the most perfect silence till they reach the stockade.*

This party will be followed closely by the assaulting body, under Major MacPherson, composed of 40 grenadiers from the 58th and 40 grenadiers from the 99th Regiments, and will be accompanied by a small party of seamen, and by 30 Pioneers from the Volunteer Militia. The seamen, and as many of the Pioneers as there are sufficient tools for, will be supplied with axes or hatchets for the purpose of cutting down the stockade. Those Pioneers who cannot be supplied with axes or hatchets are to carry the ladders, as well as strong ropes, which will be supplied by the Artillery department, for pulling down the stockade.

Major MacPherson's party will be closely followed by Major Bridge, of the 58th Regiment, having under him the remainder of the grenadiers of the 58th, to be made up to 60 rank and

* This was called the " forlorn hope," and was led by Lieutenant Beatty, who begged for the post.

file from the battalion of the same regiment, and 40 rank and file from the Light Company of the 99th Regiment, in all amounting to 100 rank and file.

A strong supporting party will be formed under Lieut.-Colonel Hulme, 96th Regiment, consisting of the whole of the detachment of the 96th Regiment, completed to 100 rank and file by the battalion men of the 58th Regiment.

The moment an entrance is made into the *pa* this party will instantly follow the preceding parties. The remainder of the force will be under the personal command of Colonel Despard, for the purpose of directing assistance wherever necessary, with the exception of 40 rank and file of the 58th Regiment under command of Captain Thompson of that corps, who will occupy the hill overlooking the *pa* and the camp, it being considered necessary to do so from the attempt made by the natives in the morning to get possession of it.*

The point of attack selected by Colonel Despard was the north-west angle, and, like most of his other decisions, was unfortunate. This happened to be a portion of the wall leisurely and strongly built by Pene Taui, who, with his own particular *hapu*, also had the honour of defending it. It was scarcely shaken by the gun-fire, for here the largest trees had been put, and few shots had been directed against it. More than all, it was exposed to the enfilading fire of two loopholed bastions, in the largest of which was laid one of the four old cannons which the fort possessed.† Axes, scaling-ladders, and ropes wherewith to hew and pull down the palisades were supposed to be carried by an advance party of twenty-eight Pioneers, but on the advice of Lieutenant Phillpotts these were left behind.

Punctually at the appointed time the men of the three attacking forces reached their respective stations without a

---

* Colonel Despard's original plan was to make a false attack on the left face of the *pa* simultaneously with the main attack, but the necessity for detaching sixty men to guard Waaka's Hill so reduced his available force that this device had to be abandoned.

† There were four guns in Ohaeawai *pa* — two iron 9-pounders, a 4-pounder, and a swivel 2-pounder. One of the 9-pounders originally belonged to the ship *Brampton*, but when she was abandoned on the reef it was taken first to Paihia Mission Station, then to Waimate, where it was used to fire salutes on great days. From Waimate it was commandeered by Heke. The other guns had been collected at various times from various sources, one at least being part of the spoil of Kororareka.

shot being fired. They were clad in their scarlet uniform, and wore the old-fashioned leather stock. Many were ragged, some were barefooted, and all carried their full knapsack, even in the charge. What happened in that charge has been told by one of the Light Company of the 58th* who participated in it :—

We formed up in a little hollow in close order, elbows touching when we crooked them ; four ranks, only twenty-three inches between each rank. We got the orders " Fix bayonets," " Prepare to charge," and then " Charge." We went along at a steady double, the first two ranks at the charge with the bayonet ; the second rank had room to put their bayonets in between the front-rank men ; and the third and fourth ranks, with muskets and fixed bayonets at the slope. When within fifty paces of the *pa* we cheered and went at it at top speed, and it was " the devil take the hindmost." I did not see a single Maori all this time—only flashes and smoke, and my comrades falling all around me. The Maoris in their sheltered pits just poked the muzzles of their guns under the outer stockade, and we could do nothing. The stockade was ten feet high, and we were helpless. One man, one of the ladder party, carried up a ladder and set it against the stockade. " Now," he said, " there it is for any one who will go up it." But who would go up the ladder ? It would be going to certain death. If any one tried it he did not live long before the Maoris got him. In our Light Company alone we had twenty-one killed in the charge. We were, I suppose, not more than two and a half minutes before the stockade, and from the time we got the first order to charge until we got back to the hollow again was only five or seven minutes. As we charged up, a man was shot dead in front of me and another behind me. In the retreat I was carrying off a wounded man on my back when he was shot dead. Then I picked up a second wounded man, a soldier named Smith,† and carried him safely out. Nothing was explained to us before

* William Henry Free, who enlisted in the 58th Regiment in 1842 and came to Hobart in the following year as a guard over convicts. He subsequently attained the rank of Lieutenant of Volunteers in the Taranaki War, and died at New Plymouth on the night of the 25th January, 1919, aged ninety-three. He was probably the last survivor of those who attacked the Ohaeawai *pa*. Shortly before his death he gave the above account of the charge to Mr. James Cowan, and it is printed in Mr. Cowan's " The New Zealand Wars."

† Probably our old friend of the comic song.

we charged. We just went at the strong stockade front under orders from a Colonel who did not know his business and who had a contempt for the Maori.

Such were the sensations and experiences of a private soldier. Here are the impressions of Major Bridge, one of the few officers who came out scathless :—

At 3 o'clock all fell in, and the attacking parties—one under my command, the other under Major MacPherson—having been told off, as well as the support under Lieut.-Colonel Hulme, we were all marched off to our respective stations preparatory to making an attack. I was posted under cover of a thick clump of trees in front of the left angle of the *pa*, the point of attack, and whilst here there was an awful pause. The defenders ceased firing, and not a sound was heard, except the occasional report of a cannon from the hill, the Colonel having ordered a few shots of shell to be thrown in before he sounded the " Advance." Then we were all to rush rapidly on the *pa* and endeavour to force an entrance. What were the thoughts of many a brave fellow whose spirit might soon be wafted into eternity ? As for myself, I only thought of my darling wife and poor old mother, and how deeply they would feel my loss if I fell in the engagement, and I offered up a prayer to Almighty God to grant me His protection for their sakes, unworthy as I am, and a full believer of my fate being in His hands. I then calmly awaited the signal to advance. After waiting about a quarter of an hour I was asked by the Brigade Major if I was ready, and I answered " Yes." Shortly afterwards the bugle sounded the " Advance," and with a hearty British " Hurrah " on we marched, and so quickly did we follow up Major MacPherson's party, according to order, that the foremost of my men were at the palisades as soon as his. For the first five or six minutes, although I always had my misgivings about our success, I thought it was all right, and that we should force our way in, but when I got close up to the fence I saw the strength of it and the way it resisted the efforts of our brave fellows to pull it down. I saw them falling thickly all round, and my heart sank within me lest we should be defeated. Militia Volunteers, too, who carried the hatchets, billhooks, and ladders, would not advance, but lay down on their faces in the fern. Only one ladder was placed against the fence, and this by an old man of the Militia, and a sailor was shot dead in attempting to climb over the palisade by it and fell inside the *pa*. Several officers were cutting at the ties with their swords* and pulling at the fence they had partially loosened, when a bugle in the rear sounded the " Retreat." This at first we thought was a mistake, and it was not attended to, for all went to work, supposing the *pa* must be taken or we must die in the attempt. After a little the call was repeated, and then all that were left were prepared to obey its summons, carrying off the wounded with us.

The native defenders of the *pa*, said to number only 130 on this day, saw the Colonel's preparations and understood them. " Stand every man firm," cried a chief, " and you will see the soldiers walk into the ovens." This was figuratively true. The story of that assault, made in the bright sunlight of a July day, is one of the most unhappy in the history of the British arms. " At this moment," says a native account, " the bugle sounded, and the soldiers came charging on, shouting after the manner of European warriors. Those of us who were on Waaka's Hill shouted also, and the whole valley resounded with the anger of the *pakeha*." Within ten minutes Captain Grant and Lieutenant Phillpotts were killed, the former shot through the head, the latter through the heart ; Major MacPherson was dangerously and Lieutenant Beatty mortally wounded.† One-third of the men were also down before the awful line of smoke and fire that belched from the trench behind the wooden wall. The defenders had their instructions to hold their fire " until the eyes of the attackers could be seen blinking," and upon the two storming-parties reaching within 25 yards of the *pa* they received nearly simultaneously a fearful volley of reserved fire from the enemy. It was this volley which killed Captain Grant and caused havoc in the body of nearly three hundred of the finest troops, throwing the two

---

* Ensign O'Reilly, as fine a specimen of a young Irishman as one could wish to see on a summer's day, was desperately wounded while hacking the flax-withes that bound the palisades, with that miserable mockery of a weapon called the " regulation " sword. His right arm being shattered, the naked sword fell into the enemy's hands, and two and a half years after the battle I had the pleasure of returning it to him at Sydney, the blade having been redeemed by old Tamati Waaka and delivered to me at the Bay of Islands.—*Lieut.-Colonel Mundy*.

† Lieutenant Beatty died at Waimate at 2 a.m. on Saturday, the 12th July.

columns into a mass of confusion. Still they went on. Every exertion which the most intrepid bravery could display was shown by both officers and men. Although they succeeded in pulling open portion of the outer fence it was only the *pekerangi*. The inner fence resisted their bravest and most desperate efforts. While the men surged and struggled in front of the wall, meeting the direct fire of the defenders from the loopholes, the gun in the bastion, loaded with an old bullock-chain in lieu of shot, was discharged at them, causing serious losses,* but the work was not abandoned until the flower of their line had fallen and the bugle had sounded the "Retire."

Colonel Despard watched the carnage with horror and amazement. In the frenzy of his despair he lost his self-control. He ordered the bugle to sound the "Retreat," and immediately afterwards demanded to know who had given the order. "You yourself, sir, did this moment," answered Ensign Symonds. The beaten men came slowly trooping back in disorder and confusion, bringing their wounded with them. At this crisis several of the men behaved in the most splendid fashion, returning two or three times to bring off their wounded comrades through a hot fire. One man, Private Whitehead, of the 58th, who seemed to bear a charmed life, carried off five or six not only of his own regiment, but men of the 99th as well. The retreat was covered in good style by Lieut.-Colonel Hulme, and when all the wounded who could be found had been brought in the Rev. Henry Williams, who was in the camp, asked the Colonel's permission to go forward with a flag of truce and request leave to remove the dead. This permission being granted, he hoisted a white handkerchief on a pole, but on approaching the *pa* he was met with a stern rebuff from the rebels, who peremptorily ordered him back, telling him to return next morning.

* For this exploit the chief Mokaraka, who had led the raid on Waaka's Hill, was responsible. He organized a party who went at night to Kaikohe and brought the bullock-chains into the *pa*. He half filled the gun with powder, then rammed it to the muzzle with pieces of chain, which in the figurative language of the Maori " wriggled like fiery eels among the soldiers."

A roll-call disclosed that forty of all ranks had fallen and eighty were wounded in the few minutes the attack had lasted. Compared with this the native loss was infinitesimal, though conclusive figures could never be obtained. And so Nga-Puhi war-runners ran through all the north, saying : " One wing of England is broken and hangs dangling on the ground."

" It would be difficult," says Colonel Despard, " to give an idea of the enthusiasm with which the troops advanced to the attack. The struggle was who should be foremost, and certainly the bravery of the British soldier was never more conspicuous than on this occasion. At one moment there was a cessation in the firing, and at the same time the outer fence began to give way, and I felt that success was certain. This was only momentary. The fire was resumed by the enemy as soon as they found that the second stockade could not be forced, and being almost all armed with double-barrelled guns, and the distance so short, it became fatally deadly. In the exertion necessary to bring away the wounded the troops continued much exposed to the enemy's fire, but this was nobly replied to by the party under the personal command of Lieut.-Colonel Hulme, who conducted it with marked bravery. The troops returned to the camp undaunted in either mind or spirit, only returning after the obstacles opposed to them were too strong to overcome, and even in the moment of repulse wishing that another opportunity of attack might be offered them.

In Colonel Despard's official despatch he expressed the following opinion :—

I must here remark that the hatchets and axes as well as the ropes for pulling down the stockade, and the ladders, were all left behind by those appointed to carry them, and to this circumstance I attribute the main cause of the failure.

In after-years, when Colonel Despard had time and opportunity to reflect upon the events of that tragic day, he considerably modified that view :—

" It would be going too far," he said, " to say that this attack would have been successful had the persons entrusted with the duty of carrying the ladders and axes performed it as they should have done."

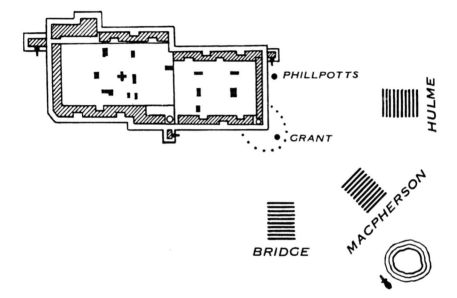

PHILLPOTTS

HULME

GRANT

MACPHERSON

BRIDGE

SKETCH-PLAN OF OHAEAWAI PA.

He then proceeds to explain that some one with the
scaling-party, obviously Lieutenant Phillpotts, had persuaded
the men to leave the ladders and axes behind them, arguing
that cutlasses would be more serviceable, and concludes
his reference to the subject with this benediction upon the
unnamed culprit : " Peace to his ashes. He was a brave
man, and one of the first to fall, close to the stockade."

As a matter of fact, the scaling-ladders had not been
entirely forgotten. One at least was brought up to the
palisades. It was reared against the wall, and a good-looking
sailor from the *Hazard* climbing to the top was instantly
shot, his lifeless body falling between the outer and the
middle wall of the stockade. In fatality and futility thus
ended the one attempt made to carry out the tactics by
which Colonel Despard then believed the *pa* could be won.

Late that evening a number of Heke's followers came
over from Kaikohe and entered the *pa*, for, having heard
that the soldiers had been beaten off, they were eager to
participate in the victory. The combined force then performed a war-dance to celebrate their success, and as they
danced they chanted this song of triumph :—

> O youth of sinewy force,
> O men of martial strength,
> Behold the sign of power !
> In my hand I hold the scalp
> Of the Kawau Tatakiha.

A song which, it is said, sounded through the still night and
amongst the hills like the roll of thunder.

That night was a sorrowful and anxious one for the
soldiers in the camp. Often the wailings of the *tohungas* in
the *pa* were heard, and in the excited state of their feelings
they were mistaken by the troops for the shrieks of tortured
comrades.* These weird sounds positively struck terror into
the hearts of the men on piquet duty, some of whom

* Of this the following native explanation is given : " And also a
great shouting and screaming was heard, which the soldiers thought was
the cry of one of their men being tortured ; but the noise was the voice
of a priest, who was then possessed of a spirit."

actually left their posts and came into camp, so horrified were they by these strange and dreadful cries. Still again through the night rang the challenge of the defiant sentinels : "Come on, soldiers; come on, and have your revenge. Your dead are with us. *Whai mai; whai mai*" ("Come on; come on ").

After a weary vigil the troops turned out an hour before daylight, but no attack was made from the *pa*. Henry Williams and Mr. Burrows came over from Waimate at an early hour, and again proceeding to the *pa* endeavoured to persuade the defenders to deliver up the dead.* This they refused to do unless Colonel Despard would sign a treaty of peace for four days, which, of course, was refused ; and in subsequent negotiations this period was extended to one month, and the withdrawal of the troops as an additional condition, a stipulation even more impossible of acceptance. Of these conferences Mr. Burrows has given the following account in his published diary :—

After a little parleying at a distance we were allowed to approach, and no opposition was at first raised to our removing the dead ; but in a short time a chief of the name of Te Haara came out of the *pa* to say that the bodies could only be removed on the condition that the Colonel withdrew his whole force at once to the Waimate, and from thence to the Bay. We replied we did not think such a condition would be agreed to, but we could name it to the Colonel, and I was leaving to do so when we were requested to seat ourselves on a log that was lying near for a *korero* (talk). There were present five or six of the leading chiefs, but not Kawiti. The first part of the conversation was directed to me, consisting of a story which had reached them that I had let our blacksmith's shop to the soldiers, and that Harry, the blacksmith, and I were helping to make bar shot, several of which had been fired at their *pa*. When I asked through what channel they had obtained such information I was told that a day or two previous they had taken one of Waaka's men prisoner. He had made his way with others to

* Colonel Despard states that one of the intermediaries in securing the recovery of the dead was that notorious *pakeha-Maori* John Marmon, " who had been a good deal about the camp, though without any employment." Marmon was an ex Botany Bay convict and whaler. He settled finally in New Zealand in 1817 and died at Hokianga, 2nd September, 1880, aged eighty-one.

the back of the *pa*, hunting for pigs ; and whilst hesitating whether they should shoot him at once or take him into their *pa* he had commenced giving them the information regarding the bar shot, but before he got to the end of his story he suddenly dashed from them. He was fired at and his cartouche-box shot away, but he himself escaped out of their hands. Of course, my only reply was that the blacksmith's shop, like all the other available buildings in the Waimate, had been taken possession of by the troops without asking my leave, and that Harry, the blacksmith, had been pressed into their service. Much more was said by them which was foreign to the subject for which we were there—namely, the obtaining possession of the dead and dying around. We were allowed to walk round and inspect the bodies, but not to touch them. I recognized those of Captain Grant and Lieutenant Phillpotts lying very near to each other close under the outer tier of defence. The latter had apparently fallen from the palisading just above where his body was lying, having been shot as he was trying to scale the *pa*. His eyeglass we found hanging on one of the sticks of the *pa*. I counted altogether about twenty-four bodies—soldiers, sailors, and marines ; several had been taken into the camp the night before. After spending a full hour and a half in trying to obtain permission to take away the dead we returned to the camp, promising that one of us would come back if the Colonel had any communication to make. As we were leaving we were asked to return next morning, even should the Colonel not agree to their proposal, when probably they would allow us to remove the dead. We were both treated with civility by them ; they asked very few questions as to the loss on our side. There was no boasting. Pene Taui, the chief of Ohaeawai, who had not joined us in our conversation, called to us from within the *pa*, saying, " Under any circumstances you will be allowed to take away the *tupapakus*—the dead bodies—to-morrow morning. Come early." We reported the particulars of our interview to the Colonel, who, of course, did not agree to the proposal of the rebels. At our suggestion, however, he agreed to remain quiet until after we had paid our next visit in the morning.*

* In a letter written on the 3rd July to his wife, who had been sent to Auckland for safety, Mr. Burrows says that in reply to the natives' demand that the soldiers should go away and peace be made for at least a month, " the Colonel offered to cease hostilities for a time. They, however, refused to allow the bodies to be taken yesterday, but requested us to return this morning. Neither Heke nor Kawiti was in the *pa* yesterday. Whether Kawiti is wounded or not we cannot tell. We were told he had gone away, but there is no believing them. Their killed and wounded must be great, but we have no means of ascertaining. They are very careful to conceal all they can."

The bodies of the dead, therefore, lay another day exposed where they fell. In the evening the rebels jubilantly danced a war-dance inside the *pa*, and as a reply the friendly natives gathered in front of the British camp, 300 strong, and shook the earth in the fury of their defiant *haka*. After it was over they fired a shot across the *pa* as a final signal of contempt. That night, though full of alarms, passed off without the expected attack.

At 10 o'clock next morning a native was seen waving a white flag from the palisade, and at the same time calling out to Mr. Williams to come for the dead. Waaka Nene answered him from the hill, proposing that the defenders should carry the bodies half-way towards the camp, and that the soldiers should bring them the rest of the way. To this they agreed, and the remainder of that day was spent in this mournful task. All the bodies were recovered except that of Captain Grant, which the rebels declared had been buried and would not be given up. This fact was reported to Colonel Despard by Major Bridge, who requested that the Colonel would ask Waaka Nene to intercede with the rebels to have the body delivered up. "This request," says the Major, "met with a most ungracious and unfeeling reception. I was told I was too fond of interfering, as every one who is rash enough to offer an opinion generally is, by him." All further efforts by Mr. Williams and Waaka Nene to recover the body were alike fruitless.

That evening the soldiers followed the remains of their comrades to their last resting-place beneath the shadow of the silent forest. A single grave was prepared at the edge of the bush, and here to mother earth was committed the bodies of the thirty young fellows cut off in the prime of life and in the midst of health, the funeral service being read by Henry Williams with all the deep impressiveness which its solemn theme must ever serve to inspire.*

---

* That the service lost nothing of its solemnity at the hands of Henry Williams may be judged by the following comment made by Colonel Despard : " While the troops remained at Kororareka Divine service was performed in the church for their benefit by Archdeacon Williams, and I must do him the justice to say that I have seldom abroad heard a better reader or preacher."

When, some days later, the remains of Captain Grant were found resting within a shallow grave inside the *pa* they were interred with those of Lieutenant Beatty in consecrated ground at Waimate,* the grief of the soldiers and sailors present being very marked, especially those forming the company of the lieutenant. " He was," says Mr. Burrows, " an officer greatly beloved by his men."

Here also was interred Lieutenant George Phillpotts, concerning whom something more should be said, for he was undoubtedly one of the characters of the campaign. He was a young man of good family, being the son of the then Bishop of Exeter, and at the time of his death he held the position of First Lieutenant of H.M.S. *Hazard*.

From all available accounts he was a strange personality : eccentric in his manner ; eccentric in his dress—unlike a sailor, constantly wearing a monocle—yet withal possessing those qualities which win general respect and admiration. A harum-scarum, rollicking tar, his sailors loved him because they knew he would never ask them to do or dare anything he would not do or dare himself. The natives regarded him with an amused affection, and called him " Toby " as an expression of their friendliness. Brave as a lion, knowing nothing of fear, he was guilty of many " blazing indiscretions " which might have broken a less popular man. He came to the Bay of Islands with the *Hazard* in the early stages of Heke's insurrection, and took part in its every incident up to the moment that he fell before the walls of Ohaeawai.

* The following appears in Dr. Thomson's " Story of New Zealand " : " In the churchyard at the beautiful mission station at Waimate are three wooden tombs, now covered with luxuriant vegetation, commemorating the names of the officers who fell at Ohaeawai ; and in the old church at Paramatta, Australia, there is a tablet to Captain Grant, of the 58th, raised by his brother officers ' to commemorate the loss of a good soldier and a warm friend.' But the non-commissioned officers, soldiers, and sailors who fell all sleep together without a memorial in the wild forest before Ohaeawai." This latter statement must now be qualified, for in 1872 the leading chief of the Ohaeawai district—Heta te Haara—made a proposal to the Government that the remains of the soldiers and sailors should be removed to the little church cemetery which has been laid out on the site of the old *pa*. This course was agreed to, and on the 1st July, 1872, the 27th anniversary of their death, the transfer was solemnly made, the Rev. Archdeacon Clarke reading the burial service at the reinterment.

He first attracted notice by wandering beyond the limits of safety at Kororareka, being captured by the insurgents, stripped of his arms, and sent back with a caution to be less reckless in the future.   In the defence of Kororareka he took a prominent part ; indeed, after the fall of Acting-Commander Robertson he became, if not the wisest, at least one of the most energetic of the European leaders.   His rashness of tongue led him to speak in the most unguarded way of the Rev. Henry Williams, even forgetting himself so far as to call him a " traitor," than which no more undeserved aspersion was ever cast upon any man.*   His impetuosity of action led him to fire the guns of the *Hazard* into the abandoned town just at the moment when the natives were assisting the settlers to remove their property to a place of safety, thereby assisting to make confusion worse confounded.   His conduct towards the missionary was strongly condemned by the Governor, and his combative propensities were hotly resented by the settlers, yet he was readily forgiven by all.   In the expedition against Ohaeawai Lieutenant Phillpotts was in charge of the sailors and marines from the *Hazard*,† and as such he was taken into the counsels of Colonel Despard on the few occasions upon which that gentleman chose to give his confidence to his subordinates.   As the result of this interchange of opinions upon the tactics to be employed against the *pa* their relations became strained.   Phillpotts disagreed with almost everything Despard did, and plainly and bluntly said so.   Contradiction was not a thing that Colonel Despard relished, and opposition was something he frankly disliked, nor was he particular how he expressed that dislike.   This had its counter-effect upon Phillpotts, who was abnormally sensitive to the rebukes of his superiors. At one stage of the attack upon Ohaeawai a proposal was

---

* This was probably due to an absurd impression which had gained currency that Mr. Williams had said the natives had no hostile intention and would not attack the town. Mr. Williams has completely answered this charge in a statement he has left amongst his papers.

† Lieutenant Clarke, of the *Hazard*, succeeded to the command of the sailors in the camp after the death of Lieutenant Phillpotts.

made to mine the palisade and blow it up with gunpowder. If Lieutenant Phillpotts did not conceive the idea, he at least approved it. He even volunteered to carry it out, and was promptly snubbed for his pains. He then, in a spirit of bravado, left the camp at midday, carrying nothing in his hand but a switch—his beloved monocle in his eye —and walked down to within a few yards of the stockade. Here he remained for some minutes, when a rebel climbed to the top of the inner row of palisades and called out to him in the best English he could command, "Go away, Toby, or else you will be shot." For this escapade, out of which he came scathless, Phillpotts had attired himself in a blue shirt and a white belltopper.*

On the day of the assault, which proved to be his last, he was attached to Major MacPherson's force, his special duty being to see that the axes, ladders, &c., were brought up to the palisade, a duty he appeared to regard as not less foolish than the whole scheme of the attack, and advised the men, who were sailors, to use their cutlasses instead. Into the assault he went with the full conviction that he would not come back alive, and before he started out his eccentricity in the matter of dress again got the better of him. During the day he was wearing a pair of black-cloth trousers with a red stripe, common to the soldier rather than to the sailor. Seeing Mr. Dumoulin, an officer of the commissariat, near the naval gun at the foot of Waaka's Hill, he called out to him, "Here, Mullins, pull these trousers off. I don't want to die a soldier." He sat down on the gun-carriage, and Dumoulin pulled the trousers over his boots. He then drew his sword, threw the scabbard into the fern, and his forage-cap after it. Having divested himself of these garments, which he no doubt regarded as encumbrances, he walked into the ranks of the assaulting

* While in camp Lieutenant Phillpotts was seldom seen in uniform; he apparently did not relish his association with the soldiers. One explanation of his immunity in this adventure is that the natives in the *pa* mistook him for a missionary—about the last thing Phillpotts would have cared to be taken for.

forces clad in a sailor's blue shirt and his flannel trousers.* He survived the first fatal volley, but was killed almost immediately the independent firing commenced, being shot, it is said, by a Maori boy when vainly attempting to break through the palisade, and falling not more than a few feet from the stockade.   His monocle was recovered with his body, and was given by the Rev. Henry Williams to Acting-Commander Johnson, of the *Hazard*, six days later.

The position in which Colonel Despard now found himself was anything but an enviable one.† His attack upon the *pa* had failed ; he was unable to continue it because his guns were ineffective, his ammunition exhausted, and he was hampered by some seventy wounded officers and men, who were lying in an exposed camp with nothing but fern beds between them and the sodden ground.   The impulse which seized him in these depressing circumstances was to abandon the attack and retire, being convinced of what he had only formerly feared, that the rebels would now do what they had hitherto refused to do—cut off his communications with Waimate and the coast, and so prevent the removal of the wounded and the renewal of his supplies.   Accordingly on the morning after the attack he ordered a retreat to Waimate.   The few tents, stores, and tools were to be burned or destroyed, and the ammunition of the Infantry was to be buried, sufficient transport for all in one journey not being available.   When the issue of this order was reported to

---

* In an interesting letter on the subject of Lieutenant Phillpotts, written by the late John Webster, of Hokianga, to the late Dr. Hocken, and now in the Hocken Collection, Mr. Webster says : " Between ' Toby ' and the missionaries there was a deadly feud. The latter called him a coward, and he retorted by calling them traitors. I saw him on the afternoon of the assault. Maning and I shook hands with him when he formed the ' forlorn hope ' with his few bluejackets. His last words I heard were, ' I will show these —— missionaries I am no coward.' "

The Mr. Maning here referred to is the late Judge Maning, author of " Old New Zealand."

† Colonel Despard does not appear to have been censured by the Governor for his rashness in attacking a half-breached *pa*, but he was justly blamed by soldiers and civilians for his tactics which proved to be so prodigal of his soldiers' lives. It was even whispered in the military clubs in London that on reading the despatches describing the event the Duke of Wellington declared that distance alone prevented him bringing Colonel Despard to a court-martial.

the native allies a few of the chiefs, headed by Mohi Tawhai, proceeded to the Colonel's tent and requested to know if what they had heard was or was not true. If true, they wanted a further opportunity of discussing it with him. A *korero* must be held. The Colonel admitted the truth of the rumour, and a conference was fixed for 3 o'clock. At the appointed hour the chiefs, accompanied by some forty of their followers, assembled to hear what the Colonel had to say. Colonel Despard, supported by several of his officers, came out of his tent and, addressing the natives, made a long and vigorous speech, in which he upbraided the chiefs for refusing to participate in the assault on the *pa*,* and charged them with avarice in demanding four new blankets for every wounded man removed to Waimate, when they well knew he had no blankets to give them. He contended that the soldiers were fighting as much for the benefit of the natives as of the Europeans, yet in this joint interest the soldiers were doing all the fighting and the Maoris none. He also complained bitterly of the isolation to which they had abandoned him, hampered as he was with his wounded ; his cattle were knocking up with the labour of hauling stores from the Bay ; and there was imminent danger that, owing to the incessant rain, sickness at any time might enter the camp and scourge his little army, leaving him entirely at the mercy of the enemy.†
Since, then, he was unable to rely upon the active

* In this there is a curious discrepancy between the European and native accounts. Colonel Despard alleges that the native allies took no part in the assault, and holds it a grievance against them that they simply looked on. The native account, however, states that when Waaka Nene found it impossible to divert Colonel Despard from his intention to assault the *pa*, he offered to make a simultaneous attack upon another face, but the offer was declined, on the ground that when the *pa* was taken the soldiers would not be able to distinguish between the rebel and the friendly natives. Further, that when the assault actually commenced, Waaka, of his own volition, took up a position at the rear of the *pa* to intercept the rebel retreat, if such should be the happy issue of the day.

† As a matter of fact, the camp was spared the visitation of sickness, and Colonel Despard was afterwards loud in his praises of a climate which kept his men healthy under the unwholesome conditions in which they were living. " Such a thing," he says, " could not have happened in any other part of the world."

co-operation of the natives, discretion dictated that he should get away while he could.

The chiefs, in reply, urged the unwisdom of retiring before the dead were recovered, which would create a most dangerous impression in the minds of neutral and enemy natives alike. They also stressed the certainty with which the enemy would find the hidden ammunition, and with it kill more soldiers. These arguments seemingly left the Colonel unconvinced, and then a flood of Maori oratory of the most vehement character was let loose upon the obdurate Colonel. It was at this stage of the discussion that the humorous incident related by Mr. J. P. Dumoulin occurred. Among the most vigorous protesters against retreat was Mohi (Moses) Tawhai, Waaka Nene's first lieutenant. Finding that the Colonel persisted in his determination, Mohi at last became angry, and employed some expressions towards the British officer that are never used in polite society. Meurant, the interpreter, unwilling to render into plain English just what the chief had said, began to temporize, but his evasion was not skilful enough to escape observation. The Colonel's suspicions were aroused ; he thought Meurant was playing him false. " Tell me instantly, sir," he demanded, " what the native says." " Nothing of any consequence, sir," replied Meurant. Thereupon the Colonel flew into one of his outrageous passions, frightening poor Meurant into a state of bewilderment. That worthy fought off as long as he could, but the Colonel would not be denied. At last, in sheer desperation, and with more regard to directness than to good English, Meurant replied, " Well, sir, if you will 'ave it, Moses says you're a hold hass."*

Colonel Despard makes no reference to this incident except to say that " Moses Tawhai made a most violent speech."

Moses, however, was capable of better things. He was tactician enough to see that having made the Colonel

* *Vide* Carleton's " Life of Henry Williams."

thoroughly angry they could do nothing with him, and so after Taonui and several others had expended their eloquence upon him Moses rose and, adopting a more conciliatory tone, said :—

It is all true what the *pakeha rangatira** has said. The fighting has all been done by the *pakehas.* They may well laugh at us, for we have done nothing. Let us now try and see if we cannot do something.

The debate proceeded for some time in this more friendly strain, and it was finally closed by Waaka Nene remarking that there had been enough talk. "Would the *pakeha rangatira* consent to remain two days longer?" To this question Colonel Despard gave a civil but evasive answer, being, as he himself admits, unwilling to let the natives think that their speeches had in any way influenced him. To be influenced by a "savage" was beneath what Colonel Despard regarded as the dignity of a British Colonel.

That night the loyal natives had a long and anxious *korero* among themselves, and next morning Waaka Nene came to Colonel Despard and gave him the most complete assurance of their active co-operation either in continuing the assault, or, if needs be, in retiring upon Waimate. Being now convinced that he could hold his allies, and that there would not be, what he feared there might be, a wholesale desertion to the enemy, Colonel Despard resolved to continue the attack, but to materially alter his tactics. The policy of attempting to breach the stockade was to be abandoned, but with such ammunition as he could procure he would employ a plunging fire, harrying the defenders by throwing shells into the *pa* instead of at it.

With this object in view, firing was resumed on the 8th and 9th, but owing to shortness of ammunition the 32-pounder was discharged only at lengthy intervals. Some skirmishes also took place between the defenders and Waaka Nene's men, though without decisive results. On the following day it was evident some important movement was pending within the *pa.* The rebels were ill at

* *Pakeha rangatira* = the white chief, the leader of the British.

ease, and those versed in native customs were not surprised next morning when the news swept through the
camp that the enemy had silently evacuated the place*
during the night.   The discovery was made shortly after
midnight by the native allies, whose suspicions were
aroused by the barking of the dogs and the complete
cessation of the sentries' watch-cry.   Tamahue, a one-
armed warrior from Hokianga, creeping cautiously up to
the wall, was confident that it was deserted.   Softly he
entered, and peering into the houses found them empty,
save for one old woman who, being deaf, had slept,
unconscious of the retreat going on around her.   Securing
her as a prisoner, Tamahue signalled to his companions
anxiously waiting outside, who entering verified their earlier
suspicions that the unusual silence was eloquent of the
garrison's hurried flight.   They then reported their discovery to the nearest piquet, who in turn sent hurried
word back to the camp.   The report of the piquets was
soon confirmed by a message from Waaka Nene.   The
Colonel then ordered a small party to proceed cautiously
down and ascertain the fact.   These noiseless seekers, to
their great joy, found their expectations realized and their
suspicions justified by the deserted condition of the fortress.
The defenders, like the Arabs, had metaphorically folded
their tents and silently sped away.   Precautions were
taken against the possibility of surprise, but there was no
intention on the part of the rebels to renew the conflict
at Ohaeawai.   Blood had been spilt, and, as in the case
of Puketutu, the place must be abandoned.   The main
body of the defenders therefore departed for Kaikohe, where
next day they were pursued by the friendly natives, who
satisfied their warlike desires by burning down a house
belonging to Heke.   The remainder of the garrison were
soon scattered deep in the safety of the bush and in the

* The Maori did not count the loss of a fighting *pa* as a disgrace, as
it may have been built only for a particular fight and on another man's
land.   The number of the enemy killed and taken prisoner was what the
Maori counted as trophies in his wars.

STORMING OHAEAWAI PA.

After the drawing by Sergeant Williams, in the Hocken Collection, Dunedin.

silence of the mountains, ready to reassemble when the word should be given.

At daylight the soldiers streamed into the *pa*, where they found evidence that the enemy had made a hurried retreat, as they had left behind them all the arms and accoutrements taken from the British dead. They also left some of their own ammunition, guns, tomahawks, and boxes full of plunder taken at the sacking of Kororareka, as well as potatoes and Indian corn sufficient for six months' supply.

A thorough examination of the *pa* revealed not only the mutilated body of Captain Grant, but that of a private soldier of the 99th, who was known to be within the fortress. Two days before the *pa* was assaulted this soldier had foolishly crept beyond the British lines for the purpose of purloining some potatoes from a native hut not far from the stockade. He was observed by the rebels, one of whom fired at and seriously wounded him. Before his comrades could come to his rescue the rebels came out of the *pa* and carried him inside. Here his hands and feet were secured, and it is alleged he was subsequently tortured, a red-hot iron being passed across his left breast and burning kauri-gum placed on his stomach. A circumstantial story, bristling with gruesome details, of how this was done was related to some soldiers at Auckland by an American named Brown six months later. The details were so complete that there appeared little doubt that the narrator had been in closer touch with the enemy than he should have been, and he was straightway placed under arrest by the authorities. He now became alarmed, and first denied that he had ever made any statement to the soldiers ; then on being confronted by the men who heard his story he changed his ground and affirmed that he had heard the particulars from another American named Woodward, with whom he had been working as a sawyer. Woodward was also arrested, and both were sent to the Bay of Islands, where it was hoped to establish that one or both had been acting against the British at the attack upon the *pa*. In this, however, the authorities did not succeed.

"I had little doubt," Colonel Despard subsequently wrote, "but that one of them had been with the enemy, as it was impossible that any but an eye-witness could have given such circumstantial detail which explained many things to us which we were before unable to account for. That some European was there I was fully convinced from many circumstances; amongst others, English words being occasionally overheard, such as 'Starboard' and 'Larboard watch.'"*

That the body of the soldier was found severely burned is unquestioned, for when it was examined by the medical officers "the marks of torture were very apparent."† It is impossible to say what actually took place within the *pa*, but as the known habit of the Maori was to give their victims the "happy despatch," and torture as practised by the North American Indian was unknown to them, one is compelled to look for some other explanation to account for the mutilated condition of the soldier's body. Fortunately, two separate accounts have been preserved which when pieced together may serve as the true explanation. The followers of Heke have left it on record that when the soldier was carried inside the *pa* he was placed beside one of the fires burning within the enclosure. Unfortunately, he was not divested of his belts, and at some time during the night the ammunition he was carrying caught fire and exploded, inflicting terrible injuries upon him, from which he subsequently died. In this way his

* During the visit which James Merrett paid to the village of Tako in 1846 he questioned the natives as to whether there were any Europeans among them at Ruapekapeka *pa*, as the troops had heard European voices shouting during the night to the people inside the *pa* to keep a sharp lookout. They said that Europeans had been among them—two particularly—but they had returned to their homes before the *pa* had been captured. There was, however, a native, Haki Moa, who had spent many years on board whalers, who was invariably in the habit of shouting his watchword in English, and that his must have been the voice which was heard so distinctly by the sentries.

† The medical officers at Ohaeawai were Doctor Pine, of the 58th, and Doctor Galbraith, of the 99th.

body came to bear marks which were afterwards mistaken for the effects of torture. The explanation as to how the body came to be burned with kauri-gum reaches us from an altogether different quarter. That well-informed native who related the story of "The War in the North" has thus stated the circumstances :—

But nevertheless the body of one soldier was burned that night, for as the people were mending the fence by torchlight there was a dead soldier lying near, and they put a torch of kauri-resin on the body to light their work, which burned the body very much and caused the report to be spread afterwards when the body was found by the soldiers that the man had been tortured. This was not true, as the man was dead before the fire was thrown on the body.

Both these happenings are well within the bounds of possibility and offer a more feasible explanation of what occurred than the supposition popular at the time that the rebels had suddenly begun the practice of torture which hitherto had been singularly foreign to their race and in which they never subsequently indulged. In course of time the story told by Brown and Woodward would seem to have dwindled into nothing more than a mischievous excursion into the realm of imagination, based upon a slender veneer of fact, and by its gradual dissolution the reputation of the Maori had been slowly rescued from an aspersion with which no one would dream of loading it to-day. The bodies of Captain Grant and Lieutenant Phillpotts were mutilated after death at the instigation of the *tohungas* and solely for religious purposes. "The foliage of the battlefield" was, according to the native account, taken to the great *tohunga*, Te Atua Wera, that he might perform the usual ceremonies and cause the people to be fortunate in war.

When Colonel Despard had at length an opportunity of examining the *pa*, nothing would convince him that the builders had not the assistance of some European skilled in the art of fortification ; and, though he was assured in the most positive terms that such was not the case, he, with his characteristic doggedness, still clung to the conviction that the work could not otherwise have been done.*

Although the result of the attack upon the *pa* was regarded as a serious reverse for the British, the effect upon the natives of their own success was not what might have been supposed. Our disaster, instead of inducing boastfulness, struck the victors with amazement amounting to awe. "We have been told," said they, "that the soldiers would go wherever they were bid—even to certain death—but we never believed it. Now we know it." Strange as it may seem, the moral effect of the ill success at Ohaeawai was thus in a measure to retrieve our previous failures at Wairau and at Kororareka.

With the *pa* in the possession of the troops,† and the rebels gone, no one knew where, no further purpose was to be served by keeping the military at Ohaeawai; and so, after destroying the palisades by fire and axe, a work which occupied three days, the troops were marched back to comparatively comfortable quarters at Waimate.‡

Colonel Despard had previously written to the Governor stating that as soon as his men were rested he proposed to march against the *pa* of the chief Te Haratua,§ situated at

* When the *pa* fell the native flag which had been flying from its staff came into the hands of Waaka Nene, who gave it to Major Bridge. It was subsequently presented by the Major to the Canterbury Museum, where it is now. While the *pa* was being examined two women of the friendly tribes quarrelled about a double-barrelled gun, which they both claimed to have found. They commenced wrestling for it, and in the struggle it went off, killing one of them on the spot. The incident caused great excitement at the moment, but in the general furore was soon forgotten.

† An officer who was present at the taking of the *pa*, after describing the manner of its fortification, says: "I think this will be a lesson to us not to make too light of our enemies, and shows the folly of attempting to carry such fortifications by assault without first making a practicable breach."

‡ Major Bridge in his diary makes this entry: "14th July (Monday).—Delighted to get back again, even to such indifferent quarters, having been three weeks under canvas and crowded with nine officers in a subaltern's small tent. Enjoyed a thorough good wash, a luxury I had not had for three weeks, during which time I had never had my clothes off."

§ Te Haratua was the *matua*, or protecting chief, of the white people at Pakaraka; but when the war broke out he allied himself with Heke, and took an active part against the Government throughout the war. He was received into the Christian Church in extreme old age, and baptized under the name of Te Wiremu.

Pakaraka, who from the beginning of the insurrection had leagued himself with Heke. He was then to proceed upon the larger manœuvre of attacking Kawiti at the unfortified *pa* in which he was reported to be resting farther inland at Waiomio. The first portion of this programme was carried out on the 16th July. The troops were marched out from Waimate on the morning of that day, and by the afternoon had accomplished the somewhat inglorious achievement of destroying an empty *pa*, Te Haratua's people preferring to fly and fight another day under circumstances more advantageous to themselves.

That evening despatches were received in camp calling Colonel Despard and Lieut.-Colonel Hulme back to Auckland. They were summoned to the capital for the dual purpose of taking counsel with the authorities as to future operations, and of holding a court-martial upon Lieutenant Barclay and Ensign Campbell, who were charged with abandoning their positions at the fight at Kororareka. Lieutenant Barclay was honourably acquitted, it being held that he succumbed to a *force majeure*. Ensign Campbell was found guilty, but in consideration of his extreme youth, short service, and the great difficulty of his situation the Court simply sentenced him to be reprimanded. Both these findings of the Court were afterwards confirmed by the General Officer Commanding, at Sydney, Sir Maurice O'Connell, K.C.B.

CHAPTER VI.

BETWEEN THE BATTLES.

WHEN Lieut.-Colonel Hulme left Waimate on the 17th July he took with him what remained of his own regiment, the 96th, and so far as the records show they did not, as a regiment, again participate in the war in the north. For a time they did garrison duty in Auckland, replacing a detachment of the 58th, which, under Captain Matson, was sent to strengthen the forces in the camp at Waimate. Before long, however, a new anxiety, the result of Heke's successes, had been added to Governor FitzRoy's accumulating troubles by the fructifying of the spirit of rebellion which honeycombed the native mind from Whanganui to Port Nicholson. Hulme and his men were accordingly transferred to Wellington, where the Lieutenant-Colonel was given the command of some four hundred troops, to whom was allotted the arduous task of checking the aggressions of those natives who, under Topine te Mamaku and Te Rangihaeata, were harrying the settlers in the Hutt Valley. Unlike the trouble in the north, this defiance of established authority in the south was almost entirely the product of quarrels about land, being the result of reckless purchases by the New Zealand Company's agent on the one hand and the excited avarice of the natives on the other. On the 24th February, 1846, the troops marched from Wellington into the Hutt Valley and occupied Boulcott's farm. So simple did the problem appear to the Governor that he believed a policy of intimidation was all that was

required to clear the valley of the marauders ; but here, as
in the north, the official expectations were rudely shattered.
The natives refused either to be scared or cajoled, and a
campaign which was anticipated might last for several days
continued with varying fortunes for as many months.*

Meanwhile the troops operating against Heke and
Kawiti settled down in camp at Waimate, under Major
Bridge, who had strict instructions from the Governor not
to indulge in aggressive tactics of any kind whatsoever.
With improved quarters, better weather, and little to do,
the soldiers made themselves completely at home, much to
the annoyance of the Rev. Mr. Burrows, who found them
ever ready to use up his fences for firewood, and just as
ready to live upon his pigs and poultry as upon the rations
supplied by the Government. Yet their life was not one
of unbroken ease, for the monotony of their daily round
was sometimes enlivened by reports brought into the camp
of how Kawiti with a large body of his followers had been
seen lurking in the forest near-by ; of how the enemy was
preparing a night attack upon the camp ; or some such
idle story which excited the fears of a few and stimulated
the ardour of others. As a consequence of these reports
the piquets were strengthened. A treble post was formed,
and orders were given to the outer piquet that in the
event of the enemy appearing he should fire and retire
on the centre post. One rather dark night the appointed
signal was given by an outer piquet, and, acting upon
orders from headquarters, the officer on duty called out
the men, and the whole camp was roused. The man who
had given the alarm was summoned and questioned as to
the grounds on which he had fired his rifle. " I saw," he
replied, " a Maori in a blanket creeping up towards me.
I fired at him and came in." The locality where the man
had been stationed was carefully searched, but no natives
were seen, and the camp retired to rest again. " On

* Hostilities in the south were opened on the 3rd March, 1846, by a
body of the 96th Regiment, acting under orders, firing upon a party of
natives.

the morrow," says Mr. Burrows, "a white cow was seen
wandering about in the neighbourhood, which had evidently
been shot in the eye. We had the poor brute put out of
its misery."

A week or two later a similar alarm was given from the
opposite end of the camp. The like process of mustering
the men and examining the author of the alarm was
repeated. This man (one of the Volunteers) had seen
"a parcel of Maoris creeping up towards him, wrapped in
blankets." On ascertaining the spot where this disturbing
vision had been seen it was at once surmised by those
who were acquainted with it that the affrighted man had
mistaken some eight or ten large boulders in the neighbourhood for the stealthy enemy stealing silently upon him. He
was taken to the spot and asked to resume the position
he was in when he made his alarming discovery. No
sooner had he done so than he exclaimed : " There they
be now, don't you see them." The highly amused company then passed over to the spot where the stones lay,
whereupon the astonished man again exclaimed : " Well,
I took them stones to be Maoris in blankets."*

In the meantime Colonel Despard fretted and fumed in
Auckland while the Governor halted between two opinions.
FitzRoy believed that the loss of Ohaeawai *pa* would
produce such a chastening effect upon the Maori mind
that the chiefs would before long sue for peace, and
that to actively continue the war would result only in a
prodigality of public expenditure and of human life which
a brief cessation of hostilities would mercifully obviate. He
was also uncertain as to what would happen in the event
of his withdrawing the troops from Waimate. The fear
which obsessed him was that the moment the soldiers
were removed the natives would swoop down upon the
mission station and wipe it out, thereby dealing a heavy
blow to Christianity and at once obliterating one of the
most important outposts of civilization in the country.
Perhaps, too, he had become somewhat mistrustful of

* *Vide* diary of Rev. R. Burrows.

Colonel Despard's reckless methods, which he had so far refrained from publicly censuring, but concerning which he must have had his private reservations. The Colonel himself had no such reservations. The Governor's reluctance to carry on the war was therefore something which, frankly, he was unable to understand.

"The New-Zealander is not a man who can be treated with any sort of hesitation. He must be talked to with a fixed bayonet," was the Colonel's dictum, in compliance with which he wished to attack Kawiti in the small *pa* of no particular strength at Waiomio, to which he had retired upon his retreat from Ohaeawai. To his representations that this operation should be commenced and carried out with vigour the Governor's reply was that he was sending out fresh peace-feelers to Heke, and he was advised that it might be necessary to include Kawiti in any arrangements subsequently made. He therefore counselled patience.

In addition to his reluctance to prejudice his peaceful overtures by precipitate action, another complication had entered into the situation which served to further perplex the Governor and incline him to a non-aggressive policy. This was the possible attitude of the powerful chief Tirarau, of Kaipara, whose allegiance to the Government was reported to be so doubtful that he might at any moment join the rebels and make a diversion against the town of Auckland. Despard's small force would then become involved with an additional enemy of unascertained strength, and it was necessary to wait and see what Tirarau's real disposition was and to make provision accordingly. Fortunately, the information given to the Governor regarding Tirarau's state of mind was wholly inaccurate. That chief was safely under the influence of the Rev. James Buller, Wesleyan missionary at Tangiteroria; and not only did he not molest the settlers or threaten the troops, but proved his loyalty to the Crown by sending word to Heke that should he make an attempt to destroy Auckland, that attempt would most certainly involve his own destruction, for never would he be permitted to pass through Kaipara territory.

7—First War.

Ignorant of the true position, however, the Governor refused to take risks, and contented himself with requesting Colonel Despard not to undertake any active operations against the rebels until he was sufficiently reinforced to do so without exposing Waimate to be destroyed during his absence.

In this passive policy he was to some extent encouraged by the wily Heke, from whom he received the following letter, in which he sought to justify all that had happened at Kororareka and at Ohaeawai, and in which to the impressionable mind of the Governor there seemed to be a suggestion of repentance :—

O FRIEND THE GOVERNOR,—   19th July, 1845.

Do you harken to me. I have not transgressed. My only transgression was in cutting down the flagstaff. I had no desire to kill the Europeans. I regard them. I went to see Mr. Williams when I learned that they (the Europeans and natives) had been skirmishing.

I then went to Mr. Beckham and requested an interview, but he refused to speak with me, and said our heads should be cut off by swords ; the great guns were also fired at us. On this account I joined Kawiti on the second day. I led my people in perfectly good order to Mawhe ; the bodies of the Europeans were not injured—no hand molested them.

I was not present at Taiamai (Ohaeawai), which was the cause of the evil of that place. It was the people of Hokianga which caused this bad work—namely, the men of Mohi Tawhai, of Arama Karaka (Adam Clarke), of Waaka Nene, of Patuone, and of Te Taonui—it was the people of Hokianga who came to Kawiti that cut up the bodies of the Europeans. I know that this is a great transgression which has been committed by Walker's people.

O Friend the Governor.

This is my good news to you. I call upon you to make peace. Would it not be well for us to make peace—to seek a reconciliation with God on account of our sins, as we have defiled his presence with human blood ?

The Scriptures tell us to pray to God, who will give us a knowledge of His laws.

I felt a regard for the soldiers, although they came with their heavy things (guns, shells, &c.) to destroy me. I did not burn the bridges on the Kerikeri Road : this was my act of great kindness to the soldiers.

If you think well of these sentences, write to me quickly in order that I may learn your sentiments. This is my second

letter to you, and I now know there is anger within you, because
you have not sent me one letter   I also know that it is Walker
who kills the soldiers, for he lets the soldiers fight, but runs
away into the bush himself.

What are the reflections respecting this affair ?   I say, do
you look into this affair, both for yourself and me.

From HONE WIREMU POKAI.

To this communication the Governor replied in the
most fatherly spirit, tendering to the rebel chief much
excellent advice, and telling him in persuasive terms that
it was for him to reflect on the town destroyed, on the
lives lost, and then to offer an atonement to the utmost
of his ability.* Nothing further happened. Heke believed
the fault, if fault there was, lay with the Europeans, and
that if any atonement was to be offered, it was by them
and to him, not from him to them. From that position
he stubbornly refused to retreat.

While waiting in Auckland, still hoping to persuade the
Governor to push on with the war, Colonel Despard busied
himself with the search for suitable carriages for his
artillery, and out of the military debris which he found
in the barracks he secured the old carriages and limbers
of the two brass 6-pounders. These had been left behind
because they were reported to be so rotten and decayed as
to be unfit for field service. Upon a more critical examination, however, the Colonel found that by replacing some
of the wheels and repairing others they might once more
be made fit for service. Two new field-carriages for the
12-pounders were also put in hand by the best artificers
the town could supply, and by the time the relieving
troops which he was sending up to Waimate were ready to
embark for the Bay these additions to the Colonel's meagre
equipment stood in the barrack-yard grim enough in their
coats of sombre paint.

Every shot and every shell that could be spared from
the ordnance stores was also collected and embarked at the
same time, but in this section of the armament there was a

* *Vide* FitzRoy's letter to Heke of the 6th August, 1845.

7*

lamentable deficiency.   There was, in fact, a serious shortage of ammunition of all classes, so much so that in all his operations Colonel Despard had to exercise the strictest vigilance to see that not a round was wasted, and frequently he was compelled to order firing to cease, or to refrain from commencing it, when good results might have been obtained by continuing it longer or beginning it sooner.

In consequence of his decision to retain the men of the 96th in garrison at Auckland, Colonel Despard had earlier in the month sent the detachment of the 58th, under Captain Matson, to Waimate, and later had withdrawn the 99th from the camp, replacing them by a detachment of the same regiment under Lieutenant Blackburn.*   By the 26th August the Colonel had collected such additions to his armament as the scanty supplies of Auckland could afford, and on that day he and a detachment of the 99th, the recovered wounded of the 58th, a subaltern officer and sixteen men of the 96th, embarked for the Bay of Islands on board the transport *Slains Castle.*†   The vessel was escorted by H.M.S. *Daphne*, which a few days previously had arrived in Auckland from Valparaiso, whither she had been sent by the Admiral of the South American Station to increase the naval portion of New Zealand's force.   Captain Onslow then became the senior naval officer in these waters.‡

* Lieutenant Blackburn was killed in the fight at Horokiwi Valley (Wellington) between the British forces, under Major Last, and the rebel natives, under Te Rangihaeata, on the 6th August, 1846.   He is buried in the Bolton Street Cemetery, Wellington.

† Colonel Despard also took with him Mr. Edward Shortland to act as interpreter.

‡ The Governor subsequently became involved in a correspondence with Captain Onslow, who wished to return to his station almost immediately.   In his letter of the 9th September, Captain FitzRoy says: " Injury has already been caused to this colony by too much haste in our hostile operations, owing to the doubts of our forces being able to remain a sufficient time.   I cannot think that you will leave New Zealand while the colony is in such extremely difficult circumstances.   Besides the rebellion in the north, the tribes near Auckland are now quarrelling, and the risk of hostile and very serious proceedings at Wellington is imminent. It is my duty to protest in the most earnest manner against your leaving New Zealand at present."

Again, on the 30th September, FitzRoy wrote to Captain Onslow, urging him not to leave New Zealand, concluding thus : " The precarious state of this colony with reference to our unfortified settlements and to the well-armed native population can hardly be estimated by a stranger."

Fine weather favoured the ships, and a good passage was made. Early on the 1st September the troops and stores were disembarked at Kerikeri, and during the afternoon they reached Waimate. Here Colonel Despard again took command, and was somewhat surprised to find that the false alarms and constant rumours of attack had induced Major Bridge to build substantial earthworks round the camp, which the Colonel at once condemned. They were of such an extensive nature that, in his opinion, three times his available force could not have manned them; but, more than all, they excited his displeasure because he regarded them as a reflection on the courage and discipline of the British soldier.

" I could never admit," says the Colonel, " that a European force of between 300 and 400 men, well supplied with arms and ammunition and four pieces of cannon, required any rampart to defend them in an open country against a barbarian enemy who never could have brought at the utmost more than double that number, without artillery, against them."

With his unchastened scepticism of the fighting-qualities of the Maori, Colonel Despard was ever scornful of the rumoured attacks upon the camp,* but to prevent the men being worried by night alarms he gave orders that in such an event the piquets alone were to turn out until the officers on duty had ascertained the cause. After this order was given the camp slept in peace at night, and during the day the soldiers busied themselves with the task of levelling the newly made earthworks which Despard ordered to be demolished, much to the chagrin of Major Bridge.

Towards the end of September Despard's native allies received an important reinforcement from the north, Nopera Panakareao, chief of the Rarawa tribe, having voluntarily brought over one hundred of his best fighting-men to assist Waaka Nene against the forces of Heke. The first public conference between these units of the race took place

* The rumours which reached the camp were not all of projected attacks and imminent assaults. Sometimes the soldiers were cheered by the intelligence that Heke had been captured, and more than once they were told that he was dead—all as false as they were doubtless alluring.

at Waimate on the 29th of the month, and after the usual ceremonial war-dance the chiefs stood up in front of their people and delivered themselves of their sentiments. Several of Waaka Nene's chiefs first welcomed the strangers in general terms ; then Waaka Nene, clothed in his best mat and carrying his favourite *mere*, spoke with the authority of one who had achieved a name in war and who could likewise claim his victories in the pursuit of peace. He modestly apologized to the Rarawas for the scarcity of food, the production of which had suffered not a little owing to the unsettled condition of the country. He then proceeded to relate his long association with the *pakeha* and the numerous instances in which he had in the past befriended them. He was still walking beside them, not, as had been alleged, for the sake of powder or blankets, but because the presence of the Europeans and the missionaries was the salvation of their race. The events of the war were next related, and pointing with his *mere* he enumerated the various hills from which Heke had retreated, reminding his hearers that they were now standing on Taiamai, a place known to all as the centre of Nga-Puhi territory. Here they would fight, and here they would die if necessary. He was not disposed to follow the enemy into the forest, but if they only came near him he would soon be stirring. Heke, he said, had written to the Governor about peace, but his heart was not warm toward Heke. He had little faith in him. If Kawiti had asked for peace his ears would be open. The *pakeha* spoke well of Heke and ill of Kawiti, but they were mistaken. Kawiti's word was his bond. He at least had not broken faith when peace was made at the death of Te Whareumu. No confidence could be placed in Heke. His five ancestors before him had been bad men, and he had followed in their footsteps. He concluded by counselling his followers to be guided by the Europeans. The war was theirs. They should act in concert with the *pakehas* and sit still until their tail (reinforcements) arrived.

Taonui followed. He repudiated all idea of peace, and spoke violently for war. Heke, he said, had attacked him while he was sitting quietly on his own land, and he had not yet obtained full satisfaction for all his relations who had fallen.

"Why talk of food?" said Nopera.* "Fern-root has always been our food in war-time." He would not return until he had brought the disturbers of the peace to their senses. He was not satisfied with simple professions of friendship towards the *pakeha*, therefore he had come to help them. The man who merely made professions of friendship was not to be relied upon. This man and that man talked of the *pakeha* being his "father." It was all deceit. Had Heke remembered the father of his ancestors, Hongi Hika, the friend of King George? "Take care," he said, "that we are not beguiled by his smooth talk. Let his actions prove his words."

Several of Nopera's followers spoke in similar strain, declaring they would not return until they had drunk of the waters of Kawakawa.†

The conference then broke up, the chiefs proceeding to discuss in private matters which etiquette had forbidden until they had first made public profession of the impulse and policy which had brought them together.

While the troops remained at Waimate the missionaries were busy as the agents of the Governor in seeking to bring the rebel chiefs to a less belligerent frame of mind. There was, they found, among the people a widespread and sincere desire for peace, but the issue was clouded by a sense of uncertainty as to how far the Governor was prepared to

---

* Colonel Despard was extremely gratified to find that Nopera had openly joined his allies. He remained for some months with the army, during which time the Colonel had every reason to be pleased with his conduct: "He is a shrewd and sensible man; silent, and thoughtful in every respect in giving his opinions; but when he did give them I always found that they contained much good sense and sound information regarding his country and his countrymen. Morning and evening devotions were practised by him and his followers, and I have seen him more than once sitting in his *whare* on a Sunday afternoon reading his Bible to himself." Nopera Panakareao was the chief who, in connection with the debates on the Treaty of Waitangi, used the oft-quoted phrase, "The shadow of the land goes to the Queen, but the substance remains with us."

† They would not return until they had invaded the enemy's territory.

go.   Heke's followers felt they could not make peace and leave Kawiti to the anger of the Governor.   Hare te Pure told Mr. Davis that Kawiti had carried the mischief much further than they had done ; yet they were the first warriors and were still *putake* (the root) of the evil, and ought not in justice to allow the weight of the Governor's displeasure to fall on Kawiti apart from them.   They were, he thought, bound to share the consequences with him, whatever it cost them.

Kawiti, on the other hand, though not adverse to peace, was known to entertain views which would prevent him accepting it on terms not honourable to himself.   He must be permitted to retire from the contest with the full honours of war, not as a combatant suffering the pangs and penalties of defeat.   The problem, then, which exercised the native mind was whether the Governor was disposed to offer only a limited or a general peace—whether his terms would impose penalties, or be graciously unconditional.

While matters remained in this uncertain condition, Kawiti, ever jealous of his own *mana*, decided that if there was to be further fighting it must be on his own land.   He remembered that so far the conflicts had all taken place within the domain of Heke, and so he said to his younger confederate :   " O, Heke, your name and fame strike the very skies.*   Up to the present the war has been carried on entirely on your territory.   Let me, I ask you, have some fighting on my territory."   To this Heke replied :   " Very well.   Go build your *pa*."   In these circumstances was commenced the erection of the formidable Ruapekapeka *pa*, colloquially known as " The Bat's Nest."   Thus while the Government and the missionaries were earnestly searching for peace the Maori was just as actively preparing for war.

To convince the rebels that the Governor would treat them with justice—even with generosity—was the task to which the missionaries devoted themselves during the next few weeks.   The first fruit of their efforts was a letter from

* *Tutuki ana ki te rangi.*

VEN. ARCHDEACON HENRY WILLIAMS, C.M.S.

After a drawing by J. McDonald.

Heke, which reached Mr. Davis on the 3rd September. It was accompanied by a request that it should be considered by Messrs. Davis, Burrows, Kemp, and Henry Williams, who were to withhold it or forward it to the Governor as their judgment dictated. It was a lengthy discursive document, in which much that did not matter was elaborated, while things of material importance were so enveloped by Scriptural quotations and religious references as to be almost obscure. In the main, however, its points were : That he was unable to restore the stolen horses and other property taken from Kororareka, as none was in his possession ; those who held this property were the Hokianga people — Waaka's Nene's people — and what they did not have had been left in the Ohaeawai *pa*. He enumerated his own losses at the hands of Waka Nene— the pigs and the cows, besides £546 of his money which was lost when his house at Kaikohe was burned after the fall of Ohaeawai. " Nothing was said about this being wrong ; it is quite right in their estimation. It was to them a savage gratification, like that of a pig when he breaks into the field of an honest man to eat his potatoes." So far as his land was concerned, he was willing to give it all up. " The thing that I put most value on is land, because it was given by God for a dwelling-place for man in this world — a resting-place for the soles of his feet, a burial-place for the strangers of the world." But if he consented to surrender his land the Governor must provide him with a ship to carry him in search of some other dwelling-place, for it is written : " If you are evil entreated in one place remove to another." It would be of no profit that the " evil people " should remain upon the land, but if they departed it would be good, for their offences would not then be seen. If peace was made with him it must also be made with Kawiti : " It will not be just that our fates should be different ; we must live and die together." In like manner, if he gave up his alliance with Kawiti, Waaka Nene must cease to follow the soldiers. Should Waaka continue with the soldiers, then he must continue

with Kawiti, because Waaka's war was a native war, waged
to avenge his ancestors, not to defend the Europeans. Here
he enumerated some of Nga Puhi's illustrious dead, and then
proceeded :—

These are the real causes of the work of the natives, which
they wish you to consider and acknowledge as a war on behalf of
the Europeans ; that the multitude may be deceived as well as
you, and that they may obtain powder ; that you may attribute
it to a true feeling within. But it is false. It is to obtain
plenty of powder for themselves that they adhere to you, that
thus they may obtain satisfaction for their dead.

Heke concluded by telling the Governor that the
capitulations could not be all on the one side : " If your
proposals, which you wish to have fulfilled in me, are
acceded to you must accede to mine." In a postscript
he added :—

If war is persisted in for the future it will assume a different
aspect ; there will be no more good. Soon you will say, " John's
work is bad." Not so ! The fault will be yours for prolonging
it. Hasten your work. Do not give heed to the words of Waaka
and his people. All that they do is to say to the soldiers, " Go
it, soldiers," but only that the soldiers may be killed while they
sit still. Their guns are to murder the soldiers. Do not suppose
this is a falsehood of mine ; it is really true.

The missionaries met on the 5th to discuss the document, when there appeared to be a general consensus of
opinion that, though far from what could have been
desired, it might, with all its imperfections, go forward to
the Governor. " Although Heke's letter is not what we
should have wished it to have been," writes Mr. Davis,
" there is evident in it a desire for peace, I think, quite as
strong as could be expected, as he appears to give up all
his land. With regard to his not wishing peace apart from
Kawiti, I think that is quite natural." With this view
Mr. Burrows was in complete agreement ; but on returning home Henry Williams appears to have looked at it
from another angle, and decided he would not send the
letter on until he had induced Heke to modify some

of his phrases, which now seemed to him unnecessarily objectionable. He wrote to Mr. Burrows and to Heke to that effect, but the modifications were never made, because Mr. Burrows did not press the chief to make them, holding strongly to the view that the letter should not be altered and should not have been delayed. In these circumstances the letter did not reach the Governor until the 25th September, nearly a month after it was written, much to the perplexity of Government House, where it was known the document was on its way.

During the following week Mr. Burrows had an interview with Heke at Titirangi, in the course of which the missionary intimated to the chief the portions of the letter to which he took more or less exception, telling him it was altogether too long and not sufficiently to the point, to which Heke replied, "You had better write and tell the Governor our conversation to-day." In consonance with this suggestion the missionary penned the following letter to the Chief Protector of the Aborigines :—

MY DEAR SIR,—   Waimate, September 11th, 1845.

Having just returned from seeing Heke I hasten to give you the heads of our conversation, which you are at liberty to communicate to His Excellency the Governor. What led me to visit Heke on Tuesday was his letter which he had desired us to read and alter if we thought proper. There were portions I was dissatisfied with, and others which I did not understand. My interview with him has given me, on the whole, satisfaction. He was much more docile than I had before found him. Upon the question of Kawiti's being included should peace be made he said that as Kawiti joined him he could not desert him, and that peace with one without the other would amount to nothing. To the reply that Kawiti had not sued for peace he said it was not the native custom for the person who was *whati** to ask for peace, but that it was commended by friends or proposed by the opposite party. He was told that the report circulated was that Kawiti did not wish for peace, but was anxious for war, to which he replied that he had not seen Kawiti, but believed he would willingly agree to terms. He pressed me much to go and see Kawiti, but as Archdeacon Williams has seen him it is

* *Whati* = broken or dispersed.

perhaps unnecessary. The Archdeacon will doubtless communicate to you by first opportunity the substance of his interview with him. He (Heke) asks what more he can say than what he has said. He, too, asked the Governor to judge his cause and to give him terms upon which peace can be made. As for the land, he says it is forsaken by them and they have no further desire for it—it is for the Governor. They have nothing else, he added, to offer. If the Governor would come and see them he thinks much good would be done. With regard to any land which might be given up in case of terms being agreed upon, I must be allowed to express my own views as to the disposal of it. I believe I did so partially when you were here. Subsequent experience, derived from frequent conversation with neutral, turbulent, and loyal natives, has confirmed me in the opinion then expressed, that no division must be made of it at present among Walker's people. The only safe plan I can devise is this : that the lands be taken by the Governor, with the understanding that they are not to be appropriated to the purpose of the Government, but to remain *takoto noa** for a season ; and to give the rebels to understand that it will depend upon their future conduct as to whether any portions of their land shall be returned to them. Heke asks, " Is not the Governor satisfied with the number of our slain ? Many of our chiefs have been killed. They have lost only three or four. How many more do they require ? "

They reckon up among themselves about 120 which they have lost from the commencement. The chief facts, however, which I think His Excellency should be acquainted with are these : That the neutral natives are anxiously inquiring, " When will the Governor have sufficient payment to satisfy him ? " Heke's seeking for peace has excited much sympathy towards him among these people, who often ask, " Is war to go on till all are destroyed ? " They say the Governor should now tell Heke on what terms he will make peace. I mention these things because they show the working of the native mind. I fear that should hostilities recommence our troops will have a much larger body of rebels to contend with than they have had yet, and that the Maoris will return to their native mode of warfare—lying in wait and cutting off as they can. From what I can gather it is not their intention to shut themselves in their *pa* should another attack be made, nor allow themselves to be surrounded, but to place themselves in the wood about the *pa*, and do what mischief they can, and retreat. Heke does not conceal the truth that they all intend to join Kawiti as soon as

* *Takoto noa* = remain in suspense.

another expedition is made. He has a small *pa* upon the top of the hill, or rather mountain, but five thousand men, were they allowed to get to the foot of it, would not so surround it as to prevent his escape. However, following him where he is is out of the question. Kawiti's position, and the nature of the road to it, Archdeacon Williams has seen. He is not inclined to make difficulties where there are none. You may be sure, therefore, that his will not be an exaggerated report.

The people Heke has about him are anxious for peace. Many of them *very* anxious. My opinion of Heke himself is not altered. He is of a restless, ambitious spirit, and I fear will not be quiet long together. My hope is that, should his party be once disbanded, he would not be able to get up another. There are some I know with him who are only waiting for a favourable opportunity to get clear, but they know not how to do it unless peace be made.

On my return to-day I saw Walker. He says peace with Heke and not with Kawiti, even if Heke were willing, would be of no avail. He spoke very sensibly upon the subject, and expressed his willingness to fall in with the Governor's views. He considers that Heke has suffered already not a little for his folly, and says that as he has asked again for peace it will be very good if the Governor thinks well.

The idea of taking [prisoner] either Heke or Kawiti is out of the question unless they be surrounded, in which case the struggle is awful to contemplate.

Heke desired me to write to you and give you the points on which we have been speaking, and especially to press the Governor coming down. His Excellency coming here would doubtless be the best thing that could be done in case of terms being agreed upon, but I only express Heke's earnest wish on this point. Some of his leading men are very pressing for peace. There was none of that bitter feeling towards Walker's people expressed by him this time which I have witnessed before. Heke asked what Kawiti had done more than he had that peace should not be made with him. I only replied that he had not asked for it, and, moreover, that he had been accused of burning and destroying the houses and property at the Bay. He said the persons who were the foremost in that were no more Kawiti's than his, but natives from all parts, many of whom had now " backed out," as he termed it.

In conclusion, he said he would wait quietly where he is until he hears what the Governor means to do, and asked me to return again as soon as I had anything to communicate. There is one thing I am certain of—that it must be war or peace.

That is, the Government must be prepared to follow them up with a sufficient force, or terms must be come to, and they must be content for the present to act only on the defensive. I do not venture an opinion as to what I consider the safest mode of procedure any further than that things appear to me in that state to render peace desirable can these men be brought to any terms which would not be dishonourable to the Government. The maxim is that when we cannot do as we would, to do as we can.

No copy of Heke's letter was sent to Colonel Despard, but the terms of it were communicated to him—probably by Mr. Burrows—and he at once wrote to the Governor urging that if peace was to be made with the chiefs, or pardon offered to them, the time was ripe for such clemency; but that any overtures of this kind should be backed up by a strong demonstration of hostility, which would dispel any idea in the native mind that such concessions were the fruit of weakness. This demonstration of hostility meant an advance " in the direction of that part of the country (Waiomio) where the particular armed rebels were then assembled." The fiery Colonel was itching to be again on the move, urging that the supine state into which they had drifted was calculated to do much mischief, giving the enemy more confidence by leading them to suppose the continued inaction of the troops was due to fear.

The Governor did not share these warlike views. He was still disposed to rely confidently upon the negotiations of the missionaries, and late in September he thus conveyed his decision to the Colonel :—

After anxiously and deliberately weighing every circumstance it does appear to me better to defer an attack upon Kawiti's *pa*, and to give time for his submission as well as Heke's, in order that an opening may be allowed for a general peace. The attack on Kawiti's *pa* would require nearly your whole force. Heke might destroy Waimate — which would be a triumph for the heathen rebels — and then join Kawiti. They might not stand to your attack, but retreat to the woods and become marauders of the worst description. The risk of these circumstances may be avoided by giving a little more time. It is impossible to doubt that forces will be sent from England, and in the event of adequate strength arriving it would be mortifying to find that we had not been sufficiently deliberate. . . . In conclusion, I deem it to be my duty to request that you will defer active offensive hostilities for a short time.

A few days later Heke's letter reached the Governor, who had already made up his mind what the peace conditions would be, and on the 29th of the month he forwarded the following communication to Colonel Despard, with instructions to have it delivered to Heke with all possible speed :—

JOHN HEKE,—   Auckland, 29th September, 1845.

I have received your letter of the 29th August asking for peace, but that letter did not reach me until the 25th of this month. You say you are willing to give up all your lands. I do not demand all. I only require portions of your land. I do not seek the destruction of yourself or children, and your companions. I only demand atonement for the evil you have caused. Without some land you cannot subsist. You ask for a ship. For what purpose do you want a ship? Where do you want to go? I cannot converse with you face to face while evil prevails. I may see you when peace is made. Kawiti shall be admitted to the terms equally with yourself—if he writes to me in time—provided that Waaka and all the men of Hokianga are fully included in a general peace. If Kawiti be included all must be included. Waaka and Tawhai took up arms for the Queen. The Governor will not desert them. I have informed the officer commanding the troops on what terms I will consent to a general peace. The terms are,—

(1.) The Treaty of Waitangi to be binding.
(2.) The British colours to be sacred.
(3.) All plunder now in possession of the natives forthwith to be restored.
(4.) The following places to be given up to the Queen and to remain unoccupied by any one until the decision of Her Majesty be signified : Parts of Mawhe, Ohaeawai, Taiamai, Te Aute, Whangai, Waikare, Katore, and Kaipatiki.
(5.) Hostilities to cease between all chiefs and tribes now in arms with or against the Government.

These terms are very moderate, because I am aware you have been greatly misled. They are very favourable to yourself and Kawiti, who have caused so much evil and distress in the land.

I cannot take into consideration the property which you say you have lost, because all the losses—your own as well as others —were caused by your own commencement, as at Maiki. I have now made known to you the conditions to which I will consent if you wish to put an end to the war. If you do not take advantage of this knowledge all future consequences will rest upon yourself ; but if you and Kawiti ask for peace on these terms it will be granted, the war will be finished, and your sufferings will cease. From me.

From THE GOVERNOR.

In compliance with a request from Colonel Despard the Governor's letter to Heke was personally conveyed to the chief by Mr. Burrows, who had previously appointed a rendezvous in the bush, some four miles from a new *pa* which Heke had built on top of Hikurangi Hill, set deep in the heart of the forest. Of the secrets of this *pa* Heke was keenly jealous, and was more than anxious that Mr. Burrows should not have the opportunity of seeing it. At the distant meeting-place, then, Heke and a number of his chiefs spent the greater part of the day talking over the Governor's terms with the missionary. The result, however, was inconclusive, for it is doubtful whether Heke's overtures to the Governor were ever anything but a subterfuge to gain time until the new *pas*, then in course of construction, were completed and the potato crops harvested. Here is Mr. Burrows's own account of the interview, and his impressions upon the general situation, given in a letter to Mr. Clarke :—

Waimate, October 10th, 1845.
At the Colonel's request I was the bearer of the Governor's letter to Heke. I sent a messenger the day before, with a request to meet me about four miles on the other side of Kaikohe. He did so. Heke read the letter twice through to himself, then read it aloud to those present, among whom were Hare te Pure and Pairama. He was very civil, but said he could not do anything with the terms without consulting the parties concerned. I found him, as usual, ready to blame others and justify himself. He said that, as far as the land was concerned, he had only a voice in that at Mawhe, and signified that there would be no difficulty about that ; but expressed the opinion that Kawiti would not yield to the terms.

He pressed me much to stay with them and see the other principal men, but as it would have taken about two or three days I could not comply with their request. They promised to communicate the substance of the letter to Pene Taui, Te Haratua, and others to ascertain their mind upon the subject. This afternoon we have received information that Kawiti refused to give up his land, and says he will fight first. Heke, I feel persuaded, will come to no terms without him. Whilst I was with Heke a messenger arrived from Kawiti, but Kawiti had not received the Governor's letter when the messenger left. He, however, had heard there was one, and something about the terms. This native hinted that Kawiti would say that he would not have his land parcelled out by the *pakeha*, and that what had been told them about the Government taking their lands was true. Kawiti had remarked that the way to have peace was for the Governor to come and see them. Heke urged the same thing. There still exists a very bitter feeling against Waaka Nene and his people. Heke says he does not think that Kawiti will make any peace with Waaka, as his people disturbed his dead which fell at Mawhe, and which he had deposited in a cave at Owhareiti, near the lake.

I trust, however, that the terms which have been offered will be the means of removing that sympathy which exists in the minds of many neutral natives for these people. They (that is, the neutral natives) say the terms are easy, but that the land is a *mea pakeke** with them. I do not expect any letter from Heke. He may write or send a message to me, or he may not.

The Governor's coming here would doubtless be the means of much good ; but he knows best what is politic with regard to English law and custom. We know what the native idea is in regard to these things. Heke has heard that a new Governor is coming. The present Governor, he had heard, was to go Home because he had been too kind to them, and the one coming would be quite the reverse. The missionaries were also to be recalled because they had persuaded His Excellency to be *ngawari*† towards them. This is just what some of our friends wish, no doubt. It is a critical time for a new Governor to make his appearance—one false step may rouse the whole body of natives ; and what if the Government at Home should violate, or cause to be violated, the Treaty of Waitangi : it will place us all in jeopardy.

* *Mea pakeke* = a tough proposition ; a fundamental.
† *Ngawari* = soft and easy—kind.

Within a few days of the receipt of Heke's letter the Governor received a communication from Kawiti, who also appeared as a suitor for peace, subject to no conditions being made regarding the land. The letter was addressed jointly to Henry Williams and to the Governor, because it was written in reply to authorized representations made to the chief by the missionary.

Ruapekapeka, September 24th, 1845.

Friend Williams. Good is your word. O friend, saluting you. Here am I feeling great regard for you. Sir, it is because you have said that peace should be made that I consent. I will not continue to disregard your wishes ; but, then, if peace is made, it must be made with respect to the land also.

Friend the Governor. Saluting you. I am willing to make peace. Many Europeans have been killed, and many natives also. Inasmuch as you have said that I must make the first advances towards peace, this is it. I do now consent to peace. This is all mine. I finish here.

By me, KAWITI.

To Kawiti a reply precisely similar in its terms to that sent to Heke was made through Henry Williams,* but the negotiations broke down hopelessly. Even had the chiefs been sincere, no peace could have been made on the Governor's terms, for by a strange blunder on the part of some of his advisers not more than a few acres of the land demanded for surrender was the acknowledged property of the chief insurgents.† Heke foiled the matter by pretending that he could do nothing, since he could not basely give away the land of other people. In any event he failed

---

* This mission was undertaken by Mr. Williams at the request of Colonel Despard. For the purpose of the conference, which was held on the 3rd November, Heke joined Kawiti at Ruapekapeka, but took little part in the *korero*, which lasted the greater part of the night. He preferred to "lay low" and listen, though he had previously written to the missionary asking him to come to Ruapekapeka so that all might hear what he had to say, and "that you may ascertain our opinion about affairs."

† Captain FitzRoy in a letter to Governor Grey—22nd November, 1845—states that private information given to him by Colonel Despard and Rev. Mr. Burrows regarding lands owned by Heke and Kawiti was defective. In that letter he supplied a further list of places which might be demanded if confiscation was ultimately decided upon.

to regard the proposals of the Governor as of sufficient importance to vouchsafe a direct reply, which somewhat favours the suggestion that he was never sincere in asking for peace.

Kawiti, on the other hand, promptly and openly denounced the terms. To him the suggestion that land of any kind should be surrendered was especially repugnant, and in bitter resentment he declared : " No ; let us fight on if they want our lands, and when we are killed they can come and take them."

To Henry Williams he wrote on the day after he received the terms :—

To Mr. Williams.

Sir, Mr. Williams. How do you do ? I cannot go to Otuihu to meet you. Had the Governor's letter been moderate I would have gone ; but his words are hard words, for they speak of taking the land. Therefore I would not go to Otuihu. Now you see it is so. I soften down, and you and the Governor harden all your words. Now you and the Governor press us to fight, and we will fight, for it was not all my evil by which I got up to fight. Many Europeans say to me : " Kawiti, your land is gone " ; therefore I got up. Now, is it not so ? You see the Governor wanted me to give up all my land to him, and I am not willing. This is all I have to say to you.

From me, Kawiti.

To the Governor he wrote on the same day :—

O Friend the Governor,—

Saluting you. This is my word to you. Will you not hearken to my word ? It was you who said I was the first to commence killing the Europeans, and that I should therefore be the first to propose peace. I accordingly gave my consent to a letter to Mr. Williams. It was he who said you were urging me to make peace. On this account I wrote a letter to you, but as you have said we are to fight—yes, we will fight. If you say, " Let peace be made," it is agreeable ; but as regards this, you shall not have my land. No, never, never ! I have been fighting for my land. If you had said that my land should be retained by myself I should have been pleased.

Sir, you are very desirous to get my land. I shall be equally desirous to retain it for myself.

This is the end of my speech. It ceases here.

From me, Kawiti.

So far, then, as the natives were concerned the peace negotiations were closed, and the word once more was: *Me whawhai tonu; me whawhai tonu* ("Fight on; fight on"). To this end they bent all their energies to complete their new *pa* at Ruapekapeka, which was to be the most formidable thing in the form of a fighting *pa* which had yet come from the brain and hands of the Maori contrivers. This work was undertaken mainly by Kawiti's immediate followers, Heke's men for the most part devoting themselves to the not less essential business of planting and gathering food with which to sustain its garrison.

Having apparently failed to provide a peace basis which would at once induce the surrender of the rebels and preserve the honour of the colony, the Governor now endeavoured to weaken the support given to the chiefs by the stratagem of offering a free pardon to all their followers who would peacefully return to their homes. As early as the 23rd July the Rev. John Hobbs had written to the Chief Protector of the Aborigines, suggesting that many natives would only be too glad to withdraw from Heke if they could be sure of a friendly reception from the loyalists. The loyal natives, on the other hand, felt reluctant to receive them, because they did not know how their action would be interpreted by the Governor. Mr. Hobbs therefore advised that the Governor should "offer an opportunity for many to escape out of the snare into which they had fallen."

The suggestion apparently had no appeal in official quarters at that time, but was carefully, or carelessly, pigeonholed until the 20th September, when it bore fruit in the following Proclamation issued by the Governor:—

PROCLAMATION.
BY HIS EXCELLENCY ROBERT FITZROY.

WHEREAS several chiefs have asked me to let them take their relatives away from Kawiti and Heke, and have asked me to pardon those who return peaceably to their own places:

I, the Governor, do proclaim and declare that every native so retiring from the rebel chiefs shall be pardoned on condition of remaining at peace.

MISSION CHURCH AT WAIMATE.

Showing graves of British officers.

What effect this belated offer of a way out had is uncertain. It is probable that it was negligible, for by this time those who had followed the chiefs through three successful fights were confident they would be victorious in a fourth, and that to abandon their cause now was to do so on the very threshold of success.

On the 2nd October the *Royal Sovereign*,* with 214 men of the 58th Regiment, under Lieut.-Colonel Wynyard, arrived from Sydney within signal distance of Auckland, and on meeting with H.M. ships *Daphne* and *Racehorse* proceeded direct to the Bay of Islands, where Wynyard received instructions from Governor FitzRoy to place himself, his troops, stores, and supplies, under the direction of Colonel Despard. By this time the Governor had made up his mind that Waimate might safely be evacuated,† and he instructed Colonel Despard to withdraw the troops to Kororareka and there commence military works which were to be of a purely defensive character. As to the peace negotiations, they were not to be abandoned, but were to continue through Archdeacon Henry Williams and Mr. Burrows, " because the natives knew them better and trust them more than any person on whom I can rely, except the Chief Protector of the Aborigines, who cannot now leave Auckland."

This reference to the Chief Protector introduces us to the man who undoubtedly was the mainspring of FitzRoy's native policy. A blacksmith by trade, Mr. George Clarke had come to the colony as one of the early catechists under the Church Missionary Society, and had rapidly

---

* The *Royal Sovereign* had on board Lieut.-Colonel Wynyard, Captain Laye, Lieutenants Dressing, Hay, Petley, and Page, Ensign Wynyard, Assistant Surgeon Philson, and 214 rank and file of the 58th Regiment. As senior officer Lieut.-Colonel Wynyard took over command of the regiment from Major Bridge. About this time an attempt was made to send by the *Regia* bullocks and horses from Sydney for the use of the military, but the greater part of these were lost on the voyage.

† FitzRoy took the opinion of Henry Williams on this point. The missionary replied that if the troops were withdrawn and did not return the station would be safe, but if Waimate continued to be a military depot and the war went on they might expect to find it destroyed at any time.

gained a knowledge of the native language and customs, and had as rapidly won the confidence of the native people. When, therefore, Captain Hobson was looking for some one to fill the new office of Chief Protector of the Aborigines, created by him, his choice fell upon this gentleman, who, with the consent of the Mission Society, assumed the difficult role of acting as the intermediary between the two races. His performance of the duty brought him into violent conflict with the New Zealand Company in the south, and with many of the white settlers in the north ; but there is no reason to suppose that he ever forfeited the confidence of the natives, and he daily grew in favour with Governor FitzRoy, who placed in him unbounded trust. In writing to Mr. Dandeson Coates, Secretary to the Church Missionary Society in London, after the fall of Kororareka, FitzRoy made this declaration of his faith in Clarke :—

In all my own dealings with the natives I have consulted fully and unreservedly with Mr. Clarke, and a more discreet, judicious, and right-minded person I have not met with in New Zealand. I have taken no step in connection with the natives in which he has not fully concurred, and I have found no man in New Zealand so generally and so well informed about such subjects. No man understood the natives, their conduct, their character, and their country, better than Mr. Clarke—a man of extreme sagacity, prudence, and discretion. Some steps that I have taken must have startled you, but, trust me, they were not taken unadvisedly.

In view of Clarke's training and environment it was but natural that he should incline to the side of leniency with the natives, in which FitzRoy's philo-missionary predilections made him a ready sympathizer. Hence it was that the war policy of " wait and see " was evolved which so roused the anger of Colonel Despard, who first deprecated its " hesitation," and then roundly denounced its " supineness."

The evacuation of Waimate was commenced on the 22nd October, when Colonel Despard, with the 99th and 96th detachments, marched with two field-pieces to Keri-keri, the point of embarkation. Two days later Major Bridge led out the remainder of the force, leaving the mission station so sadly dilapidated as the result of its military occupation that the friendly natives felt constrained to come and *tangi* (cry) over it. On the day following the departure of the 58th the *North Star* and the *Slains Castle* carried the men across the bay to Kororareka,* where they disembarked and camped on the beach in front of the blackened ruins of the deserted town. Once Colonel Despard got his men on the move he would gladly have converted his march to Kororareka into an advance upon the enemy, but in view of the imperative orders from the Governor that no hostile movement of any kind was to be made the Colonel had reluctantly to content himself with the less exciting task of establishing a permanent camp, which was to be the base of future operations if such should be deemed necessary. With this work he was well advanced when the colony was startled by the intelligence that Governor FitzRoy had been recalled, and that Captain Grey, Governor of South Australia, had been transferred to New Zealand.

The manner in which this announcement was received in the colony varied according to the particular interest it seemed to serve or appeared to prejudice.† The supporters of the New Zealand Company were naturally overjoyed at the success of their campaign of malice, for ever since FitzRoy had refused to punish Te Rauparaha and

---

* Colonel Despard's force which landed at Kororareka from Waimate was 650 strong. They had a battery-train of three 24-pounders, with two 6-pounder field-guns and two 12-pounder carronades mounted on field-carriages ; with seven small 5 in. mortars which had been cast in Sydney. Waaka Nene and the friendly natives occupied a special camp near the force. It was found that not every house in Kororareka had been utterly destroyed by the fire, and such as could be patched up were repaired and occupied by the soldiers, they being found more comfortable than the leaky tents. Colonel Despard was under orders from the Governor to re-erect the flagstaff on Maiki Hill, but this does not appear to have been done. Plans of a redoubt and two blockhouses were prepared by the Captain of the Engineers, and these were in progress when the news of Governor FitzRoy's recall reached the colony. The work was then stopped by Colonel Despard, in the hope that the policy of the new Governor would be more in consonance with his own, and that the force would be ordered to take the field rather than remain confined to a camp.

† Our Governor is recalled, and Auckland is all in a bustle at the intelligence. I dare say many think now as they thought before, " This Governor has only to go away, and the new one to come, and their coffers will be filled with gold."—*Bainbridge.*

Te Rangihaeata for their share in the affair at Wairau the company and its claquers had never ceased to manœuvre for his downfall. The missionaries were as naturally dismayed, for FitzRoy had trusted them, consulted them, and had brought his policy into as close sympathy with theirs as a secular and a religious policy could well be. Some feared they would not get another Governor like him, but Henry Williams, in his bluff, downright manner, expressed the opinion that FitzRoy was well quit of the whole business, and that he must be exceedingly thankful to be relieved of what he called "a most unpleasant Government." The natives, both friendly and rebel, were exceedingly alarmed when they learned of the impending change, for long before the official announcement of FitzRoy's recall had been made rumours* that it was imminent had swept over the colony, and in contradistinction to FitzRoy's policy of mildness the natives were told that the new Governor was to be a man of different stamp, one who would rule them with the proverbial rod of iron. There was to be nothing *ngawari* about him, a report which more and more tended to unsettle the already excited native mind. FitzRoy himself took the position philosophically. Knowing the influences which had been operating to secure his dismissal, he was cheerful in the consciousness that under his guidance the colony was steadily recovering from the staggering blows it had received. He was not disposed to nurse a grievance, but busied himself in preparing to hand over to his successor, of whose appointment he heartily approved.†

Captain Grey made his official landing at Auckland on the 18th November from the East India Company's

---

* The *Hannah* (Captain Salmond) arrived at Wellington from Sydney on the 4th October, 1845, bringing the news of Captain FitzRoy's recall. There were also rumours that Sir George Gipps, Governor of New South Wales, and Sir Maurice O'Connell, Commander-in-Chief, were about to visit New Zealand, anticipating that Captain FitzRoy might leave before the arrival of his successor.

† Captain FitzRoy's early impressions of his successor may be interesting. Writing to George Clarke on the 15th, the day after Grey arrived at Auckland, he says: "I have had a good deal of conversation with Governor Grey, who seems anxious to collect information and is open to reason. He seems but delicate, which is in favour of kindly feelings. I think him more *ngawari* (soft and pliable) than *pakeke* (hard and unbending)."

ship *Elphinstone*, and was the recipient of the warmest of welcomes not only from his predecessor, but from the populace and a large number of leading chiefs whose presence had been assured by the kindly forethought of Captain FitzRoy. Here is a somewhat quaint account of the event left to us by Mr. Bainbridge, the tutor at St. John's College :—

Tuesday, November 18th.—A very grand day at Auckland. Governor Grey landed at 11.30, and the preparations in consequence were very extensive, as far as military, clerical, medical preparation could be made. At 8 in the morning the ships were beautifully ornamented with colours, as far as each could furnish. Never has Auckland Harbour presented such a gay scene. The *Elphinstone* (East India Company's sloop-of-war, the vessel which brought the new Governor), the *Racehorse*, and the *North Star*—every little vessel did its best, and hung out as well as it could. The departure of the Governor from the *Elphinstone* was signified by a general salute from the ship and the fort. The military was drawn up on the beach, and most of the " quality " followed in the rear. I had the pleasure of seeing Tamati Waaka, the native chief and hero who has proven himself so loyal, accompanying Mr. Clarke to the Government House. He was dressed in a cocked hat and epaulettes just like an English General, sword, &c., complete.* After due ceremony of swearing in the new Governor a levee was held, and a great number of the élite of Auckland passed through the room, bowing and scraping before the Governor as they went.

Upon assuming office Grey quickly realized that he stood in the face of critical times. Although he now had what FitzRoy never had, ample money with which to carry on the Government, and a promise of a large and a speedy reinforcement, his native difficulties appeared likely to increase rather than to diminish. As the result of his predecessor's urgent appeals for help the coast of New Zealand had suddenly become crowded with ships-of-war. Within the past few months there had been six representatives of the British Navy in the vicinity of Auckland, together with transports and storeships laden with men and munitions. This enormous and apparently miraculous accession to the fighting strength of the colonial forces both

---

* These clothes had been given to the chief by Governor FitzRoy when he (the chief) was on a visit to Auckland a few weeks previously.

astonished and alarmed the natives, who saw great ships-
of-war arriving as birds which flew in from the sea. Nor
was the significance of the change lost upon them. The
Ngati-Whatua tribe in the neighbourhood of Auckland, the
Ngati-Paoa at the Thames, and the powerful numerous warlike tribes on the Waikato and the Waipa Rivers were all
in a state of extreme excitement and alarm at this new and
surprising development. Throughout the whole Island, in
fact, the tribes were fortifying *pas* in their strongest holds,
awaiting the issue of the contest with Heke, and the first
acts of the new Governor towards themselves.* A policy
of strength and vigour was therefore necessary to close the
war with Heke, and to this end Grey determined immediately
to apply his new and powerful agencies of men and money.

Rapidly discharging such business as awaited him at
Auckland, he hurried off to the Bay of Islands, there
personally to inquire into the military state of his new
administration. He reached the Bay in the *Elphinstone*
on the 22nd November, and on the 24th landed at Kororareka in the midst of military and native ceremonial. The
salute, the inspection of troops, the levee, and the war-
dance† being concluded, the Governor entered upon a general
survey of the position. He found the troops under the

* I find the greatest distrust regarding the intentions of the British
Government upon the subject of claiming all lands of the natives not
actually in occupation and cultivation exists amongst many of the most
influential and hitherto friendly chiefs at the Bay of Islands. They are
tolerably well acquainted with the details of the discussion which took
place in the House of Commons at the end of June last regarding the state
of New Zealand, and their apprehensions are avowedly based upon what
transpired during the debate to which I am alluding.—*Grey to Lord Stanley.*

† With the intention of doing especial honour to the new Governor,
Waaka Nene appeared on parade dressed in the naval uniform which he
had worn at Auckland—epaulettes, laced trousers, cocked hat plus a
Colonel's plumes, embroidered naval belt, and sword. He conducted
himself with perfect propriety until the war-dance commenced ; then the
thin veneer of civilization disappeared, and he was a native once again.
Suddenly he began to perform the evolutions of the *haka*, flourishing his
drawn sword above his head, shouting at the top of his voice the while.
His dark, tattooed face contrasted sharply with the fine gold epaulettes,
his grimaces were altogether foreign to the traditions of his dress, and
when his sword-scabbard, getting between his ambulating legs, nearly
threw him to the ground the sedate British officers were inclined to think
the exhibition ridiculous. As the performance went on, however, the
humour of it dawned upon them ; they could not restrain their risibility,
and as one of them has said : " He amused us all most exceedingly."

command of Colonel Despard to consist of detachments of the 58th and the 99th Regiments, comprising about 670 men.

They were quartered upon the barren peninsula on which Kororareka stands, from which there is no road practicable for troops to the mainland. The forces were in this situation wholly separated from the country occupied by the rebels, except by water communication, and they had no boats with them. They were, therefore, for all practical purposes wholly useless, and they were employed in clearing ground upon which it was proposed to erect fortifications for the purpose of protecting the flagstaff and town of Kororareka when it might be rebuilt.

Though far from satisfied with the disposition of the troops, Grey greatly pleased Colonel Despard by assuring him that the policy of procrastination which had hitherto characterized the war was at an end; "and," chuckles the Colonel, "whoever has been the guiding-star in that line is no longer to be so." The work of fortifying Kororareka was to cease, and the Colonel was directed to devote his energies to making preliminary preparations for an advance against Kawiti's new *pa*, should subsequent developments necessitate such a step. Grey also announced his intention of holding a conference, with a view to arriving at a mutual understanding with the chiefs resident in the vicinity of the Bay, at the earliest possible moment. That moment was somewhat delayed by stress of weather, which prevented the assembly of the natives on the appointed day, but by the 28th so many tribesmen had arrived that the tent erected for their shelter was discovered to be too small for their accommodation, and the meeting was held in the open air. Standing amongst the ruins of the deserted town, Grey, after again affirming the good intentions of the British Government, and assuring the assembly that the terms of the Treaty of Waitangi would be sacredly observed by that Government,* called upon the chiefs

* I have in the most public manner, in the strongest terms, and upon repeated occasions assured the natives that I have been instructed by Her Majesty most honourably and scrupulously to fulfil the terms of the Treaty of Waitangi; that their welfare and happiness was an object of the most lively concern to the Queen, and that it would be my most earnest desire to carry out Her Majesty's most gracious wishes in their favour; and I am satisfied that these declarations on my part have produced a very favourable impression upon many of the most influential of the chiefs.—Vide *Grey's despatch to Lord Stanley.*

likewise to discharge their duty by upholding the treaty in this hour of crisis. As the rebel chiefs Heke and Kawiti had not yet given a satisfactory reply to his predecessor's peace proposals he would not close the negotiations immediately ; but should no evidence of their acceptance reach him by the following Tuesday evening he would break off all communication with them. Then the war must go on. In unmistakable terms he declared in that event his policy must be "he that is not for us is against us." Neutrality would no longer be recognized as a permissible attitude, particularly that class of neutrality which kept the chiefs out of the war but permitted their followers to join the enemy. To Grey it did not appear proper that any of the chiefs who had recognized Her Majesty's authority, and for whose benefit and protection that authority had been exerted, should pretend, during the period of an active rebellion, to declare for neither party, but quietly remain watching the event of the contest. Such a system gave to the rebels an appearance of strength which they did not really possess, and to the Government an appearance of weakness injurious to it. It, moreover, prevented many others from joining the Queen's forces, from the conviction they naturally felt that all those who pretended to be neutral would, if any reverse should overtake the troops, undoubtedly declare for the party of the rebels. These, and other considerations equally vital, induced the Governor at once to put an end to the system of pretended neutrality, and to treat as enemies all such chiefs who did not openly declare for and as openly assist the Government. The chiefs were therefore required to range themselves on one side of the conflict or on the other. The Government must know who were its friends and who its foes. In his despatches to Lord Stanley, describing this meeting, Grey says :—

I thought it right at once to test the real sentiments of these so-called neutrals, and I therefore, after my arrival at the scene of operations, explained generally to the natives that I should not recognize any neutrality on the part of any chief ; that

I should require the whole of the neutral chiefs to render me any assistance that I might call upon them to afford ; that if they failed to come to see me and to offer me any assistance that I might require, or any information upon the state of the country, I should certainly consider them as rebels, and treat them as such.

In reply to this spirited declaration, which broke in upon the Maori ear with a new note of firmness, many chiefs made speeches, all of which were uncompromisingly against a premature peace.　There was no division in their counsel that the war against Heke must be continued until he was brought to submission.　Their word was that a peace made before his complete subjugation was effected would last only until he felt strong enough to again begin aggressions against the authority of the Queen, for " he was a man of many thoughts," and no dependence was to be placed upon his word.

The conspicuous absentee from this gathering was Pomare, who, though generally reprobated, was considered valuable as an ally to the British because of his undoubted influence as a chief.　His immediate friends, particularly Te Whareumu, used every exertion to induce him to meet the new Governor, but whether from a real or feigned fear Pomare resisted the pressure, urging that he might again be taken prisoner by the British.　Towards this attitude Grey did not conceal his displeasure, and his remarks on the subject of neutrality probably had more pointed reference to Pomare than to any other chief who was hovering on the fringe of the war.

When the neutral chiefs became aware of these altered sentiments on the part of the Government, Grey wrote to Stanley :　" The whole of them, with the exception of two,* visited me and promised to afford the Government any assistance that might be required, and stated that they looked on the rebels as rogues and robbers ; that they were most heartily afraid of them ; and that they trusted most sincerely the

---

* These were Pomare and Waikato.　Te Whareumu, Pomare's nephew, subsequently waited upon the Governor and apologized for the absence of his uncle.

Government would inflict upon them the punishment they deserved. Indeed, I never heard more sensible or just remarks than many of the leading chiefs made upon the motives and conduct of the rebels."

Having thus secured the complete allegiance of a large body of friendly and neutral chiefs, Grey's next task was to ascertain definitely where Heke and Kawiti stood in the matter of the peace terms. With these terms he himself was not in entire agreement,* but he hesitated to withdraw them, fearing that his motives might be misunderstood and his action regarded as a breach of faith. He therefore decided to continue them as the basis of peace, which must be accepted or rejected. Accordingly the following letter was sent to both chiefs :—

KAWITI,—   Kororareka, 27th November, 1845.

The new Governor, who has arrived at Kororareka, has heard that some letters have passed between you and Governor FitzRoy, and that Governor FitzRoy had promised if you would accede to certain conditions that he would not take further proceedings against you. Now, the new Governor says if he does not hear from you by Tuesday next that you have agreed to the conditions offered to you by Governor FitzRoy he shall consider that you have refused these conditions, and he will hold no further communication with you.

From me,
GEORGE CLARKE, Jun.

To Kawiti, at the Ruapekapeka.

The copy of this letter sent to Kawiti was entrusted to one of his nephews for delivery, the Rev. Mr. Burrows undertaking to see that Heke received his. The chiefs by this time had separated, Heke having returned to his *pa* at Hikurangi, Kawiti remaining in his fortress at Ruapekapeka. They were thus deprived of the benefits of immediate communication and consultation, and therefore their letters in reply may be taken as an indication of their individual and independent sentiments. Heke's letter was characteristic of the man and his environment. It was a wordy effusion,

* Grey fully stated his objections to these terms in a despatch written to Lord Stanley on the 15th December, 1845.

which skilfully evaded the point of accepting the terms. It was written under the influence of his own vain and ambitious spirit, supported by the turbulent disposition of many of the young men by whom he was surrounded, who by individual acts of aggression had placed themselves beyond the pale of the law, who still believed themselves more than a match for the British soldier, and who were anxious to increase their renown by driving the white settlers from the country.   In official circles no more harsh interpretation was put upon the letter than that it was "unsatisfactory."   To the friendly chiefs, who better understood the native idiom, it meant only one thing—the definite and unequivocal rejection of the Governor's terms.

Kawiti, on the other hand, was more conciliatory.   He, too, had in his camp many restless young men of similar disposition to those by whom Heke was surrounded and whose counsels were all for war.   Over against their influence, however, were set more humane considerations.   He had lost two sons, besides many relatives in the war, and his own family were extremely urgent for peace.   He therefore wrote a letter in which he plainly said peace might be made provided he was not asked to give up the land at Katore, because the rights over that district rested with the people of Kawakawa, not with him.   This refusal, however, was not to be taken as closing the negotiations,* for he added in a postscript : " This is my regard for you.   Do not suppose that this is the end."

Then an unfavourable turn was given to events by an unexpected circumstance.   A messenger arrived at Ruapekapeka from Hikurangi, bringing the terms of Heke's letter ; and when Kawiti saw that Heke's reply was more unfavourable than his own he at once began to hedge, and endeavoured to cover up his retreat by sending a second letter more belligerent in tone.   In this communication he sought to cast the whole blame upon Waaka Nene and the

---

* When Kawiti's nephew delivered this letter to the Governor he also brought a verbal message to the effect that perhaps Kawiti would send His Excellency " another little word."

Nga-Puhi with him, who, he said, were fighting merely to gratify an ancient grudge, and in which he demanded that the Governor should make concessions as well as the rebels.

From the Ruapekapeka,
Saturday, 29th November, 1845.

SIR, THE GOVERNOR,

Salutations to you. Formerly I was a good man to the Europeans, but Nga-Puhi were so eager to fight with me. They are the people who formerly killed Europeans. If this war were solely yours and the natives had not taken part in it with you our peace would have been made ; but as for native fighting, perhaps it cannot be made straight, because Waaka is constantly naming his dead. You do not understand this. Waaka's fighting is not for your dead. No ; it is for those who were killed long ago—on account of Hao, of Tuahui, Tihi, and Poaka. These were killed long ago. Sir Governor, the thought is with you regarding Waaka that he return to his own people at Hokianga. Do not be hasty about the land. Land is heavy (enduring), but man is light (perishable). Friend, I have no desire to write to you, but you may write if you are pleased with my letter. Sir, if you say that we do fight, it is well. If you say " Cease," it is well ; but do not say that you will not yield some portion of your thoughts.

From me,
From KAWITI.

The belligerent spirit was once more in the ascendancy at Ruapekapeka, and the despatch of these letters was followed by a movement which resulted in the two chiefs again acting in concert. The collection of large stores of food and ammunition was commenced ; the finishing touches were put upon the defences of their fortified places, and emissaries were sent to all parts of the country seeking to fan the flames of rebellion wherever they might happen to find them latent.* Knowing this, Grey came to the conclusion that the correspondence of the chiefs was only a device to gain time, and that if time were given them to complete

* One of their methods of propaganda was to make a model of the Ohaeawai *pa* with fern-sticks, to show how the victory there had been gained. The Rev. Richard Taylor states he saw several of these in the interior being carried southward by messengers from the north.

Rev. Richard Davis, C.M.S.

their arrangements they would simply at their own conveni-
ence commence operations against the troops and settlers,
choosing themselves the point at which to make the attack.
He therefore directed that further and more peremptory
letters be sent to them, demanding a statement in plain
words whether or not they accepted the terms.

On the morning of the 1st December Te Whareumu, the
grandson of Kawiti and the nephew of Pomare, waited on
the Governor and told him an arrangement was about to
be concluded which would enable Kawiti to accept the proposed terms by giving up Katore, the piece of land he had
always professed himself unable to part with, inasmuch as
Pomare and other principal chiefs who had joint claims with
Kawiti to the land had agreed to relinquish these claims
in favour of the Government ; and that they would also
compel, by force if necessary, those of the friendly natives
and others who were interested in it to in like manner
relinquish their claims. In making this communication Te
Whareumu pressed the Governor to give them further time
to enable Kawiti and Pomare to consult with Heke and his
friends, as it was useless to hope the one would make peace
without the other. The confederacy could not be broken
except by mutual consent.

These overtures were flatly and promptly rejected by
Grey. In the first place, he pointed out that the British
Government would not permit of any arrangement under
which natives who had committed no crime could be required
to give up their possessions, or even a joint interest in them
which they might have with Kawiti. What was expected
was that Kawiti and those who were in arms against the
Crown should relinquish any claims they might have to the
lands nominated in Governor FitzRoy's terms, without any
reference to the interests of others. Secondly, that no delay
beyond the date named for submission could be permitted.
Kawiti, he said, was well aware that if he made peace his
example would soon be followed by many others, and that
if he had any fears that by so doing his personal safety
would be endangered he would find asylum on board the

8—First War.

North Star, where he could remain until tranquillity had been restored.

These decisions were speedily conveyed to Kawiti, and on the afternoon of the following day Te Whareumu again waited on the Governor to say that a messenger had come down from Ruapekapeka with intelligence that Kawiti had agreed to accept the terms ; that a letter to that effect would follow in the evening ; and that in the meantime Pomare was anxious to have a time named when the principal rebel chiefs could collectively meet the Governor to express their joint acceptance of the terms, and hear from His Excellency himself the line of conduct he would expect them to pursue in the future.

Grey, who was supremely distrustful of what all this meant, declined to commit himself to any line of action until he had actually received Kawiti's and Heke's letters of plain and simple acceptance of the terms. Nor would he nominate a place of meeting with the chiefs. He was on board the *North Star*, and there they might come to him if so disposed.

True to promise, a letter came from Kawiti that evening, but it was so ambiguously worded as to be quite unintelligible. Te Whareumu was sent for and asked his opinion of the letter. He said it was intended to express a general assent to the terms proposed in so far as concerned Kawiti's own claims to the land at Katore.

With this view Grey did not concur, and he directed Te Whareumu to return at once to his uncle, Pomare, and tell him if no explicit acceptance was received by the following day that would end the matter. In the meantime the *North Star* would be moored in the Kawakawa River, and there the chiefs could come and make their submission if they were sincere in their desire for peace.

Almost simultaneously with the receipt of Kawiti's superambiguous letter came a communication from the Rev. Mr. Burrows, stating that on the previous day he had seen Heke, who, as usual, had much to say, but little to the point ; that His Excellency might possibly receive a letter from the chief next day, but in all probability it would be only another evasion, as Heke, while professing to accept the peace terms himself, sheltered behind the pretension that they could not be accepted by Kawiti. In this attitude the missionary did not believe Heke sincere ; that any peace he might contemplate was not to be a permanent one ; and that unless kept in a constant state of alarm by the troops he might at any time launch an attack upon the friendly natives, towards whom he was particularly resentful. Mr. Burrows further stated that Heke did not like the tone of decision adopted by the Governor, and that to test whether it was real or only assumed he would probably not send his reply to His Excellency's demand until after the date named had expired. He would then see what the Governor would do.

On Wednesday, the 3rd December, Heke's letter reached the Governor, and on the following day Kawiti sent his last " word," but not until he had been made aware of Heke's sentiments. These letters were a revelation. Hitherto the communications which had come from the chiefs had been tinged with a spirit of boasting and arrogance, but they had at least been courteous. Now a complete change was observable. Both rebels replied in the same strain, their letters being filled with language not only defiant, but most offensive and personally insulting to the Governor.* Heke's letter concluded with a defiant note struck in a wild war-song :—

> Oh ! let us fight, fight, fight. Let us fight.
> Fight for the land that lies before us.

What circumstance caused this change in the tone of the chiefs is uncertain, but it left no doubt in the mind of the Governor as to what his policy should be. All hope of a peaceable arrangement with the rebels must be abandoned. It was now war to a finish.

* This is on the authority of Colonel Despard, who was with the Governor at the time, and no doubt heard the letters read, translated, and discussed. As published in the blue-books the letters are unexceptional, though not very intelligible, which may be due to the deletion of the offensive portions, a practice sometimes adopted in connection with public despatches.

8*

CHAPTER VII.

THE BAT'S NEST.

FEW men were more tenacious of purpose when once they had reached a decision than Governor Grey. Having now decided that the rebellion must be crushed, he proceeded to take such steps as were necessary to crush it. Orders were accordingly issued to Colonel Despard to complete the preparations begun for an attack upon Ruapekapeka *pa*. In this policy of aggression there was to be no temporizing with either time or opportunity. The Colonel was to act with due despatch, and in the perfection of his plans he was to employ every available man and to utilize every available gun. Immediately after issuing these imperative orders the Governor sailed for Auckland, there to arrange for the raising of Volunteers, the despatch of supplies to the troops, and to submit to his Legislative Council a Bill for the suppression of the indiscriminate sale of arms and ammunition to the natives. This was a measure the necessity for which had been foreseen by FitzRoy, but he had hesitated to take the bold step, fearing its enactment might estrange the friendly natives, without whose support his position would have been even more helpless and hopeless than it was. The vigorous mind of Grey also perceived the need for intervention; and, confident that the strong forces, both naval and military, at his command would enable him to maintain the authority given by the legislation, he determined upon having the

Ordinance passed without delay. Accordingly there was introduced into the Legislative Council an Arms Importation Bill,* which conferred upon the Governor the power of regulating by Proclamation everything relating to the importation and sale of warlike stores. At first its operation was limited to Auckland, the principal seat of the mischief. Up to this point a lucrative trade had been driven by the Auckland merchants, who were openly selling to the friends of the rebels guns and ammunition which were soon to be turned against the British troops and, for anything they knew, against their fellow-colonists. It was also known that during the previous six months large supplies of ammunition had been obtained by the rebels in exchange for kauri-gum, so that the conditions were clamant for reform, even though it meant the taking of great risks. The effect of the prohibition upon the native mind was not, however, that which had been generally anticipated. Naturally the rebels were annoyed —so, too, were the Auckland shopkeepers—but the friendly natives welcomed it. They were beginning to see that an unlimited supply of arms tended greatly to multiply trouble among a high-spirited race like themselves, many of whose customs both generated and vitalized a spirit of feud. So far, then, from displaying resentment towards the measure they regarded it as a wholesome contribution to the cause of peace, and from that moment its success was assured.

Colonel Despard entered upon the enterprise entrusted to him by the Governor with energy and enthusiasm. In company with Sir Everard Home he made a flying reconnaissance to the navigable head of the Kawakawa River, where he learned of a suitable base for future operations at a spot occupied by the *pa* of Tamati Puku-tutu, a loyal chief who had been pressing the Governor to begin hostilities against Kawiti, with whom he had long been at variance. On the day following the Governor's

* This measure was passed by the Legislative Council on the 13th December, 1845.

departure an order was issued to the whole of the troops at Kororareka to hold themselves in readiness to embark at the shortest notice. On the 8th the advanced division of 300 soldiers, supported by a party of Bengal Artillery* and some seamen gunners from the *Elphinstone*, under the command of Lieut.-Colonel Wynyard, embarked on board the *Slains Castle* and proceeded to the junction of the Kawakawa and Waikare Rivers, where they anchored beside the *North Star*, which had preceded them by three days.

It was Colonel Despard's intention to push these men forward in boats that day, but time and tide were against that operation. They were therefore disembarked and encamped on the site of Pomare's ruined *pa*, the transport meantime returning to Kororareka for the remainder of the force. These, under the personal command of Colonel Despard, reached the point of disembarkation on the following day, when it was discovered that after providing transport for such guns, ammunition, and stores as were indispensable there were not sufficient boats to carry more than 150 men, a number scarcely large enough to defend the guns in the event of an attack. While pondering a solution of the dilemma in which he again discovered himself for lack of transport, there came to the aid of the Colonel the chief Te Whareumu, Pomare's principal adviser, who has already been referred to as making intercession to the Governor for his superior. Te Whareumu informed the Colonel that the only access to Pukututu's *pa* was not, as he had supposed, by water, but that there was a native track across the hills which was practicable for troops, and over which he was prepared personally to guide them. The Colonel — at first suspicious — finally decided to place himself in Te Whareumu's hands, as in the absence of boats the mountain-track appeared to offer the only way out. Lieut.-Colonel Wynyard, with the guns, stores, &c., and 150 men, was ordered to proceed by water to the point of rendezvous, while the Colonel himself, accompanied by

* These men were on board the *Elphinstone*, and Governor Grey took the responsibility of diverting them from their original destination.

Te Whareumu, took boat across the Kawakawa* to a small
pa on the north-west side, and then marched at the head
of his 160 bayonets by the inland route.

The track was both serpentine and undulating, and
though passable for light troops was impassable for wheeled
traffic of any description. Here it skirted the river, there
it swept into the forest or down into deep ravines; but
from every hill they ascended they saw the green valley
lying before them, with the silver river meandering to the
sea. At the end of an hour's march they climbed the last
hill, from which the eye swept across a rich and fertile
district where everything grew with a refreshing luxuriance.
Two miles farther on they came to Pukututu's *pa*, nestling
amidst its gardens at the foot of a gentle slope which rose
from the floor of the valley.

"I was very much struck," says Colonel Despard, "with
the neatness of the cultivated ground in the neighbourhood of
this *pa*. The common potato was planted in great abundance,
as well as the sweet potato. Not a weed was to be discovered
amongst them. Onions and cabbage were also much cultivated, and the peach-tree was to be seen in every direction at
this season in full bloom. I also observed the vine growing in
great luxuriance, with large clusters of young fruit, but I should
much doubt its ripening to any perfection. When returning
by this way a month or five weeks later there was as fine a
basket of cherries brought to me as I ever saw in Europe."

The remainder of the ordnance division arrived about
two hours later; and, leaving Lieut.-Colonel Wynyard in
command, Colonel Despard returned to the ships for the
purpose of pushing on with the despatch of stores and the
speedy embarkation of the remainder of the troops at
Kororareka. This, with the aid of H.M.S. *Racehorse*, was
safely accomplished next day, 250 men of the 58th and
99th marching by the Maori track, the remainder proceeding
by water. By the 12th December the whole force was
assembled in camp at Pukututu's *pa*, its effective strength
being then 631 officers and men.

* Their starting-point was the present Taumarere.

So far as the British had any knowledge of the rebels, they were at the moment divided. Heke was resting in his newly built *pa* at Hikurangi, some twenty miles in a south-westerly direction from Kawiti's position. His actual adherents assembled in the *pa* were not supposed to be numerous — some two hundred in all — but the report of every native chief who was consulted was that his position was so inaccessible as to be beyond the reach of artillery, and so strong as to defy attack without it. Kawiti was sitting quietly in his recently constructed fortress at Rua-pekapeka. This stronghold was built upon a mountain lying nearly due south from Despard's camp, but separated from it by some ten miles of rough and difficult country. Because of its peculiar situation and its unusual strength it was regarded as the Gibraltar of Maori fortification, and its ability to resist the British attack was a topic keenly discussed in every native settlement throughout New Zealand.

As in the case of Heke, Kawiti was known not to have retained a large body of followers about him, but the attached and unattached retainers of both chiefs were busy collecting supplies of food and ammunition against the day when they surely would be needed. Moreover, it was no secret that the emissaries of the chiefs were abroad spreading the gospel of rebellion among the disaffected tribes, and the measure of success which they would achieve was something which no one could accurately assess. Grey believed that they could never at any time be able to assemble a force of greater numerical strength than seven hundred ; but this much was certain : any reverse to the British arms would immediately bring large accessions of strength to the ranks of the victorious enemy. Under these two rebel leaders there were a number of minor chiefs actively participating in the rebellion, and, so far as they were known, these men were—

Chiefs of the Nga-Puhi tribe acting under Heke : Whe, Te Haratua, Hare te Pure, Hautungia, Te Awa, Kuao, Pene Taui.

Chiefs of the Hineamaru tribe living on the Kawakawa River and acting under Kawiti : Te Haara,
Tahua Hori Kingi, Maru.

Chiefs of the Kapotai tribe living on the Waikare
River and acting under Kawiti : Kokouri, Hikitene, Haumere, Tukerehu.

Upon these men developed the responsibility of organ-
izing, arming, and feeding the forces who came under the
banner of their leaders.

In making his advance upon Ruapekapeka Colonel
Despard had the choice of three routes — they could
scarcely be called roads, for at the best they were nothing
better than sinuous native tracks, quite impassable for
vehicles, and nearly so for men. For the purpose of determining which presented the fewer difficulties the Colonel,
assisted by Captain Marlow, of the Engineers, made a
personal reconnaissance of two of them, finally selecting
one which, though the more circuitous,* was capable of
being speedily made passable for drays and artillery. Upon
the work of converting this rough bush track with its
walls of high fern and dense *manuka* into a practical dray-
road a body of Pioneers† and soldiers was employed, and
so heartily did they work under the direction of Captain
Matson, of the 58th, and their own immediate officer,
Captain Atkyns, that in less than a week its steep hills,
swampy valleys, and timbered ravines were reported to
be passable for men and guns as far as Waiomio, the
point at which Colonel Despard had decided to make his
next halt.

With this work well in hand Colonel Despard turned
to face another problem, that of bringing up his heavy
battery guns. What promised to be a task of no small
magnitude proved simple in the hands of the sailors. By
their energy and ingenuity two 32-pounders and one

* The second road, though preferable in many respects, was intercepted by a wide and deep ravine, which it was not thought practicable
to bridge.

† These men were Volunteers who had enlisted in Auckland.

18-pounder were placed in boats and safely floated to the camp. In the same manner the heavy shot and shell were brought up the river, and although this work was not without its incidents and anxious moments it went on smoothly under the skilful direction of Sir Everard Home, who undertook the duty of supervising the delivery of supplies. The carriage of the guns and ammunition over the newly formed road proved a much more strenuous business, for there was again an aggravating shortage of drays and draught cattle, even after the utmost resources of the district from Auckland to the Bay of Islands had been exhausted.*

On the 12th December H.M.S. *Castor*, thirty-six guns, arrived at Kororareka from China, Captain Graham, her commander, having been appointed to the position of Senior Naval Officer on the New Zealand Station. Two days later the *Elphinstone* followed with the Governor on board. Grey then remained continuously with the force during the campaign, imposing upon it not only the benefit of his experience as a soldier, but not less the impress of his forceful and magnetic personality.

While these preliminary movements were proceeding, life in camp proved to be much as it had been at Ohaeawai. There were the same wet days, the dripping tents, the damp beds, and general discomfort for the men, and this sense of uneasiness was frequently accentuated by untimely alarms† and fearsome rumours of impending attack. By the evening of the 21st the supplies and men in camp were considered sufficient to warrant the first step in the

---

* After five months' preparation these necessaries for the movement of troops were not provided. " In this branch of our armament," says Colonel Despard, " we were very defective. When all the bullocks which could be collected were brought into camp there were only sufficient for six drays, and there was also one three-horse cart."

† On the night of the 15th one of the sentries, who had managed to imbibe more liquor than was good for him, amused himself by promiscuously firing off his gun at imaginary enemies. The camp was turned out, and when the cause of the alarm was ascertained the bibulous private was confined for the night. Next day he was tried by a court-martial and found guilty of being drunk on duty and of creating a false alarm. For these offences he was on the 17th flogged in the presence of the whole of the troops.

advance being taken. Thanks to the active co-operation of the naval officers, the force had in the intervening days been considerably reinforced by detachments from the ships, and in its various units it now numbered about one thousand five hundred officers and men.

The Naval Brigade consisted of 280 men, with a due proportion of officers. In this brigade were included a number of gunners sufficient to work all the guns supplied by the men-of-war, as well as men to serve the rockets, this unit being in charge of Commander Hay, of H.M.S. *Racehorse*.

The Infantry Brigade was made up of detachments of the Royal Marines, about eighty in number, including those joining from the *Castor*, under Captain Langford; the 58th Regiment, under Lieut.-Colonel Wynyard; the flank companies of the 99th Regiment, under Captain Reed; and the Volunteers from Auckland, under Captain Atkyns. The whole brigade numbered 750, exclusive of officers.

The artillery comprised two 32 - pounders, one 18 - pounder, two 12-pounder howitzers, two light 6-pounders, supplemented by a good supply of Congreve rockets, under Captain Egerton, of the *North Star*. There were also four small mortars, which by virtue of their lightness proved most serviceable, being conveniently shifted from point to point, and where absolute accuracy of aim was not required they did excellent work in throwing shells into the *pa*.

To this force must be added the native allies, under Waaka Nene and his immediate lieutenants, Nopera Panakarcao, Mohi Tawhai, and Repa. With the exception of about one hundred men who had been detached to watch Heke, the native allies were in full force, the Governor having directed that they should be supplied with rations from the camp, thereby overcoming the difficulty they must have experienced in providing themselves in a hostile country with an ample and regular commissariat.*

* Prior to this the native allies had fought without food or pay from the British.

At 7 o'clock on the morning of the 22nd December the
first division, consisting of about three hundred and fifty
soldiers and one hundred and fifty seamen, under Lieut.-
Colonel Wynyard, left the camp and took up a position at
Waiomio, five miles distant. The site of this camp was
well chosen, being upon elevated ground, easy of defence
in case of attack. It also possessed what Colonel Despard
deemed to be an invaluable advantage, but which in truth
was quite illusory. It was situated at the junction of the
Hikurangi and Ruapekapeka Tracks, and it was assumed
by the Colonel that if Heke contemplated joining Kawiti
he must travel by the former, and would therefore find
his advance cut off by the presence of the British troops.
Colonel Despard was inexperienced enough in the habits of
his enemy not to know that it was impossible to cut off
the march of the natives in war-time merely by occupying
their usual paths. When on the march each native carried
his own clothing, arms, and ammunition, while frequently
the women carried the food. They were not concerned
about wet feet, and were able to camp wherever fortune
might bring them at the end of the day. They were
thus independent of all beaten tracks, and so it proved
in Heke's case. He evaded the British troops and joined
Kawiti just as soon as he desired to do so.

The remainder of the force followed on the next day,
but their progress was slow and laborious, rain having
fallen in the meantime, rendering the road almost impassable. With them the first division had taken up three
guns on the previous day, and these had been hauled
over the soft road with increasing difficulty ; but now the
heavy guns had perforce to be dismounted and placed in
drays, which were dragged through the mud by exhausted
bullocks, the stores being transported by the not less
exhausted men.*

---

* Major Bridge states that owing to the difficulty of transport Colonel
Despard had decided not to take the 32-pounders up to Ruapekapeka,
a decision which the Major characterizes as " more folly." The Governor,
however, intervened, and the guns were taken up in drays drawn by eight
bullocks, supplemented by the power of sixty seamen and soldiers hauling
on drag-ropes.

The 24th was spent by the Governor and the Colonel in reconnoitring the ground beyond Waiomio in the full and fervent hope that they would be able to complete this stage on the next day. Orders were therefore issued that the troops were to march out in the early morning, notwithstanding that it would be Christmas Day. Against this order there was much grumbling among the soldiers in camp, who saw no need for haste, since the enemy was showing so little disposition to run away. That night it commenced to rain and continued unabated for two days, whereupon, much to the gratification of the troops, the order to advance was countermanded.

On the 27th, the weather having moderated, a division seven hundred strong again moved towards the desired goal, camping on an elevated and commanding position three-quarters of a mile from the enemy whom they had come so far and through such travail to seek. The distance, though only five miles, took some hours to complete, for in its low places the road was a quagmire, while on the hill-sides it was treacherous for man and beast. Under these circumstances the stores moved more slowly than the men, and when the latter reached their immediate destination they were without food, tents, or accessories of any kind.

Immediately upon their arrival at the new camp the Governor, who had accompanied the soldiers on the march, and the Colonel went forward to more closely examine the enemy's position. They discovered that the *pa* was situated on a narrow ridge along which they had been advancing from Waiomio, and which had begun to be thickly wooded, especially in the ravines, while on the higher levels it alternated between wooden hills and open spaces. The actual site of the *pa* was clear of trees and sloped towards the British camp, so that from the camp, which was pitched on a high knoll, there was an uninterrupted view of the *pa*. The most disconcerting fact discovered was that between the camp and the *pa* there lay a deep and abrupt ravine with thickly wooded sides, which unless bridged would cause endless delay in crossing. To bridge it quickly the Colonel had no adequate appliances, and time was too pressing to permit of delay. He therefore determined upon turning the ravine by cutting a track through the bush for half a mile or more. To do this was a labour of some magnitude,* but when completed it promised substantial advantages of a safe and speedy passage for the drays and guns, which in the light of all his past experiences were attributes which Colonel Despard was ripe to appreciate.

As to the actual distance of the *pa* from the ravine a difference of opinion arose between the Governor and the Colonel, and to test the point the Rocket Brigade was brought up and ordered to throw a rocket into the *pa*. The attempt failed in the desired purpose, but achieved an unlooked-for result. The first rocket used was a 24 lb. spherical case, but from some defect in either its construction or direction it exploded over a patch of fern far short of the walls of the *pa*. Instantaneously a heavy fire of small arms came from the fern patch, revealing the fact that the enemy was there lying in ambush, waiting for an incautious advance on the part of the British.

While these incidents had been proceeding Mohi Tawhai moved with his men across the ravine and took up an advanced position beyond the first belt of trees. Here he built a small stockade for the protection of his men 1,200 yards from the rebel *pa*, and in this position he was subsequently supported by a small body of the military, whose strength in the camp had been increased by a detachment of the 58th just arrived from Norfolk Island.†

"A most timely reinforcement," comments Colonel Despard, "as our men were beginning to be a good deal harassed from the difficulties of the road, which being much cut up by the rainy weather it frequently required sixty men in addition to a team of eight bullocks to each gun to get it up the hills and through the woods, besides being afterwards obliged to stop till some large tree was cut down, perhaps six feet in diameter."

* Some of the trees to be hewn down were from 4 ft. to 6 ft. in diameter.
† This reinforcement consisted of 1 Captain, 4 subalterns, and 108 men.

BRITISH CAMP BEFORE RUAPEKAPEKA PA.

After the drawing by Lieutenant Page.

The 28th being Sunday the natives on both sides refused
to make it a day of hostilities.   Not so the British, a great
portion of whom were employed assisting the drays and
dragging at the guns.   Before daylight next morning Waaka
Nene and Mohi Tawhai led their men into the clearing
nearest to the *pa* and took possession of the open ground
800 yards from the *pa*, where they could be in even closer
touch with the enemy.   Sending intelligence of what they
had done to Colonel Despard, he pushed forward 200 of the
Infantry to support them in holding a position upon which
he now decided to place his big batteries and his camp of
attack.   Up to this time no systematic camp had been
formed, chiefly because of the difficulty experienced in getting
up the tents from the lower camp.   These it was now decided
to discard, and to shelter the men in hutments constructed
of native scrub, of which there was on every hand abundant
supply.   This work was pushed on with vigour, and on the
30th an intermittent fire was opened on the *pa* by the
32-, the 18-, and 12-pounders, which had been established in a
battery on a knoll in front of the camp, and excellent practice
was made by both gunners* and the Rocket Brigade.   These
shells and rockets, plunging into the *pa* with unerring aim,
created consternation among the defenders, who ran out
to escape the concussion, only to return again to put out
fires and repair any damage done to their defences when
firing ceased.   Of these tactics Major Bridge is mercilessly
critical :—

This is not the way I hoped to see the *pa* attacked.   There
is no use in firing a shot till all the guns, ammunition, &c., are
up and everything prepared to carry on the attack with vigour.
An incessant fire should be kept up by all the guns and rockets
till the *pa* is set on fire or so battered that by taking immediate
advantage of the confusion a part of the force might rush in
before the natives could return to their defences, whilst the
remainder should be so posted as to cut off their retreat into
the woods.   Also, how deplorable it is to see such ignorance,
indecision, and obstinacy in a commander who will consult no

* Lieutenant Bland, of H.M.S. *Racehorse,* and Lieutenant Leeds, of
the *Elphinstone.*

one, or attend to any suggestion made to him, and also in consequence has neither the respect nor the confidence of the troops under his command.   Every one looks disheartened at such a beginning and apprehensive of the result.

To this sporadic fire of the British Kawiti replied with two shots from two guns in the *pa ;* but they were speedily silenced by the better practice of the naval gun, and one of them was afterwards discovered dismantled by a shot from the 18-pounder.

That night a mizzling rain fell, and in the midst of it the camp was twice turned out in response to an alarm by the nervous piquets, who, imagining Maoris were creeping upon them, fired at what eventually proved to be nothing more than a brace of inquisitive pigs.   Next morning a thick fog enveloped the camp and *pa*, but no surprise tactics were attempted by the British.   The rebels were not so idle.   A small party came out from the *pa* and crept close up to the Pioneers who were at work in the bush, and seeing one of their number, a negro, leave the main body to go in search of water, they poured in a heavy fire upon him, hitting him in three or four places, and then decamped.   The friendly natives immediately sallied out in an endeavour to intercept their retreat, and a sharp skirmish was the result, in which the chief Repa had three fingers of his left hand shot away. The unfortunate Pioneer was found in the scrub and brought into camp alive, but died a few hours afterwards, the first British casualty of the expedition.   At 9 o'clock the fog lifted, when the guns again began their somewhat listless fire which so roused the indignation of Major Bridge.

When the sun broke through the clouds Kawiti for the first time since the enemy came to his gates hoisted his flag on the staff set up within the *pa*.   This was his challenge to the British fire, and his declaration that he was ready to fight.   The flag itself was of red and white material, and on the white section were depicted the sun, moon, and stars, which, doubtless, had their significance in his mind, but what that significance was is now uncertain.   In any event the flag proved objectionable to Colonel Despard, who indicated to Lieutenant Bland that he would like to see it brought down. Bland cheerfully accepted the commission, laid his gun, which was already loaded, and with the first shot struck the staff near the ground, bringing it down with a crash, equalled only by the hearty British cheer which rewarded the marksman's sporting success. Kawiti tried no more experiments with the flag which so belied the celestial emblems with which it was adorned. Indeed, there is every reason to believe the incident had the most profound effect on the mercurial minds of the natives inside the *pa*, who forgot their successes and suddenly became seized with a superstitious fear, a fear that was heightened by a curious phenomenon visible in the heavens on the following day. A young moon with a bright star near it was distinctly seen while the sun shone in the fullness of his splendour. This some of the friendly natives interpreted as a good omen for the British, urging that it was Kawiti's flag gone up into the sky. Others, however, read into it a different meaning. They saw in it something favourable to Kawiti, since the star was on his side of the moon and not on that of the enemy. Kawiti may or may not have troubled about the heavenly portents, but he certainly saw in the fall of his flag the beginning of the end, and he made it publicly known among his people that he intended to give the soldiers one day's battle and then cry "Enough." This decision was speedily conveyed to Heke at Hikurangi, whereupon he immediately wrote to his comrade a letter, quaintly worded, urging him valiantly to continue the struggle to the end. Heke was not at this time being daily " roasted with iron " as Kawiti was, and could well afford to be valorous :—

SIR RUKE*,—

    I have great friendship for you, for surely the heart knoweth not the hour when the soldiers will come. There is an appearance of want of energy. Let there be no sign of fear ; but, sir, be on your guard against the practices of deceitful persons, of deceitful white men. Take care that the judgment

* *Sir Ruke*—supposed to be one of Kawiti's names.

fail not ; let it not be trampled on by the many.* Let it not
decay, but persist. Let not the slack of the fishing-line be in
the damp till it rot. Oh friend, oh sire, put aside this folly,
the end thereof is child's play, but keep a sharp lookout for the
dust of that thing—the soldiers. Do try to remember the one
word, one only word—the one day, one only day. Let it be
warm ; let it not be cold. Let the small and great strive to
exalt the one word of Kawiti, for he is our only father.† If
you are bold enough to attack that thing—the soldiers—and
fail, lo, I come to my father and to all of you.‡ Be careful,
careful, exceedingly careful. Be firm, firm, constantly firm ;
unyielding, ever unyielding. Oh sire, let us not be pointed
at as a cat's paw for Nga-Puhi to gain wealth by.§ If we do
fail, continue to the last. Oh tribe, behold the house of strife.
Enough, Amen. This is my regard to you all. Go, this my
letter, to hearken to the cry of the rockets. When you fire
the gun's mouth hasten to me.‖

The New Year was ushered in by a smart skirmish
between the rebels and the native allies, brought on by
the latter, who were seeking payment for Repa's fingers.
The fight lasted only a few minutes, but in that time
Waaka Nene's brother, Wiremu Waaka Turau, shot one
of the enemy with Repa's gun, and this being considered
" sufficient unto the day " the friendlies came back to the
camp well satisfied with their morning's work.

Since occupying the camp in front of the *pa* Colonel
Despard had been steadily advancing to position after
position, which brought him to within what he considered
striking distance of the fortress. On the morning of the
1st January, 1846, the most important of these advances
was made when he pushed forward a strong detachment
into the only wood that now divided him from the enemy.
In the centre of this wood he discovered a spacious area
cleared of trees, though covered with fern. Calculating
that the distance was not greater than 400 yards from the

* Advice to keep his own counsel, and not be swayed by the voice
of the many.
† This was meant to flatter and encourage Kawiti.
‡ Meaning that if Kawiti needed assistance he would come to his aid
§ A suggestion that if they were defeated Waaka Nene and the other
Nga-Puhi chiefs would share their land.
‖ When you begin the attack let me know.

walls of the *pa*, he decided that here he would erect his breaching battery, the screen of bush in front being so thick as to encourage the hope that the men might work at it free from observation or attack. Accordingly a strong stockade was commenced, of sufficient height to prevent the enemy bullets dropping over, and of sufficient dimensions to house a battery of two 32-pounders, the $4\frac{1}{2}$ in. mortars, a magazine, and a guard. By evening the work was so far advanced as to almost preclude the possibility of its guard being driven out. While the soldiers worked the native allies watched, and that to some purpose, for as the walls of the stockade rose within the clearing the sentinels on watch at the *pa* saw them, and it was decided to stop this new menace if it was at all possible so to do. During the afternoon of the 2nd January a strong force sallied out from the *pa*, bent on driving in the working-parties and destroying the fruits of their labour. The native allies, being upon the spot, asked that they might be permitted to take the situation in hand, with this further request that the soldiers would stand aside, since there was a danger that in the excitement of the fight they might not distinguish between friend and foe. Keeping his Infantry as a reserve, Colonel Despard agreed to give the friendlies a free hand.* Firing commenced at long range, but with Waaka Nene in the centre, Nopera and Mohi Tawhai on the wings, the allies' line moved rapidly forward, firing steadily the while, but meeting a fire which compelled them to find cover in the most approved native style. For some hours the firing continued and the fight ebbed and flowed with all the elements of uncertainty, but towards dusk the friendlies, having been continually reinforced by their own people, began to assert their superiority,† and succeeded in driving the rebels into the *pa*, with seven of their number killed

* Lieutenant (afterwards Colonel) Balneavis states in his diary that Colonel Despard's object was to test the sincerity of his native allies, whether they were in earnest or not.

† The native allies also fought with the additional advantage of superior Government ammunition.

and thirteen wounded, their own casualties being only
five wounded. Their elation at this success found vent in
vehement speeches and a stirring war-dance when they
returned to camp. To this incident in the campaign
Major Bridge makes the following reference :—

While the fight was going on I was put out with a strong
piquet of 200 men to occupy the stockade, which was about half
completed, and arrived there during the action. The balls were
whistling over our heads in the stockade, the skirmish between
the natives being in front and on the right of it. After sunset
all Walker's people came in and went to their *pa* on the right
of our encampment, and we were left to pass the night on the
bare ground, with a fence on one side of us and only a small
trench on the other. After placing my sentries we all lay down
and kept ourselves as quiet as possible, and, although dark,
we heard the enemy searching for their dead, and those in the
pa talking over the fight. They acknowledged to having got
the worst of it, lamenting that more of Waaka's people had
not been killed ; but the chiefs were trying to encourage them
by telling them they would be successful to-morrow, or the
next day they fought—exhorting them to be strong, to be firm
and brave, and they would serve the *pakeha* as they had done
at Ohaeawai.

With a view to preventing any renewed attempt on
the part of the enemy to sally out under cover of the
woods Colonel Despard resolved on having a second stockade erected to the right and in advance of that which
the enemy had sought to destroy, which would eventually
shut him in on the side next to the encampment. Into
this battery it was proposed to put one of the 18-pounders
and one howitzer, so placed that their fire would range
along the western face of the *pa*, upon which also was to be
concentrated the fire of the larger guns. Should circumstances demand it, these guns were equally capable of
being directed against the south-west angle, which flanked
the part intended to be breached.

Colonel Despard now had the sites of three batteries
fixed. The first in front of his camp, 650 yards distant
from the *pa*, and containing one 32-pounder and one 12-
pounder howitzer ; the second, 344 yards away, and in it

was to be placed one 32-pounder, one 12-pounder howitzer, and the $4\frac{1}{2}$ in. mortars ; the third, no more than 150 yards away, was to contain one 18-pounder and one 12-pounder howitzer, the latter two batteries being protected by high stockades. The erection of these stockades proceeded without further interruption from the enemy, their construction, with their walls, their gun-emplacements, and all their internal equipment, occupying some seven days.* During these seven days there were frequent and heavy rains which swamped the camp and, penetrating the grass huts, drenched the men and their beds of fern. On the 6th Major Bridge records : " A miserable, wet day. The piquets came in in miserable plight." But amidst it all the work went on.

The smaller battery was armed as Colonel Despard originally intended, but within the larger one there were placed eventually two 32-pounder naval guns, as well as the howitzer and the mortars. Here the Colonel had proposed to mount only one such gun, considering that the other 32-pounder was sufficiently effective where he had already placed it. The Governor, however, was insistent upon the nearer battery being more heavily armed. In this he was supported by Captain Graham, who offered to provide the gun if the Colonel would avail himself of the offer.

To these persuasions Colonel Despard yielded rather than consented, and the Governor and Captain Graham started for the Kawakawa camp† to superintend the delivery of the gun. The sailors of the *Castor* brought it smartly by boat from the ship. To facilitate the getting of the

---

* The apparent indifference of the rebels to these proceedings and their failure to harass those engaged in the erection of the batteries may cause some surprise. The explanation, no doubt, is that they were relying on a repetition of the tactics adopted at Ohaeawai—a brief bombardment and then a storm—when they knew they could get the soldiers in their own time and in their own way.

† The camp at Pukututu's *pa* was now treated as a depot, and was guarded by forty sailors, thirteen soldiers, and a number of Pukututu's natives, who were supported by a 6-pounder gun. They were under Lieutenants Johnson and Holmes, R.N.

gun from the level of the river to the high bank above, Lieutenant Johnson procured an old Maori canoe, which he cut in two. The gun was then lashed inside the larger half, a 5 in. hawser was clapped round the bows of the canoe, with a clove-hitch round the muzzle of the gun. A relay of handspikes was prepared to place under the canoe, and the brawny arms of two hundred sailors pulling on the hawser did the rest. They dragged it bodily through the brushwood, over every obstacle, right up to the gate of the *pa*. The sailors then gave three rousing cheers, turned the gun out of the canoe, placed it on its carriage, and fired it three times to impress the natives that it was ready for action.

Application was made to Mr. Dumoulin, the commissariat officer in charge, for the use of one of his four bullock-drays to convey it to Ruapekapeka. To grant the request would, Mr. Dumoulin knew, seriously interfere with the due delivery of supplies and almost certainly involve him in official censure. Seeing, however, that the request came from the Governor and the senior naval officer, he decided to comply with their wishes and gamble on the consequences. "The gun," says Mr. Dumoulin, "was on the dray by daylight on the following morning, the carriage being dragged by bluejackets. On arrival at the camp Colonel Despard became savage. I was sent for and asked : ' How dared I give conveyance for the gun without his orders ? ' I explained, and was told to go back."

Mr. Dumoulin went back a little relieved to find he had escaped so lightly, but comforted in the knowledge that if more were said he would be firmly supported by one who had already taken the Colonel's measure.

Having now received his full complement of guns, together with an adequate supply of shot and shell, Colonel Despard felt that so soon as the finishing-touches were put to his stockades he would be able to begin in earnest the general attack he had so far been compelled to withhold. As a necessary preliminary the Pioneers were on

the 6th January detailed to hew down the screen of forest
in front of the stockade so as to expose the threatened
wall of the *pa*.*   This work occupied the greater part of
three days, but by dusk of the 9th a clear view was for
the first time obtained of the doomed fortress.   What the
attacking force now saw was a fighting *pa* conventional
in type, yet with many remarkable differences.   Its
measurements were roughly 120 yards long by 70 yards
wide, and much broken in flanks.   Its first lines of defence
were two rows of palisades, each constructed of young
trees from 12 in. to 20 in. in diameter ; its interior lines
consisted of a series of smaller stockades, systematically
arranged around the defenders' dwellings.   The outer poles
were set deep in the ground, and rose 15 ft. above it.
Between these two rows of palisading was a ditch 4 ft.
deep, with earthen traverses left in it, the excavated earth
being thrown up in a solid bank behind it to form
an inner rampart.   At frequent intervals the exterior wall
was loopholed close to the ground, so that the defenders
might lie in the trench in comparative safety and yet pour
in a deadly fire upon an approaching enemy.   From an
exterior survey these features were more or less evident, but
there were other singular methods adopted of strengthening
the *pa* which did not meet the eye until after its capture.
Writing of these Colonel Despard says :—

In the interior nearly every hut was stockaded, with a deep
excavation underground, into which the inhabitants could retire
and shelter themselves almost entirely from both shot and
shell.   The earth taken out from these excavations formed a
low rampart to support its stockade, thus rendering each hut
a little fortress in itself.   There was great ingenuity displayed
in this sytem of the defence, more probably than had ever
been before exhibited by any race of savages we have yet been
acquainted with.   The chief Kawiti's hut attracted particular
attention.   It was remarkably neat, with a low veranda in
front and an extensive excavation underneath, as well as being
strongly stockaded, on the side exposed to attack, by upright
timbers, with others laid horizontally behind, and supported
by an embankment.

*" Rather an injudicious proceeding," comments Major Bridge, " to
open up the wood so much until the battery is quite ready to fire."

It was to this *pa* that Heke and his followers came secretly on the night before Colonel Despard's main attack was launched, and they were present at its fall two days later. This was in complete accord with the British strategy of the campaign, which aimed first at keeping the chiefs apart, and then at driving them together so that they might both be destroyed by the one blow. When the Governor finally decided that he must attack Kawiti at Ruapekapeka, Heke was in his new *pa* at Hikurangi, twenty miles away. To keep him there was the policy of the Governor, who seems to have intervened and over-ridden Colonel Despard whenever he felt so disposed. In this connection, too, he did what Colonel Despard would never have done : he trusted his native allies. He sub-mitted his proposal to the friendly chiefs, and requested them to attend to its execution. After consultation among themselves the chiefs thought well of the suggestion, and recommended that Taonui, one of Waaka Nene's lieutenants, should be detached with one hundred of his followers for this duty.

On the 19th December Taonui received his instructions from the Governor, which were that he was to watch Heke closely. If he left his *pa* to join Kawiti, Taonui was to fall upon his rear and harass him at every turn, without com-mitting himself to an actual encounter ; then, as the rebels neared Ruapekapeka, he was to press them closely, and, if possible, drive them in upon Kawiti in a state of confusion, the ostensible purpose being thereby to reduce Heke's prestige in the eyes of his countrymen. Taonui was then to take up his station on the side of the *pa* opposite to that on which the attack was being made, in the hope of cutting off what the British leaders were vain enough to expect would soon become a precipitate retreat.

The first portion of this duty Taonui carried out with the utmost fidelity. He built a small *pa* near Heke's, from which the rebel chief was under constant observation, but even this vigilant surveillance was not sufficient. Heke was too clever for the watch-dogs of the friendly Nga-Puhi, and on the 5th January Taonui arrived at the Ruapekapeka camp to report that Heke had slipped out of his *pa* and eluded his every effort to find him. As usual, all sorts of rumours were afloat, but it was commonly believed that this freedom would be used by Heke either to attack the settlers or to break in upon the British lines of communication. Accordingly a company of sixty friendly natives was sent off by Taonui to Hokianga to protect the settlement there from any designs Heke might have in that direction,* while one hundred of his force was sent to Pukututu's *pa* to protect the British rear should Heke attempt marauding operations against the slow and cumbrous vehicles of transport. Heke, however, had no designs such as these. He, like Kawiti, believed there was no need for tactics of that kind, since of a surety the soldiers would walk up to the walls of the *pa*, where they could be shot down with much more certainty and comfort than in a bush skirmish. In these circumstances he was content to join Kawiti, which, with about sixty followers, he did on the 9th January, doubtless having been well advised that the British preparations were approaching completion.

Of this reinforcement Kawiti stood in sore need, for already there were evidences of dissension among his retainers. Early on the preceding day the British had observed a party of about eighty men leave the *pa* and, crossing the hills to the left, disappear from the scene. Whether they were a force coming out to attack the supply columns or to procure supplies for themselves was a matter for conjecture, which was not set at rest until 10 o'clock that morning. Then there appeared to be a mild commotion inside the *pa*. Its garrison was observed running in and out and manning the trenches, and immediately a flag of truce was seen, carried by a woman who

---

* The war-brig *Osprey* was also sent as a precautionary measure to Hokianga.

walked towards the friendly natives stationed in front of
the big stockade. This proved to be the wife of the rebel
chief Tahua Hori Kingi, a half-caste girl, whose mother
was with Waaka Nene's people.

"The poor thing," says Major Bridge, "came to tell our
natives that she wished to get out of the *pa*, but that they would
not let her. She said the party that went over the hills this
morning would not come back again. A chief accompanied her
of the name of Haara, who appeared very much disgusted and
asked : ' What more do you want ? You have been a month
here roasting us with iron, and you are not satisfied yet.' He
was told we should not be satisfied till they had left the *pa*
and we had possession of it. The Governor sent a message to
Kawiti to request he would send away all his women and children, as he had not come there to hurt them, and to express
his sorrow that a woman and child had been killed in the *pa*
on the 1st of the month. I fancy they are leaving the *pa* by
parties, and that they will shortly all bolt ; but I hope not
before our batteries open on them, as it is better that we should
drive them out than that they should go of their own accord,
just to show them what we can do and to take the conceit out
of the rascals."

There was a good deal of firing by the sentries on
the night of the 8th, and the camp was turned out many
times to no purpose. In the morning there was further
excitement, caused by the report that thirty rebels had
left the *pa* to attack the ammunition-train which was
bringing up the last of the shot and shell for the 32- and
18-pounders. Strong escorts were accordingly sent off to
give the drays safe convoy, and then the final touches
were put upon the preparations, which every British soldier,
with Major Bridge, devoutly hoped would serve to "take
the conceit out of the rascals."

Colonel Despard now had under his command and immediately before the *pa* the following troops :—

NAVAL.

	Officers.	Men.
H.M.S. *Castor, North Star, Racehorse,* H.E.I.C.		
Elphinstone—Commander Hay, R.N. ..	33	280

BRITISH STOCKADE, RUAPEKAPEKA.

After the drawing by Major Bridge.

MILITARY.

	Officers.	Men.
Royal Artillery, Royal Engineers—Captain Marlow, R.E., Lieutenant Wilmot, R.A.	2	0
Royal Marines—Captain Langford	4	80
58th—Lieut.-Colonel Wynyard	20	543
99th—Captain Reed	7	150
H.E.I.C. Artillery—Lieutenant Leeds	1	15
Volunteers from Auckland—Captain Atkyns	1	42
	68	1,110

NATIVE ALLIES.

Under Tamati Waaka Nene, Patuone, Mohi Tawhai, Nopera Panakareao, Repa 450

Mr. Philip Turner was the Commissary-General.

ORDNANCE.

Three naval 32-pounders, two 12-pounder howitzers, one 18-pounder, one 6-pounder brass gun, four 4½ in. mortars, two rocket-tubes.

Pitted against this force the enemy within the *pa* was supposed to number some five hundred, made up of various elements of Nga-Puhi and some adventurous spirits of the Ngati-Kahungunu from the south.

On the morning of Saturday, the 10th, all was ready, and at 11 o'clock the attack began on a scale never before witnessed by the Maori, and of which in all probability his imagination had never conceived. What had happened at Puketutu and Ohaeawai was mere child's play compared with the onslaught to which they were now subjected. From every gun and Cohorn mortar at the Colonel's command there came a rain of shot and shell which never ceased during the whole of that day to batter at the western wall and to plunge shells into the centre of the *pa*. "Rockets, mortars, ship's guns, long brass guns," says a native account, "all burst out firing at once. We were almost deaf with the noise, and the air was full of cannon-balls. The fence of the fort began to disappear like a bank of fog before the morning breeze.

NEW ZEALAND'S FIRST WAR.

So now we saw that the soldiers had at last found out how to knock down a *pa*."

Severe as this fire appeared to be, and disastrous as it undoubtedly was to the outer wall of the *pa*, the casualties within the *pa* itself were comparatively few.* By one of those strange freaks of fortune which sometimes guides a missile in its course a rocket decapitated a woman, but left uninjured a child she was carrying on her back. Two men were killed by rockets, and one man had his leg carried away above the knee by a round shot which broke through the fence and sent him reeling in the dust. This man was a Ngati-Kahungunu warrior from the south, who was on a visit of adventure to the rebels of the north. When he realized what had happened he good-humouredly remarked : " Look here, the iron has run away with my leg. What playful creatures these cannon-balls are," and so saying he fell back and died like the brave warrior that he was.

For the rest the men, women, and children sheltered in the shell-proof pits, where they were comparatively safe from injury. But as the day wore on the defenders were out of all patience with the mortar-shells. " They came tumbling into the *pa*, and they would hardly be on the ground before they would burst with a great noise, and no sooner would one burst than another would burst, and so they came one after another so fast that the people in the *pa* could get no rest and were getting quite deaf. These guns† are a very vexatious invention for preventing people from getting any sleep, but they never killed any one." That the fire was " vexatious " enough the British officers judged by the fact that towards 3 o'clock in the afternoon numbers of natives were observed leaving the *pa*

---

* Many of the shells did not explode immediately, and after the defenders had recovered from their first surprise they derived a good deal of amusement and excitement by extracting what they called the *wiki* (fuse) from the shells as they lay fizzing on the ground. From the shells so intercepted they obtained a considerable supply of powder.

† The natives called the mortars " pot-guns," owing to the shortness of the barrel.

with loads on their backs, and returning for more. To
the British the whole movement bore the appearance of
an impending evacuation, and in a sense it was.

The ultimate end of such a bombardment was soon
apparent to the keen intellect of Heke, who, seeing the
shaken fence and the harried condition of the people, said
to them : " You are foolish to remain in this *pa* to be
pounded by cannon-balls. Let us leave it. Let the soldiers
have it, and we will retire into the forest, and draw them
after us where they cannot bring their big guns. The soldiers
cannot fight amongst the *kareao*.* They will be easily killed
amongst the reeds, as if they were wood-pigeons."

Yielding to this advice, Heke's own people withdrew, but
Kawiti stoutly refused to leave his *pa* without first making
a fight for it. During all this time the defenders had not
returned a shot. They had carefully reserved their fire, in
the full anticipation that sooner or later the *pa* would be
stormed by the impetuous soldiers. Nor were they entirely
wrong in this assumption. Towards 4 o'clock in the afternoon it was plainly to be seen that the outer palisade
was seriously breached, though the inner walls were scarcely
injured. No sooner was this apparent than the impatient
and impulsive Despard ordered up a party of 200 men for the
purpose of making an assault upon the damaged points.
Then occurred one of the most dramatic incidents of the day.
Tamati Waaka Nene and Mohi Tawhai, hearing that the
Colonel proposed to repeat his fatal tactics of Ohaeawai,
doubled over to the spot where the storming-party was
assembled, and in the most vigorous language, accompanied
by equally vigorous gestures, protested against any such
scandalous waste of human life. As a reply to Despard's
resentment of such an interference with his prerogative as
commander, Mohi Tawhai took up his station in the centre
of the road along which the soldiers must pass, and standing
with outstretched arms and legs he exclaimed : " How many
more soldiers do you want to kill ? " declaring at the same

---

* *Kareao* (*Rhipogonum scandens*), the common supplejack.

time with angry voice and quivering hands, "You shall not pass by me."

Seeing the chiefs so much in earnest the Colonel adopted a more reasonable attitude, and requested them to give him their opinion on the situation. They told him that if he attempted to storm the *pa* he would only lose his men, as he had done at Ohaeawai; but if he waited until to-morrow he would get it for nothing. It was only a bundle of sticks, and not worth the sacrifice of a human life. In a few days the enemy, they were confident, would be gone, and the *pa* could be destroyed at leisure.* For once the arrogant Colonel listened to sane advice. The storming-party was sent back to the camp, and the gunners ordered to keep up a dropping fire on the breaches throughout the night to prevent the adroit defenders effecting extensive repairs.

During that night the officer in charge of the outer piquet, Lieutenant Balneavis, thought he observed an unusual silence in the *pa*. In the morning he communicated his impressions to his superior officer, Captain Thompson, who directed him to report to Colonel Despard. This he did, but received little encouragement in his theory that the enemy had either left the *pa* or were attempting to entice the soldiers into an ambush. "I was in some measure doubtful about the

* This incident as narrated above has become one of the disputed points of the campaign. It is supported by the independent testimony of Major Bridge, Mr. Dumoulin of the commissariat, by Captain Collinson of the Royal Engineers, and by the native account. It subsequently reached the Australian papers and was published there, much to the annoyance of Colonel Despard, and in reply he has said: "I never had the slightest intention of assaulting the *pa* at Ruapekapeka. So far from having any desire to hurry on the attack, I had not even formed my resolution half an hour before the assault began, and then it was in consequence of my having personally discovered that a great and deciding advantage was within our reach if laid hold of instantly, that the breach was at the moment undefended, and that if we could enter and take possession of some of the works within it before the enemy, who had retired to a distant part of the *pa* to avoid our shot, could arrive to defend it we could hold it. This was done, and the result proved its correctness." Colonel Despard, however, has a way of putting things on paper which scarcely represents the facts, as witness his first official despatch on the fall of the *pa*, which could do no other than convey to the un-initiated reader the impression that the *pa* had been taken "by assault" in the face of a vigilant and prepared enemy. There is surely a difference between taking a *pa* by assault and walking into an empty one.

enemy having retreated during the night," says the Colonel, and in that opinion his judgment, for once, was correct. The enemy had not retreated, but merely temporarily vacated the *pa* for a purpose which could not with justice be construed into flight. Anxious glances were next morning none the less turned upon the *pa* in the hope that the belief in the enemy's departure might be justified.

The day being Sunday it was thought in the camp that hostilities would not be actively pursued, and when the men were ordered out for church parade it appeared as though that impression would be confirmed. This opinion the rebels evidently shared, and towards 10 o'clock those who still remained within the *pa* and were converts to the Christian faith quickly emerged from the subterranean shelters and joined Heke's followers to hold their own religious service away from the scene of strife in the quiet of the bush. So confident were they that the sanctity of the Sabbath would be observed that they did not post sentries to keep guard over the breached palisade. Kawiti, who was not even nominally a Christian, cared nothing about religious services ; but he, too, believing that the Christian soldiers would at least observe the *ra-tapu** as a day of rest, and being wearied with his weeks of working and watching, retired with a few companions to the back of the *pa* and fell asleep in one of the trenches. Kawiti was about to discover, to his discomforture, what many another Maori discovered before their wars were over, that " the soldiers did not mind Sunday at all when any harm could be done on it ; but when there was nothing else to do they always went to prayers."

The unusual quiet within the *pa,* which had already been noticed, was now even more pronounced, a circumstance which did not fail to attract the attention of the friendly natives, who shrewdly suspected what had happened. A party of these, led by Wiremu Waaka Turau, Nene's brother, started out from the camp to investigate. Creeping through the fern and scrub with a stealth which only those who are reared in the wild can employ, they were soon seen standing

* *Ra-tapu* = Sunday, or sacred day.

in the breach, peering through the broken palisade, and then waving to their comrades to follow them. Waaka Nene and his people instantly set off across the intervening slope, but not before they had despatched a messenger hot-foot to advise Colonel Despard. This messenger spread the glad tidings as he went, and in a flash the camp resounded with the cry, "The *pa* is empty!" Many of the soldiers, believing this to be so, ran off without waiting to pick up their arms, and entered the *pa* in a perfectly defenceless condition.

Lieut. - Colonel Wynward, who was the first British officer to appreciate the possible advantage in the situation so suddenly developed, immediately responded to the signals of the friendly natives by calling out the inlying piquet, and taking it down himself left Major Bridge in charge of the camp. Colonel Despard, who was in the advanced battery when Waaka Nene's messenger found him, on being made aware of what was passing, directed Captain Denny, of the 58th, to bring up 100 men, and then moved on rapidly himself to the breached palisade. Captain Denny was soon at his side, and "with that intrepidity for which he was well known" he immediately entered the breach at the head of his men. Scarcely had the soldiers got inside than the alarm was given by one of the friendly natives incautiously ringing the bell which hung in the *pa*. This awoke Kawiti and his handful of followers, who had been soundly sleeping while the web of fate was being spun around them. Starting up from the trench they poured in a heavy volley of rifle-fire upon the soldiers, and then another. This, however, was the limit of their resistance. Pushing on rapidly the soldiers had gained the protection of the intervening houses and inner stockades, and began to return the fire, which grew more and more intense as the supporting parties arrived. Kawiti and his eleven followers then beat a retreat through a door at the rear of the *pa*, abandoning in a few minutes what up to that moment they had believed to be an impregnable fortress. The fortunes of the contending parties had now swung to the opposite poles : the rebels must strive to recover their *pa*, the British must fight to hold what they had won.

The Sunday morning service which Heke and his people were holding in the silences of the bush was rudely interrupted by the sound of Kawiti's volley, and great was the consternation when he himself arrived, breathless, with the intelligence that the *pa* had been surprised. Calling on the rebels not to allow their fortress to be taken without a struggle, Heke and Kawiti led their people from prayers to battle. Hiding behind the rocks and trees they began to fire on the *pa*, in the hope of enticing the soldiers into the open. Through a door in the east fence of the *pa* went a few sailors eager for the fight, and were shot by snipers in the trees. This indiscretion was responsible for the greater number of the British casualties; but, undeterred by casualties, the soldiers and sailors went out and fought the Maoris in their own fashion, from tree to tree. A hot engagement ensued. The rebels fought gallantly and desperately to regain their *pa*, keeping up a dangerous fire upon the soldiers for upwards of four hours. In this their zeal defeated the strategy of their leaders, for when Heke saw that the troops were coming through the *pa* he laid an ambush, instructing his main body to gradually retire and so entice the eager soldiers towards him. But the blood of the Maori was up, and his infatuation was still further excited by the rumour, originating no one knew how, that Kawiti had been taken. The fight for the *pa* was now almost forgotten in the new necessity to rescue their chief, and so these braves stood their ground, losing many men the while. Heke, at last, sent word to them telling them to fall back; but this they refused to do, saying that as Kawiti had been taken they would die where they stood. Being reassured on the point of Kawiti's safety they at length withdrew, but the stratagem was too long delayed. The British officers had by this time obtained some conception of what bush fighting meant, and were able to restrain their men from pressing the pursuit too far. In

9—First War.

other directions the attackers were held in check by an incessant fire from the loopholes of the *pa*, from which volley after volley was poured by the troops inside, and in yet another quarter a charge was repulsed after a stiff hand-to-hand encounter. Slowly, as the day wore on, the attackers were pushed back, until, for them, the fight became not one to reconquer the *pa*, but to recover their killed and save their wounded. This they did by putting up a barrage through which the soldiers could not penetrate, and when late in the afternoon all had been gathered in, their fire slackened and slowly died down as they withdrew, a defeated and disconsolate band, into the shelter of the bush.

" We had thus," says Colonel Despard, "gained in little more than twenty-four hours the strongest fortress which the New-Zealanders had ever erected, and one which the natives throughout the colony, our immediate allies excepted, hoped would have resisted our utmost efforts. Their whole attention was turned to what the result of this attack would be, and had it been different to what it was there is no doubt but our enemies would have been multiplied fourfold."*

The British casualties were twelve killed, mostly men from the *Castor*, and thirty wounded. The dead were buried on the spot, where they lie to-day in their obliterated and long-forgotten graves.

The native losses were never accurately ascertained, but at least twelve chiefs were killed, and their total casualties were doubtless heavy.† That night the *pa* was occupied by Lieut.-Colonel Wynward and 250 men, but

---

* Lieutenant Balneavis thus comments in his diary on the *pa*: " Ruapekapeka was found a most extraordinary place—a model of engineering, with a treble stockade, and huts inside, these also fortified. A large embankment in rear of it, full of underground holes for the men to live in ; communications with subterranean passages enfilading the ditch. Two guns were taken, a small one and an 18-pounder, the latter dismantled by our fire. It appeared that they were in want of food and water. It was the strongest *pa* ever built in New Zealand.

† A native named Kihe was wounded, and captured when the *pa* was taken. It was from him that the British learned that Heke had been present when the attack was made.

no attempt was made to recapture it. Next day the soldiers and sailors were busily employed in pulling down and burning the palisades not only of the *pa*, but of their own miniature stockades.

Scarcely had the excitement in the camp consequent on the fall of the *pa* somewhat abated than it blazed up again as the result of sensational rumours that treasonable documents had been discovered, and that the writer of them was known. Some one searching the native houses had stumbled across a number of letters written to both Kawiti and Heke by Henry Williams. These were at once taken possession of and handed over to the Governor. Grey was at this time, for some unexplained reason, rapidly acquiring the antipathy towards the missionaries which culminated in his mischievous " blood and treasure " despatch of the 25th June, 1846, and the discovery of these letters was something eminently suited to the mental attitude he was cultivating towards the mission, and particularly towards its Archdeacon. His treatment of the whole matter, however, was extremely disingenuous, if nothing worse. He read the letters, and then caused it to be notified by Proclamation that the letters were treasonable; that the writer of them was known ; but that, in view of all the circumstances, he did not propose to prosecute the matter further, and he had ordered that the letters be destroyed.

By pursuing this course Grey first succeeded in creating the impression that the letters were in fact treasonable ; he allowed it to become widely known that the writer was Henry Williams ; and then, by burning the letters, sought to destroy the best evidence that they were not treasonable—viz., the documents themselves.

Accepting the Governor's Proclamation at its face value, a fiercely worded article was published in *The New-Zealander*, an Auckland newspaper, in which the writer demanded that, whatever clemency the Governor in his wisdom might show to the rebel natives, none should be extended to

" those European traitors who have been clandestinely
conspiring against the peace of the colony and insidiously
instigating the excited natives to direct open rebellion."
The writer then proceeds :—

Cowards and knaves in the full sense of the terms, they
have pursued their traitorous schemes, afraid to risk their own
persons, yet artfully sacrificing others for the sake of their own
aggrandizement, while probably at the same time they were
most hypocritically professing most zealous loyalty. . . . It
has been rumoured that investigation of these epistolary proofs
and documents would have implicated some whose station and
previous character ought to have dictated more correct and
scrupulous behaviour towards the Maoris and more consistent
gratitude towards the Queen's Government. If such be the
fact, we deem it to be the more powerful reason why the
Governor should really know the truth, and, however he might
deal leniently for past offences, his knowledge of the character
and extent of these treasonable acts would operate most power-
fully against future repetition.

Unfortunately for the Governor and his journalistic
champion, others also read the letters. Several of these
communications were actually written at the request of
the authorities and in the interests of peace. The one to
which greatest exception was taken was forwarded at the
express wish of Governor FitzRoy, but in the campaign
of calumny it was grossly distorted. The Archdeacon
was accused of having addressed Kawiti, a rebel, as his
" friend." What he actually wrote was " My foolish
friend," and this in the course of a reminder that no
letter had come from him offering to make peace with
the Governor. In other respects the letters were such as
one would expect a man with Henry Williams's record
to write, kindly and humane epistles, penned by one to
whom personal and national honour were the highest secular
considerations, and who never ceased to regard the rebel
chiefs in the light of wilful and erring children. Here,
however, is the opinion of one who was intimately and
officially concerned with the whole incident, and his first-
hand knowledge of all the circumstances places a new and

valuable light upon one of the most unpleasant incidents
of the war :—

Grey and Williams were very antagonistic, and Grey would
have liked to shoot home a charge of disloyalty if he could have
done it. Williams cared greatly for the Maoris, but he cared
more for the honour of his country. He was no more a traitor
than Lord Roberts himself, but he was not sufficiently guarded
in his dealings with Heke after the war had begun ; but,
remember, Heke was almost a boy in his family. No doubt
Williams was not wise to write letters to a man in arms
against us. I was at Ruapekapeka when some of them fell
into Grey's hands, and read them all. They were partly in the
way of religious advice, and for the rest they were counsel of
moderation intended to prevent the recrudescence of old Maori
barbarities. The chivalry of our first war with the Maoris owes
not a little to the influence which Henry Williams brought to
bear on the opposing chiefs.

Here we have the testimony of George Clarke, jun., who
was acting as interpreter to the Governor at the time.
His word is unimpeachable as to the character of the
letters, and in its exposure of Grey's partial and unjust
treatment of them it affords an interesting instance of how
a truly great mind can sometimes descend to pettinesses
which would be beneath many a one of more common
mould.

Having now accomplished all that he could accomplish
in the neighbourhood of Ruapekapeka, the Governor,
accompanied by Captain Graham, and Captain Young
of the *Elphinstone*, left the camp on Monday morning, a
number of the sailors following on the succeeding day.
As the ground on which the camp stood had become
saturated by the almost incessant rain which had fallen
during the previous fortnight, and pools of water and
stretches of mud were unpleasantly frequent, Colonel Despard was anxious to break up his establishment as speedily
as possible, fearing, as he did at Ohaeawai, that the
uncomfortable conditions under which they had been living
might induce an epidemic of sickness among the troops.
To do this quickly, however, was to be an undertaking

comparable only with the exertion required to put the camp where it was. There was still a considerable quantity of shot and shell and other stores to be carried back, for which no wheeled carriage was available. The services of the soldiers had therefore to be requisitioned, each man being required to be the bearer of something in addition to his own arms and accoutrements. The heavy guns were dismantled and loaded into drays, but the aid of the soldiers was still required to drag the light guns and the carriages of the heavy ones. With this division of labour the Colonel was able to break up his camp on the 14th and to fall back as far as Waiomio. On the following day the march was resumed in similar mode, and during the afternoon the whole force reached Pukututu's *pa*, the soldiers accepting their additional duties as burden-bearers with the utmost alacrity and good grace.

Colonel Despard now received instructions to leave a detachment of three hundred men at the Bay of Islands and to embark the remainder of the force with all possible speed for Auckland. During the afternoon of the 15th and the two succeeding days these dispositions were in course of being carried out. The guns and stores were embarked in boats and sent down to the shipping. The men were marched back by the same road as that by which they had advanced a month before, cheered by the fact that they had disposed of " Johnny " Heke for some time to come. The detachment of three hundred men from the 58th Regiment was landed at Victoria,* making a base of Mr. Busby's house, the British Residency of former days, which had suffered severely at the hands of the natives after the fall of Kororareka. One 6-pounder was left with this small outpost, and, all else having been safely embarked, the main body, with its guns and stores,

---

* Owing to the absence of proper quarters and covering, sickness began to make itself manifest among these troops in the following May, when Major Bridge applied to have them transferred across the harbour to Wahapu, where a more comfortable post was formed. Of this camp Major Bridge has left an interesting sketch, which is in the possession of the Department of Internal Affairs.

BRITISH TROOPS ENTERING RUAPEKAPEKA PA.

After the drawing by Major Bridge.

sailed for Auckland on the 18th, where they arrived and disembarked on the 20th.*

The war in the north being now considered at an end, and regimental business requiring the presence of Colonel Despard in Sydney, that officer, on the 26th January, took his departure for Australia, " much," as one caustic officer has remarked, " to the satisfaction of the troops in New Zealand."†

RETURN OF KILLED AND WOUNDED OF THE FORCE UNDER COMMAND OF COLONEL DESPARD, 99TH REGIMENT, ACTING-COLONEL ON THE STAFF, DURING THE ASSAULT ON KAWITI'S PA ON THE 11TH JANUARY, 1846.

	Killed.	Wounded.		
—	Rank and File.	Midship-man.	Rank and File.	Remarks.
Seamen from Her Majesty's ships	7	1	14	Severely.
Royal Marines	2	..	3	,,
58th Regiment	2	..	9	,,
,,	..	..	1	Slightly.
99th Regiment	1	.	1	Severely.
Volunteer Pioneers	..	..	1	Slightly.
	12	1	29	

Wounded during previous operations : Two Volunteer Pioneers, one since dead.

* The *Driver*, the first man-of-war steamer to come to New Zealand waters, arrived at Auckland on the 21st January, and there was then in Auckland Harbour a schooner carrying 100 soldiers of the 58th Regiment, under Major Arney, who had arrived from Norfolk Island on the 19th.

† Thanks and rewards were given to the troops for this last campaign. Colonel Despard, Lieut.-Colonel Wynyard, and Captain Graham, R.N., were made C.B.s; Captain Marlow, R.E., Captain Denny, 58th, and Lieutenant Wilmot, R.A., got Brevet rank ; and, finally, Tamati Waaka Nene was given a pension of £100 per year.

List of Seamen and Marines killed and wounded at the Attack made on Kawiti's Pa at Ruapekapeka on the 10th and 11th January, 1846.

Her Majesty's ship *Castor*—	Killed.	Wounded severely.
Seamen	7	10
Marines		2
Her Majesty's ship *North Star*—		
Seamen	1	2
Marines		..
Her Majesty's ship *Calliope*—		
Seamen		..
Marines	1	1
Her Majesty's sloop *Racehorse*—		
Seamen		1
Marines		..
Hon. E.I. Company's ship *Elphinstone*—		
Seamen		1
Artillery		..

Midshipman Murray, of the *North Star*, was wounded in the face.

List of Native Chiefs killed at Ruapekapeka.

Te Whau, of Ngati-Tu, Ohaeawai : A *toa rangatira*, a chiefly warrior.

Houmatua : A chief—a brave ; son of Te Atua Haere, of Ngati-Tautahi, and cousin of Heke.

Rewiri Nohe : A chief—a brave—of Ngati-Tu, Ohaeawai, a nephew of Te Whau.

Piripi te Pae : A chief of Ngati-Waiharo, Mataraua, a cousin of Heke.

Rimi Piheora : A chief of Te Roroa, a nephew of Pamuka.

Ripiro : A chief of Kapotai, Waikare.

Wharepapa : Son of Ripiro, of Kapotai.

Te Horo, of Kapotai.

Hauraki : A chief of Ngati-Hine, a relative of Kawiti.

Te Maunga, of Ngati-Hine, of Waiomio.

Tuhaia : A chief of Ngunguru.

Te Aoro : A chief of Kapotai, Waikare.

CHAPTER VIII.

THE LAST PHASE.

WITH the fall of Ruapekapeka fell the hopes of Heke and Kawiti. There was nothing left now for the rebels but to sue for peace. In this they were unusually expeditious for Maoris, but the hopelessness of their case proved an irresistible incentive. For some days after their defeat they had wandered about the bush destitute of food and with the sorrows of forlorn men upon them. When the resumption of hostilities was discussed their hungry people had asked, "Can shadows carry muskets?" The prospect of leading a spectral army was no more to the humour of the chiefs than it was to the humour of the spectral army to be led in a hopeless cause. They thereupon resolved to sue for peace, and to make, if possible, Pomare the medium of their penitent appeal. They accordingly presented themselves at his *pa* at Karetu as applicants for food and shelter, as suppliants for intercession. His erstwhile victorious compatriots having passed through the door of defeat, and being in a sense fugitives in their own land, Pomare had now no doubt as to which side he was on. He therefore at first refused to receive the rebels into his *pa*, but directed them where they would find some food. Being, however, informed of their desire for peace, he communicated with Waaka Nene, who also at first was dubious as to the correct attitude to adopt towards them, since their rebellion was against the Governor and not against him. As a tentative step he sent a trustworthy member of his force to Pomare's *pa* to inquire into the correctness of the report which had reached him, and as to the sincerity of the rebel protestations for peace. This messenger was, on arrival at Karetu, invited to an interview with Heke, Kawiti, Hikitene, Hare te Pure, and other of the insurgent chiefs, from whom he heard in the most positive language their desire for an immediate peace, their self-reproachment for having rejected previous offers, their condemnation of their own conduct, and their justification of that of the Governor. They were willing, they said, to procure peace on any terms, even to the giving-up of their lands, and would take no denial. They even named the country they were willing to give up to the Government, but suggested as an act of indulgence that the smallest corner might be returned to them for the support of their children. If the Governor would not give peace and pardon on these terms, then they must become wanderers in the bush, but they had no thought of remaining a public menace by continuing the struggle.

This report was in due course made to Waaka Nene, together with a request from Kawiti for a personal interview, which Waaka declined, fearing that his doing so might in some way compromise him with the Government. He, however, suggested that letters should be written by the chiefs to the Governor, offering personally to become the bearer of their communications and to use his good offices with His Excellency on their behalf. Accordingly the following letter was composed to explain the circumstances under which the application for peace came to be made :—

FRIEND,—   Te Karetu, 19th January, 1846.

Governor Grey, this is my word to you concerning this thing. Friend, our hearts are dark on account of the visit of Kawiti to Pomare's *pa*. We thought he came without any particular object, but he came to avail himself of your former offers. Friend, on this account we were afraid, as his belly was full (satisfied with) of fighting. Therefore I and Pomare spoke to Kawiti and Hikitene and all the chiefs. I said to them :

THE LAST PHASE. 267

"Let your peace with the Governor be made in good faith."
To which they all replied : " Peace shall be made ; peace shall
be made." After this conversation John Heke said : " Oh
elder, oh sire, oh Kawiti, I consent. If the Governor had
been here it would have been well ; but as he is not accessible
by us Pomare must be our intercessor, and Matiu will assist him.
You and I will wait here for the Governor." Kawiti answered :
" Peace shall be made with the Governor, and peace shall also
be made with Waaka."
This is all. It is finished.
From us,
MATIU (MATTHEW) WHAREUMU.
POMARE.

Supplementary to this communication, the following letter
was written by Kawiti, but it is notable that no letter
was sent by Heke, nor does Kawiti appear to write on
his behalf :—

FRIEND,—   9th January, 1846.
Our esteemed friend the Governor, I salute you. Great
is my regard for you. This is the end of our—yours and
mine—converse, which I give now to you. Friend Governor,
I say, let peace be made between you and I. I am filled with
—I am satisfied with—I have had enough of—your riches—your
cannon-balls—therefore I say, let you and I make peace. Will
you not ? Yes ! This is the termination of my war against
you. Friend Governor, I, Kawiti, and Hikitene, do consent
to this good message. Friend, this is my object in going to
Karetu to see Pomare, to make peace with you. This is the
end of mine to you. It is finished.
To my esteemed friend,
To the Governor,
KAWITI.

Having secured the writing of these letters, Waaka Nene
then approached Commander Hay,* of H.M.S. *Racehorse*, who
undertook not only to forward them to the Governor, but
saw that Waaka was given a passage in the Government
brig *Victoria* for Auckland, whither he went to intercede

* By the rules of his service Commander Hay was required to forward
his communication to his superior officer, Captain Graham, of the *Castor*,
who in turn sent it on to the Governor. In this there was a delay which
caused the letters to be delivered to the Governor after Waaka Nene had
seen him, instead of prior to the interview, as intended.

on behalf of the penitent rebels. His arrival was as welcome to the Governor as it was unexpected, for Grey was not only delighted to hear from such a reliable source of the happy turn events had taken, but he was particularly anxious to discuss with one so deeply interested a phase of the peace terms which had been giving him great anxiety.

Grey had become fully convinced that Heke and Kawiti would not be content to long remain the Ishmaelites of their race, and that no great time would elapse before they must become suitors for peace. He must therefore be prepared with an answer which would be at once just to the rebels and satisfactory to the colony whose existence they had so seriously jeopardized. Rightly or wrongly, he had reached a decision that, upon offering their complete submission to the Government, those natives who had been concerned in the rebellion should be at once given security for their persons, leaving the question as to the forfeiture of their lands to be settled by the Imperial authorities ; at the same time permitting it to be understood that, in view of Her Majesty's great regard for her native subjects in New Zealand, it was certain nothing would be more pleasing to Her Majesty than ultimately to grant them a full and unconditional pardon if their future conduct was such as to warrant so generous an indulgence.

In arriving at this decision Grey was influenced by three important considerations. In the first place, he desired to leave the position in such a way that he might retain some hold over the future conduct of those who had been concerned in so many outrages. He also desired to make it plain to the native population generally that in the event of their engaging in active rebellion they would forfeit their lands, and that in future those guilty of the crime of insurrection could count upon being severely punished. Lastly, he was particularly anxious that the gracious act of a free and unconditional pardon should come direct from the Queen, counting upon it being received with greater regard from that high quarter, while at the same time it would tend to exalt Her Majesty in the estimation of the native race as a whole.

These conditions were properly appreciated by the Governor's officers, but in his consultations with them they felt bound to point out to him that he was precluded from consummating any such arrangement as this by the fact that his predecessor's instructions to Colonel Despard in the previous June had expressly stated that the lands forfeited by the rebels would be divided among the loyal natives. These instructions clearly presupposed the confiscation of land in the event of the rebellion being put down; that such land would be divided among those natives who aided the Crown, as compensation for their services; and that, as directed, Colonel Despard had repeatedly and publicly proclaimed the fact. To now vary that arrangement would amount to a serious breach of faith with those whose services had so materially contributed to the success of the Crown.

This line of argument came as a startling surprise to Grey, who up to that time had not heard of these instructions. Upon perusing them he felt that, as they had not been revoked, the Government might possibly be bound by them up to the time of his arrival in the colony. Beyond that he did not believe the colony was committed, for his own repeated declarations to the natives that he would not allow them to acquire land by conquest from each other fully exonerated him from any participation in his predecessor's policy. As, however, the rebellion had been one continuous act he was at a loss to determine what lands should be forfeit in the predecessor's Governorship and exempt from forfeiture in his own. This was a riddle so difficult of solution that to attempt it would be but to invite failure. He therefore determined to take the bold course of altogether disregarding the instructions issued by FitzRoy which had been so suddenly sprung upon him. The promise contained in those instructions he conceived to be so impolitic, so liable to be misconstrued in its administration, of so little real advantage to those for

whose benefit it was intended, and so contrary to the
course which he thought Great Britain should pursue in
the circumstances, that he was able to satisfy himself no
one could reproach him if he refused to be in any way
associated with it.

Further discussion with his officers equally convinced
him that his own original proposal was as impossible of
adoption. He now saw that if he accepted the lands
which the rebels were willing to surrender and held them
pending a decision by the Imperial Government the friendly
natives would distrust his motives. They would probably
not understand the difference between his holding the lands
temporarily and his retaining them altogether, and they
might not unnaturally assume, in not fulfilling his predecessor's promise—that the Crown would not accept any
of these forfeit lands, but would divide them among the
friendly natives—he was considering the interests of the
Government and ignoring theirs.

When, therefore, Waaka Nene made him acquainted with
the complete submission of the rebels, and the unconditional surrender of the whole of their lands, Grey resolved
to cut the Gordian knot by frankly telling the chief
that he would at once grant to the rebels a free and
unconditional pardon ; that he would not fulfil Governor
FitzRoy's promise to divide the lands, but that he would
leave it to the Imperial Government to say in what manner
the loyal natives should be rewarded for their services.
To do otherwise, he explained, would be to place Waaka
Nene and those associated with him in a false and mis-
leading position by laying them open to the charge that
they had been contending for revenge and private gain,
not for the higher purpose of re-establishing peace and
good order. He further pointed out that if he did bestow
the forfeited lands upon the friendly chiefs, that would not
end the war, but simply change its direction ; for there
could be no doubt that so soon as the British forces were
withdrawn the original possessors of these lands would return
and attempt to recover them by force of arms. That

simply meant a new crop of internecine strife ; and, even
if his worst fears in that connection were not realized,
he foresaw that it would be impossible so to divide the
lands as not to give rise to incessant quarrels and feuds
among the loyal chiefs themselves.

This line of reasoning appealed to Waaka Nene pro-
foundly. Knowing native character as he did, he saw
how clear Grey's vision was. He remembered how ten-
aciously his countrymen clung to their lands and all that
was associated with them. How long they remembered
an injury ; how closely they hugged an ancient grudge.
He was probably not familiar with the cynical dictum of
Machiavelli, that "a son will sooner forgive the death of
his father than the loss of his inheritance " ; nor with the
centuries of hatred which had followed upon the confiscation of land in older-settled countries. He was, however,
deeply sensible of the black and bitter crop of enmity
such a course would plant in New Zealand, for he saw
with the sure sight of a statesman that while Heke and
Kawiti might be content to surrender their lands to the
Government it would remain as an eternal stab in their
hearts that those lands should pass into the possession
of their traditional enemies. After giving the matter a
few moments' earnest consideration he entirely assented to
Grey's pronouncement, declaring with obvious satisfaction, as
he grasped the Governor's hand : "You have saved us all."

When Waaka returned to the Bay of Islands as the
bearer of the Governor's magnanimous terms he was
naturally received with great joy by the rebels, whose
jubilation was renewed when the following Proclamation
reached them to confirm the good news :—

PROCLAMATION.

Colonial Secretary's Office,
Auckland, 23rd January, 1846.

THE Government directs it to be notified to the chiefs in the
northern part of New Zealand, and to all others concerned,
that the rebel chiefs having been defeated and dispersed by

Her Majesty's troops on the 11th instant when the *pa* at Ruapekapeka was taken and destroyed, and having subsequently made their complete submission to the Government by letter, and through Tamati Waaka Nene, who on his own part and that of the other friendly chiefs interceded warmly on behalf of the rebels, the Governor has thought proper to give effect to Her Majesty's earnest desire for the happiness and welfare of Her native subjects in New Zealand by granting a free pardon to all concerned in the late rebellion, who may now return in peace and safety to their houses, where, so long as they conduct themselves properly, they shall remain unmolested in their persons and properties.

It must be distinctly understood that nothing contained in the foregoing portion of this notice shall justify any natives retaining in their possession horses stolen from Europeans. Such horses must forthwith be returned to their proper owners, and those natives who continue to retain them in their possession may rely that whenever they may be apprehended the Governor will cause them to be handed over to the proper authorities to be dealt with according to the law, without any reference to the period of time that may have elapsed since the horses were stolen.

By command.
ANDREW SINCLAIR,
Colonial Secretary.

Kawiti immediately wrote to the Governor a letter in which there is behind the words themselves an evidence of his proper sense of gratitude and of his genuine satisfaction that once more the *pakeha* and Maori were at peace:—

Ratareka, 29th January, 1846.
This is my absolute consenting to make peace with the Europeans on this day. Exceedingly good, O Governor, is your love towards us, and I say, also, good is my love towards you. That is the joining (by peace) for ever, ever, ever!
From me,
KAWITI.

There was not the same spontaneity or willing acceptance in Heke's reply.* He still wished to be considered a man of some importance, with whom the Governor was personally to treat. Although the fighting might be over

* Kawiti, who entered the war with less éclat than Heke, appears to have emerged from it the more noble of the two.

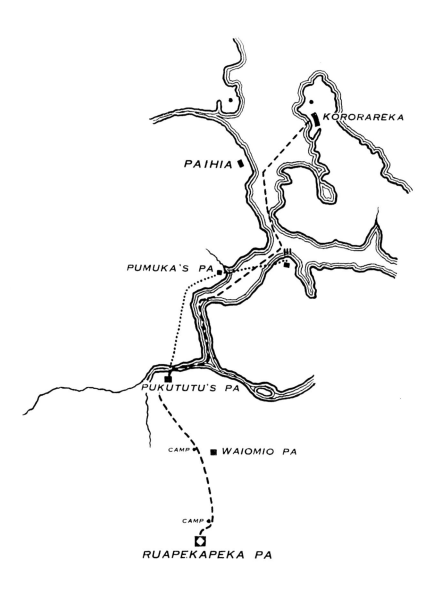

KORORAREKA

PAIHIA

PUMUKA'S PA

PUKUTUTU'S PA

CAMP

WAIOMIO PA

CAMP

RUAPEKAPEKA PA

COLONEL DESPARD'S ROUTES TO RUAPEKAPEKA PA.

THE LAST PHASE. 273

there was still room for argument ; it was just as fitting that the Governor should acknowledge his shortcomings as that Heke should be pilloried for his mistakes. In this self-conscious spirit, then, he wrote his letter* :—

FRIEND GOVERNOR FITZROY, FRIEND THE NEW GOVERNOR,—
I say to you, will you come and let us converse together either at Paihia, or at Waitangi, or at the Waimate, that my thoughts may be right towards you concerning the stick (flagstaff) from which grew the evil to the world? Walker and Manu (Rewa) and others say they alone will erect the staff. That will be wrong ; it will be better that we should all assemble—they, we, and all the many chiefs of this place and of that place, and you too, and all the English also.
Now, this I say to you : come that we may set aright your misunderstandings and mine also, and Walker's too. Then it will be right; then we two (you and I) will erect our flagstaff ; then shall New Zealand be made one with England ; then shall our conversation respecting the land or country be right.
Mr. Busby ; the first Governor ; the second Governor ; the third Governor ; the Queen : salutations to you all.
From
JOHN WILLIAM HEKE POKAI.

Grey treated this letter with studied disdain. He regarded Heke as a person no longer possessed of any influence, and that to further acknowledge him would be to lend him an importance in the political scale of which he was not worthy. In his despatch to Lord Stanley, Secretary of State for the Colonies, Grey thus surveyed the events of the few previous weeks, and justified his action in granting a free and unconditional pardon to the rebels without reference to the Imperial Government. His greatest justification, however, has been not the explanation he made to his chief, but the continued peace and happiness which his action promoted.

* When Heke saw that peace was sure to be made he went away to Tautoro, and said he did not want peace to be made, but that if the Governor came to him and asked for peace he would consent. Heke is a man of many thoughts. So Heke kept at a distance at his own place, and never made peace with the Governor or Waaka, until Waaka at last came to him ; and then Heke said, as Waaka had come to him, there should be peace, but that until the Governor came also and asked for peace he would not consider it fully made.—*Native account.*

10—First War.

A more favourable opportunity than the present of restoring tranquillity and peace to the country could not have offered itself, as those natives who had assisted the Government throughout the war, and the consideration of whose interests I had always feared would materially have embarrassed any attempt at a complete settlement of the existing disturbances, came forward to intercede with the Government on behalf of the rebels. And upon my stating to Waaka Nene my opinion that himself and the other friendly chiefs must forgo any claims they might have upon the lands of the rebels arising out of promises made by my predecessor—firstly, because they would best promote their own interests in pursuing this course, and, secondly, because I could not conscientiously fulfil these promises—he at once assented, and expressed his readiness to leave to the consideration of Her Majesty any reward that himself and the other friendly chiefs might be thought worthy to receive for the services they have rendered.

The aspect of affairs in the northern part of the Island, evidently, therefore rendered it proper for me to lose no time in granting a free pardon to all those who had been concerned in the late rebellion.

The natives generally had been drawn from their homes, and in espousing the side of one party or the other had abandoned in a great measure their usual pursuits ; and the laxity of morals which invariably follows war, and the collection of men in large numbers, were producing evils which it was most desirable to put an end to with as little delay as possible by inducing the natives to return to their own districts.

In as far as the rebels were concerned, no advantage could be gained by the continuance of the war, as they would have only been driven into the remoter fastnesses, from whence they could with comparative impunity have committed depredations upon the European settlers ; whilst, on the other hand, by pardoning them and allowing them to return to their former habits of barter with the Europeans and to occupy their villages in the vicinity of the coast they could be readily punished on any future occasion when they might merit it.

The effect also on the whole Island of a generous and liberal line of policy towards the rebels, after the severe defeat and punishment they had received, was likely to be very beneficial. I therefore considered it advisable to issue the notice, a copy of which is enclosed, stating for the information of the rebels that I thought proper to give effect to Her Majesty's earnest desire for the happiness and welfare of Her Majesty's native subjects in New Zealand by granting a free pardon to all concerned in the late rebellion, who might return in peace and safety to their homes, where so long as they conducted themselves properly they should remain unmolested in their persons and properties.

The interest of the northern natives was now to settle down and endeavour to adapt themselves to the conditions inevitably attending a *pakeha* Government. At first this was no simple matter, for the waywardness engendered by the two years of war was not easily eradicated from a national character at all times volatile. Their social fabric, such as it was, had been sadly shaken. Planting had been neglected, because the commandeering by rebels and loyalists alike had made cultivation unprofitable. Food was therefore poor in quality and scarce in quantity. This condition of quasi-starvation resulted in several mild epidemics of various kinds, which were responsible for a heavy mortality among the poorly nourished people. In some cases populations were reduced by half, and the mission churches and schools which for years had been flourishing centres of civilization were almost emptied.

The Christian missions, which prior to the war were the only uplifting influences among the Maoris of the north, though not overwhelmed by the catastrophe, found themselves gasping for breath. Their congregations were widely dispersed and sorely distracted, and when the body was in daily peril and want it was difficult to induce the people to devote much attention to those things which appeared good for the soul. The gloom of the fatal storm was dense, and it required a healthy optimism at times to discern a ray of hope in the sky. But through it all the missionaries bravely struggled on, exerting themselves at every turn to secure the blessings of peace, and but for their restraining influence it is incontestable that throughout the war the rebel forces would have been counted not by their hundreds but by their thousands. Their position as intermediaries between the Government and the rebels placed them in an extremely delicate situation, and one not of their own seeking. Its arduous

10*

tasks were, however, discharged with courage and with honour, there being no instance recorded in which they refused to go where they were asked, or in which the confidence of either party was betrayed or abused. Their influence in steadying the people was not, however, their only service, for it must stand to their eternal credit that they humanized the war. When we contrast this rebellion with the former sanguinary conflicts in which the Maori engaged it becomes remarkable for the almost entire absence of acts of wanton cruelty or of dark revenge, while there were not a few instances of generosity and kindly feeling shown by one foeman towards another. This taming of wild and savage passions, this softening of the asperities of barbarous acts, had its origin in the teaching of the missionaries, and is an abiding instance of how great a change was wrought in the native mind by the inculcation of the mild precepts of the Gospel. To no one in this respect is humanity more deeply indebted than to Henry Williams, one of the most misunderstood yet none the less one of the greatest men who ever influenced the destinies of New Zealand.

In addition to the calamity of war and the scourge of epidemic the non-combatants were for the most part but indifferently housed. Many of the regular villages had been broken up, the people, having fled from the disturbed districts, congregating in temporary cantonments. Here their huts were the abodes of wretchedness, a condition of domestic misery keenly intensified by the fact that they were worse clad than they had been for years.

Moral as well as physical standards had suffered in the meantime. The native regard for the Sabbath, and all that this implied, was perceptibly weakened by the failure of the army to strictly observe it. In this respect the habits of the loyal natives suffered more than those of the rebels, since they had been brought more closely into contact with the dissolute soldiers ; not the least regrettable feature of this association was that drunkenness spread among them to an alarming extent.

Added to these discomforts of the body there was the uneasiness of mind induced by the knowledge whispered abroad that Earl Grey, the then Chief Secretary for the Colonies, had instructed the Governor that all waste lands in the colony were to be regarded as the demesne of the Crown—an act of virtual confiscation and a breach of the Treaty of Waitangi which to them seemed incredible after all they had heard of the sacred nature of its contracts. Nor was this state of doubt and apprehension relieved by the sudden seizure of Te Rauparaha, the great southern chief, by Governor Grey, and the unfounded rumour that the chief had been as quickly hanged. In the absence of authentic information regarding this much-discussed incident the confidence which many of the rebel leaders had been induced to repose in the Government by the Governor's peace Proclamation was almost instantly destroyed by the not unnatural fear, in such distracted times, that what had been Te Rauparaha's fate yesterday might be theirs to-morrow. Into these wider sources of unrest there also entered a local incident, which for a time gave rise to grave anxiety. A number of Waaka Nene's people continued to hold the Mawhe district, in spite of the Governor's Proclamation that no land should be taken, and in spite of the remonstrances of many of their friends. This obtrusion into his territory proved extremely aggravating to Heke, and if persisted in might well have provoked another outbreak of hostilities. Thus, although there was no war, it was not possible to claim that there was peace.

Under these circumstances, so fruitful of distrust and unrest, the rumblings of the aftermath were heard for several years, and then a series of events took place which made for permanent peace.

Upon the cessation of hostilities Heke had removed to his home at Tautoro, where he lived the restless spirit he ever was, but keeping within the four corners of the law. For some time he adopted an attitude of aloofness towards both the Governor and towards those chiefs who had allied themselves with the Government. With the former he was angry because he had not thought fit personally to discuss the peace terms with him ; the latter he regarded as enemies who were unforgivable because they had been instrumental in bringing about his defeat.

Heke still had a considerable force about him, some of them being chiefs of various districts—Tauranga, Rotorua, Hawke's Bay, Cook Strait, and Taranaki—men who had joined his cause from mere love of fighting and adventure. They were a reckless and a daring set, who were not disposed to let trifles stand in their way. It was therefore a grievous error to suppose, as the Governor in common with many others supposed, that Heke's influence among his own people had disappeared, the fact being that he had more followers at this time than he ever had, and he was being treated with infinitely greater respect than either Waaka Nene or Kawiti.

Among this dangerous element the belligerent spirit was kept alive by the confident belief, acquired as the result of intercourse with unscrupulous Europeans, that a war was imminent between Britain and America, or between Britain and France, and that they might depend upon the assistance of either nation so soon as one or both became the enemies of Britain. They were also anticipating a serious native rising under Te Rangihaeata along the shores of Cook Strait, which would necessitate the detachment of large bodies of troops from the north, leaving them, in the face of divided forces, a clearer field for their own warlike enterprises. There, too, were rumours to the effect that Ngati-Maru and Ngati-Tamatera, on the River Thames, were about to launch an attack upon the town of Auckland ; indeed, Heke and his comrades appeared to be of the opinion that the troubles of the Government were only about to commence, and they were quietly waiting to see what line of conduct it would be politic for them to adopt when the Governor and his troops became involved in the suppression of that wider crop of insurrection which seemed ripe for the harvest on every hand. Heke still declared that nothing less would satisfy him than that the French and American flags should fly

THE LAST PHASE.   279

beside the Union Jack on Maiki Hill, and he had not relented one jot his hostility to the establishment of a Customhouse at Kororareka.

This was Heke's attitude of mind for some months after the promulgation of the Governor's peace, in which he at first appeared to acquiesce, but to which he had not as yet, in reality, given a willing and binding consent. His posture towards the peace and the Government at this period has, however, been more particularly stated by Hariata, his wife, and by himself, and it will not be inappropriate to here place before the reader the terms in which they sought to justify his still untamed and rebellious spirit.

Shortly after the Proclamation of peace James Merrett, who had been employed formerly as an interpreter to the forces, conceived the idea of personally interviewing both Heke and Kawiti, neither of whom he had previously seen. In the case of Heke the difficulties were great, for there was but scant information as to his whereabouts, and in the unsettled state of the country it was a task fraught with the elements of risk to journey from village to village in search of him. He at last heard that Heke was about to pay a visit to Whangaroa, in the north, and thither Merrett went in the hope of meeting him. To facilitate his introduction Merrett compiled a letter in the native language, purporting to come from some one with whom Heke had previously been on intimate terms, and so worded as to create the impression in Heke's mind that the bearer was the agent of the Americans. Armed with this counterfeit communication Merrett reached Whangaroa, only to find that Heke had not arrived, while his movements were shrouded in the greatest uncertainty. His visit was not, however, destitute of good fortune, for there he met Hariata, Heke's wife, who was waiting for her husband, and who in the interval was seeking to preserve her beauty by submitting her chin to the tattooing-chisel of her brother Charles, who had considerable skill in that fast-failing art. To Merrett, Hariata appeared to be a woman of excellent proportions, about two or three and twenty years of age ; her manner was exceedingly agreeable, with a quiet, pleasing smile in the expression of her lips. Her clothing was English print, with a native mat thrown loosely over her shoulders. When a girl she was so attractive that a captain of a merchant vessel is said to have offered her friends £70 to be allowed to marry her. She had been well educated by the missionaries, and she was at this time acting as secretary to her husband, who employed her to write all his letters.* She, in fact, impressed her visitor as one possessing all the qualities consistent with superior breeding and training. " I met her," he says, " returning from church on a Sunday. Her dress was plain, but her *tout ensemble* the picture of neatness. She had a Testament in one hand, while the other held an umbrella, with which she sheltered herself from the heat of the sun."

Hariata at once accepted Merrett's letter of introduction at its face value, whereupon they freely discussed the political situation, and here is Merrett's own account of what followed :—

I asked if it was true that Heke was still bent on fighting. She said it was not true ; that he did not wish to continue the war if the Governor chose to treat with him face to face. " He is willing to make peace," said she, " and I myself wrote a letter for him to the Governor expressing his wishes. I confined myself to civil language, and it was a good letter. It is true that Heke said afterwards that he would not make peace, but that occurred in this manner : Pomare gave him a bottle of rum which intoxicated him, and while he was in this state Pomare teased him by telling him the Americans would kill him for making peace with the English ; that he was much annoyed at what the others said, and that he did at the time make use of violent language. Heke wishes the Governor to treat him as an honourable enemy, and shake hands with him ; and that, in return for His Excellency's treating him with consideration, he will himself, with his own hands, assist in raising the flag of Great Britain."

* Before Merrett left Heke's *pa* the chief called to his side another native, to whom he dictated a letter in reply to the one Merrett had brought. From this circumstance, and from the fact that his wife acted as his secretary, Merrett formed the opinion that Heke himself was not able to write, which was wrong.

Hariata then proceeded to recount to her guest Heke's justification for his conduct. He had, she said, many reasons for commencing the war.* One was that he had been assured the French and American vessels would never visit the Bay as they did in former days before the British flag was hoisted. He wished both these nations to have their flags flying as well as the English, as he was friendly to the vessels of all nations. He had other reasons. He had been deceived; but if the Governor behaved to him as he expected he should he would reveal to His Excellency the parties who had fomented the rebellion. He had been told by the Europeans that the peace promulgated by Governor Grey was not sincere; that the Governor was only waiting for more troops to commence fighting a war of extermination. Heke, in his desire to meet the Governor and make peace with him, had appointed several places of meeting, any of which the Governor might have chosen, but his advances had been declined. All reasonable conditions of peace he would accede to, though he might not so express himself to all Europeans who spoke to him about it. He knew that Governor Grey was not like his predecessors; that he had his own opinions, and did not allow Mr. Clarke or Mr. Williams to speak for him, and therefore, as he knew no one but the Governor himself had any right to speak, he did not intend to make any inferior Europeans the medium of communication with him. All the missionaries and other Europeans were, in Heke's judgment, merely slaves to the Governor; then, as the Governor only could propose terms, and was the only chief among the white men, he would treat with no other than His Excellency himself.

Curious to know Hariata's own feelings in the matter, Merrett asked her if she wished for more war. With a

* Charles Hongi, Hariata's brother, joined in the conversation. He asked Merrett if he did not think the New-Zealanders a braver race than any the British had conquered, because the soldiers had taken other places but had not taken this. He asked if the soldiers who fought Bonaparte and the Frenchmen were no braver than those in New Zealand. "The sailors are brave," he said, "for they go joking and laughing to fight; but the soldiers must fight, because they are afraid if they run away their officers will kill them."

truly feminine expression she replied : " Oh, no ! A rocket went so close over my head at Ruapekapeka that it nearly frightened me to death. Let us live peaceably ; the war may soon be ended. Let the Governor treat Heke kindly, and he will find my husband will repay his goodness."

Thus did Hariata confide in her visitor, believing his credentials to be genuine. But she did more. She gave Merrett confidential information as to the whereabouts of Heke, and found for him a guide upon whom he could rely. Next day Merrett started off with his native boy for a village named Tako,* which in due course he reached. Not without some trepidation he strode into the *pa*, where he was received with doubtful mien by the " fierce warriors," who sprang to their feet as he entered. Producing his forged papers, they held a brief consultation upon them, and then proceeded to announce the arrival of the stranger to Heke.

" In a short time," says Merrett, " they returned with Heke preceding them. I had never seen him before, but I felt certain he could be no other than the man I wanted. He approached, seized me by the shoulder and shook me roughly, and, speaking quickly and angrily, he asked me what made me come there, and what I desired. He evidently wished to intimidate me, but he was mistaken for once. I threw the letter on the ground and said abruptly : ' There is an explanation for you.' He looked at it with hesitation, and I observed a slight nervous tremor on his hand and lip as he took it up, opened and read it, while he sat apart from the rest of the chiefs, who none of them asked him a single question or spoke a word while he was so engaged. I fancied I perceived in his countenance a latent suspicion of my errand. He turned his eye stealthily on mine once or twice while he was reading the letter, and I was marking as coolly as I could the effect it produced. Its sentences were few, but so worded as to be ambiguous to a native, and its meaning wrapped in mystery. I saw, however, I had not failed in my estimate of the native character, for this extremely shrewd native was completely puzzled, and my success was complete. I had taken care to recommend the bearer of the letter to his particular hospitality, and when he had finished he rose, shook

---

* There were seven horses at Tako, and Merrett mentions that the natives were thus early acquiring their well-known love of horse-racing by constantly amusing themselves pitting these animals against each other in trials of speed.

TAMATI WAAKA NENE.
After the etching by J. McDonald.

me by the hand, ordered food to be cooked, a house to be
prepared for me, and gave strict orders that I should not be
intruded upon.* When his warriors saw me so cordially received
many of them came forward and shook me by the hand. They
also welcomed me, and, seating themselves, I was soon surrounded by numbers. A desultory and interesting conversation
now took place between us. It related principally to the war.
We laughed and joked ; they brought me food, and I was elated
at the success of my enterprise.

"Heke returned to the spot where we had been conversing,
and, seating himself by my side, began to talk, and, as near as I
can recollect, the following is the sum of his conversation : ' Has
the Governor gone to Port Nicholson to fight Te Rauparaha ?
Is he going down there to make the rockets fly about ? Why
did he not come to speak to me before he went ? I have
appointed places of meeting. He should have chosen one of
those I mentioned for a conference between himself and me.
I will come to no terms until he speaks to me face to face. If
he wishes the flagstaff put up, let it be put up by myself, the
Governor, and Waaka simultaneously. If we are all present
when it is put up, well and good. I will not allow Waaka to
put it up without my consent being obtained. I have heard
that the Governor intends to make Waaka the great chief of
this part of the Island, and that I am not entitled to consideration. I shall certainly never recognize any power which may be
invested in Tamati Waaka, should he be delegated to propose
terms of peace. The final arrangement of the quarrel must be
between me and the Governor alone. The Governor does not
possess the strength to do as he pleases. My voluntary consent
will establish peace, but soldiers cannot compel me to do it.
I have beaten them at Kororareka, as I beat them at Okaihau
(Puketutu) when they attacked my *pa*. They retreated in their
boats to Kerikeri, and I buried their dead. At Ohaeawai we
killed great numbers of them when they assaulted our *pa*.†

* Merrett was something of an artist, and during this visit he made
several sketches of Heke, Hariata, and Charles Hongi.
† During the course of the evening Merrett was shown a sword which
he was told had belonged to Captain Grant, killed at Ohaeawai. It had
the name of Buckmaster on the blade. Merrett asked those about him if
it was true that a portion of Captain Grant's body had been cooked.
They immediately answered, without the slightest reserve, that it had,
but only after he was dead. Merrett also asked them why they had
burned the soldier alive at Ohaeawai. They replied that nothing of the
kind occurred. Merrett then wished to know whose cries they were
which were heard during the night. They replied that the cries proceeded from a soldier who was much burned after he was wounded, by
his cartridge-box igniting while lying by one of the fires ; that he suffered
great pain, and was crying out incessantly.

There they were obliged to leave their dead in our trenches, and make a hasty retreat; while we, not thinking the place tenable against the great guns of the sailors, effected an orderly and safe retreat, and left them an empty fortress as a payment for the loss of their chiefs and people. Then the blood first flowed in gushing streams from the white men, but our own people were hardly scratched. At Ruapekapeka they desecrated the Sabbath, which we, in our ignorance, supposed would pass without fighting. We left our *pa* to avoid the shot and shells while morning prayers were read by one of the teachers. Had we been in the *pa* at our guns the madness of the soldiers in trying to carry it by assault would have been seen, for there would have been worse slaughter than at Ohaeawai. The Europeans cannot say they were strong because they took Ruapekapeka; and, after all, there were only twenty-five of our people killed. The white men have only two points of superiority over us— namely, their guns and rockets; but we shall be more than a match for them when we skirmish with them in the bush, as in future we shall if necessary.' "

After witnessing the arrival of a large party of Heke's allies, and a war-dance, which proved to be a stirring sight, Merrett took his leave of the still rebellious chief, whom he left in the mood of one who was savagely nursing his injured vanity. This condition of embittered reserve he continued until October, 1846, when owing to the magnanimity of Waaka Nene a conference was held at Kaikohe which cleared the way for a more satisfactory state of things.

During the previous September the Governor received a letter from Waaka Nene, in which that chief, after congratulating Grey upon his successes against Te Rangihaeata in the south, intimated that he had a strong desire to visit Heke so that they might discuss their differences together. He pointed out that he had already held a similar conference with Kawiti, and that if only the Governor would consent to his meeting Heke he felt confident the result would be beneficial, "for," he said, "this is a good arrangement, an arrangement to save men." Grey willingly gave his consent to the proposed interview, and in a letter to Mr. Gladstone, the then Chief Secretary of

State for the Colonies, he gave an interesting review of his attitude towards Heke at this period :—

Government House,
SIR,— Auckland, September 19, 1846.

I have the honour to transmit a copy of a letter I received yesterday from our most faithful ally, Thomas Walker Nene. This letter is important, inasmuch as the old man voluntarily proposes that I should permit an interview to take place between himself and Heke, which interview, it may reasonably be hoped, will result in the complete and final adjustment of the various differences still prevailing between the chiefs of the northern part of the Island. My difficulty hitherto in dealing with Heke has been that I knew him to be a violent excitable character, little respected by any of those natives who knew him well, and owing his reputation in the distant parts of the Island solely to his unlooked-for successes against our troops when the war first broke out in the north. Many of his relatives have lately stated to me his extreme anxiety to obtain my good opinion and to aid in any way he could the views of the Government. He was, however, anxious that this should be done without any complete and perfect reconciliation taking place at the same time between himself and Waaka Nene and our other allies in the north. I always declined in any way to connect myself with him until his differences with the other chiefs had been adjusted, as a different line of proceeding on my part might have made our allies suspicious of me, and might have impaired throughout the Islands the belief it is so necessary all the chiefs should entertain, that an ally is never deserted or overlooked by the British. Now, however, that some communications have evidently taken place between Waaka Nene and Heke, and the old chief himself suggests an arrangement which would be exceedingly advantageous, I intend to assent to the proposed interview taking place, and I am about to confide the management of this very delicate affair to Captain Graham, of Her Majesty's ship *Castor*, who, fortunately, happens to be at this moment at the Bay of Islands, and who has frequently rendered me important assistance and is in every way well qualified to conduct this business. There can be no doubt that from the general repute which Heke has acquired (however unjustly) his name is the cause of constant apprehension and continual disquiet to many persons, and the security which will be felt by these individuals if it is known that he has made a public declaration of his attachment to the

Government and of his desire to assist its views, and is completely reconciled to the northern chiefs, renders it an object of much importance not to pass by the opportunity which has thus presented itself.

Letters were accordingly sent to Heke, Kawiti, and Waaka Nene, inviting them to a conference at Kaikohe on the 7th October. A few days later Heke rode into the settlement in full dress as a chief, and informed the Rev. Mr. Davis that he had received a most satisfactory communication from the Government, and requested to be furnished with pens, ink, and paper that he might send an answer to the Governor. On the day appointed, Heke, Kawiti, Waaka Nene, with a small band of followers, and Captain Graham, as the representative of the Governor, arrived at Kaikohe, and the conference was duly held. Unfortunately, no official record of the proceedings appears to have been published, but the Rev. Mr. Davis tells us that "the meeting was very satisfactory to all parties. Thus has peace been once more restored to this distracted district."

The next link in the chain of peace-making was not forged until eighteen months later. Captain Edward Stanley, in command of H.M.S. *Calliope*, reached the Bay of Islands in February, 1848, and expressed to Major Bridge, who was in charge of the military station at Wahapu, a desire to meet and shake hands with Heke. Major Bridge inquired of Mr. Burrows if he could arrange such a meeting, but the missionary had his reservations on the point, being unwilling to further mix himself up in political matters. Waaka Nene was then appealed to, and he undertook to bring the meeting about if it was possible to do so. For this purpose he left Kororareka and journeyed to Te Ahuahu, where Heke was then living. The arrangements, however, were not completed as quickly as was anticipated ; but on the 14th February Waaka wrote to Major Bridge announcing that Heke had consented to the interview :—

FRIEND THE MAJOR,—

Hone (Heke) and I am here at Te Ahuahu. We are waiting for you and the Captain of the man-of-war to come and see Hone Heke. Come to-morrow, and likewise bring some tobacco. Come; do not you delay. Bring some tobacco. O Captain of the *Calliope*, let there be plenty of tobacco.

From WAAKA NENE.

By this time, however, Captain Stanley had been compelled to sail from the Bay, but Major Bridge undertook to pay the visit on his behalf. Accompanied by Mrs. Bridge, he proceeded to Waimate, where they were most cordially received by Mr. Burrows, who completed the arrangements for the meeting in his house. Heke received the Major with great ceremony and considerable dignity. He impressed Bridge as " a fine-looking man, with a commanding countenance, and a haughty manner which appears habitual to him."*

The conversation was long and intimate, Heke expressing himself as most anxious to maintain the peace, and especially to meet the Governor in order that he might convey to him personally his conciliatory intentions and to shake him by the hand.

The satisfactory nature of the interview was reported by the Major in a letter to the Governor on the 23rd February, 1848, in which he concluded his narrative by expressing the fervent hope that His Excellency would be

* Of those who came into personal contact with Heke and have left their impressions of him, perhaps the most unfavourable picture of the chief is that given by Lieutenant George Johnson, of H.M.S. *North Star*. Lieutenant Johnson was present at the interview between Heke and Sir Everard Home at Paihia on the 28th January, 1846, and of Heke he says: "This chief is the worst of all the chiefs. Young, brought up among the mission, he has benefited only by being able to read and write well. He has a most debased mind, bloodthirsty and eager for power, and has not a settled plan, but is bent on mischief. In his younger days he was always dreaded as a vicious scamp. If he had not Europeans to worry he would get up a fight among his own tribe. His person is very disgusting : an ugly, wide mouth; drunken eye; a broad, stout fellow, upwards of six feet high, full of bombast, turns his knowledge of the Bible into ridicule, never gives a reason for any act he commits, has great fears, and never sleeps without a watch round him. Even on this (Paihia) beach on which the mission station is planted he has a native sentry walking about, armed." Of Kawiti, whom he met a few days later, Lieutenant Johnson formed a very high opinion.

able to meet Heke, as such a conference would be productive of much good, and would comply with the wishes of both Europeans and natives throughout the northern districts. Grey fell in with the suggestion made by Major Bridge, and on the 4th March, 1848, he wrote to Earl Grey :—

In compliance with the wishes expressed by Major Bridge, I intend to take an early opportunity of visiting the Bay of Islands so as to permit of Heke making me those explanations which he professes his anxiety to have an opportunity of doing.

The preliminaries for this meeting were skilfully arranged by Mr. Burrows, under whose auspices Heke one morning met Grey at breakfast at the missionary's house at Waimate. Here they had an interview which was not lengthy but cordial, the incidents of the past being discreetly left undiscussed. As a mark of respect and as an emblem of peace Heke presented the Governor with his greenstone *mere*, which is now preserved in the British Museum.

Though reconciliation and peace were now accomplished facts, Heke made one more bid for notoriety by writing a lengthy letter to Queen Victoria, setting forth his views and his wrongs. This communication Grey forwarded to the Chief Secretary of State for the Colonies, but accompanied by a suggestion that it would be inadvisable to have the letter acknowledged by the Queen, since such acknowledgment would lend to Heke an importance both dangerous and undeserved. To ignore him was the surest means of reducing him in the estimation of a following who still believed him capable of great things.

In August, 1850, Heke died when still in the prime of life, being then only forty years of age. Two years before he began to suffer a decline in health, consumption claiming him as one of its victims. Under its decimating influence he passed through two critical illnesses, from the second of which he may be said never to have recovered. When he found himself permanently weakening in vitality he left his place at Tautoro and went to

reside at Kaikohe in order that he might be near to the
medical and other assistance for which his case seemed to
call. Though thus in decline he still had enough of the
Old Adam in him to play the gay Lothario, having
shortly before his removal to Kaikohe consummated an
alliance with a second wife. This act of infidelity caused
a violent altercation between himself and Hariata, his true
spouse, when they met at Kaikohe, and as a fitting conclusion to the argument the lady beat him severely and
used him roughly. " This, although he was a fierce and
violent man, he quietly endured " ; but the treatment is
said to have somewhat hastened his end. As, however,
the second wife did not venture to intrude herself upon
the domestic circle at Kaikohe the breach was soon healed,
and Hariata faithfully and affectionately tended him all
through his illness, and after his death she never ceased
to mourn him.

His last public act was one of violence. Still persisting
in his prerogative as a chief, he sent a party of his
followers to take a young woman as a wife for one of his
young men, from a household who were of his own family
and friends living in the settlement. His ambassadors were
repulsed, and returned without the woman. This defeat,
ill as he was, threw Heke into a fit of rage, and in the
violence of his anger he threatened to kill the reluctant
bride. Next morning he mustered his force, armed them,
and, riding at their head, proceeded in person to the
home of the girl. This his followers surrounded, each man
having a loaded musket. Heke then sent word to the
family that they might elect to surrender the girl or be
blown to pieces. Discretion proved to be the better part
of valour, and the girl resignedly bent her neck to the
yoke. This act of lawlessness proved to be Heke's last.
He returned home from the excursion much exhausted, and
immediately took to his bed, from which he never rose
again. At this stage, and to the end, he was closely
attended by the Rev. Mr. Davis, who tells that in a little
time his savage, sullen temper passed off and he became

peacefully minded. The change was almost sudden, but none the less the lion became the lamb, and in this state he remained, with very little exception, to the day of his death.

He was four months ill, and I paid him every attention in my power; but though he was attentive to what I said to him, and particularly in having prayer, yet he was always backward to speak on the real state of his soul. My last interview with him will never be forgotten. He was fast sinking into the arms of death, and my duties having called me from home I had not seen him for nearly a week, but as soon as he knew I was present he took me by the hand, which he long held with a firm grasp, and fixed his eyes on me during nearly the whole time I was with him, beaming with affection. On the Sunday before he died he was much exhausted, but expressed much affection. His mind appeared to wander. I told him to keep his mind fixed upon Christ. He replied : " It is there fixed." These were his last words to me. After I left him, late in the evening, his people being with him, he would not be content until they all assembled in his presence for a late evening service, which was conducted by a Christian native. His own people asked him in his last hours where he would recommend them to live after his decease. He replied : " In everlasting life." The question was repeated, and the same answer was returned.*

After death the body lay in state in the approved Maori fashion, both the corpse and the immediate surroundings being highly ornamented. The body was covered by a scarlet cloth elaborately fringed at the edges, a strip of black crape was tied over the eyes, and the head dressed with beautiful white feathers. On his right side lay his trusty musket, on his left his favourite *paraoa*.†

Knowing it to be Heke's desire that he should receive a Christian burial, Mr. Davis made a formal request to the presiding chiefs that he might be permitted to dispose of the body in that way, but was refused. Feeling that it would be vain to persist, he called the people round him, and putting on his surplice he took his station at

---

* *Vide* a letter written by the Rev. Richard Davis to the Rev. J. N. Coleman, M.A., dated the 6th May, 1851.

† *Paraoa* = a weapon made from the bone of the sperm whale.

the foot of the bier. There he read such portions of the funeral service as were suitable,* and gave them, to the best of his power, an address appropriate to the occasion. The body was then disposed of according to native custom.

The coffin was committed to the care of a few men chosen for the purpose, whose sacred charge it became until the following summer, when it was conveyed away to a distant cave, the precise locality of which is not certainly known to the natives generally to this day, but supposed to be a cavern in the volcanic hill Te Putahi.† Here in his secret burial-place the turbulent Heke was laid to his final rest, and so passed from the scene one of the men who made Maori history.

" Heke was a singular man," says the Rev. Mr. Davis, who had better opportunities of judging him than most. " He was proud and aspiring. In his youth he was wild, wicked, and cruel, and during the latter part of his life he was turbulent and tyrannical. At this settlement we had but little peace, for when he was away and we were quiet the dread of his return embittered our peace. Since his death we have enjoyed unusual quiet, and, I hope, with feelings of thankfulness."

Kawiti appeared to feel his position more keenly than Heke did. For months after the fall of Ruapekapeka he lived, bent down with grief, in a few huts at Waiomio, with no more than twenty-five people in his train, but still a great personality among the tribes who owed him allegiance, and who were at any time ready to respond to his call. He was therefore still an element of danger should the passion for war again become dominant in his character. During his visit to Tako, Merrett had learned that Heke was shortly to make a pilgrimage to Rua-pekapeka for the purpose of removing the bones of his

---

* Mr. Davis altered the words " We therefore commit his body to the ground," &c., to others more suitable to the circumstances.

† Mrs. Williams, in a letter dated the 6th November, 1851, says: " Heke's body was brought with great state last summer to Pakaraka, nd his tomb is in these woods, in a native reserve."

dead,* and that he was to call on Kawiti on the way. Here, then, was an opportunity for Heke, with his increasing numbers, to persuade the old warrior to again join him against the Europeans, for, as his own relations were concerned equally with those of Heke, the grief of the old man might be excited by the ceremony, and under the persuasions of Heke he might be induced to continue the war. This, at least, was the opinion of Merrett, though, fortunately, it was far from the fact. Kawiti was intensely embittered against Heke. He accused him of numerous instances of cowardice and of screening himself and his people at the expense of others, and had vowed that on no consideration would he again join Heke in breaking the peace which had been made. Ignorant of the true state of his mind, Merrett decided to visit him, as he had already visited Heke at Tako, with a view of, if possible, persuading him against again involving himself and his people in war. On reaching the *pa* of Tamati Pukututu, at the head of the Kawakawa River, he there enlisted the services of Parata, the son of Pukututu, and grandson of Kawiti. Parata had not seen Kawiti since the beginning of the war, but as peace was evidently resolved upon he agreed to accompany Merrett and seek a reconciliation with his grandsire. Not the least important part of their mission was to induce the old chief to abandon his place in the wilderness and come and live with his grandson, for once domesticated among the British allies Heke's designs upon him might be considered as "scotched." On this errand the two started off for Waiomio, and for the rest Merrett may be permitted to tell his own story :—

Parata was a little nervous on the subject of his reception by a grandfather whom he had so lately been in arms against. We were received in the usual manner—throwing the spear, &c.,

* Merrett says : " The number of chiefs killed on the side of Heke and Kawiti since the commencement of the war is estimated from all accounts I have received from various chiefs at between sixty and seventy. The slaves would be the proportion of about three to one. At present there is little doubt Heke could enter the field with eight hundred men."

SIR GEORGE GREY.

Governor of New Zealand, 1845–53 and 1861–68.

followed by a war-dance. There were seven or eight rude huts in the centre of the road to Ruapekapeka, on the bare summit of a hill, quite away from all forest land, and these with about twenty-five persons composed his whole retinue and establishment. Nevertheless his influence with the tribes connected with him is sufficiently great to raise a large body of followers when he requires them. My friend Parata was the first to speak, which he did as follows : " I am but a young man. I have, therefore, but little to say. The speech of a young man is of but little importance in the estimation of the elder men, but I have heard that my grandfather has said there is to be peace among us. I am glad of it, for you are my relations. I fought for the Europeans, for their cause is just. I am not sorry for what I have done, and I tell you now, if it is to be daylight, and it is to be peace, I shall be well pleased. If it is to be night, and it is to be war, I am also well content. If it is to be peace, I shall come and visit you in kindness. If it is to be war, you are strangers to me, and I shall be a stranger to you for the future."

Kawiti, after a lengthy song, spoke to the following effect, although there were so many similes in it to which neither Parata nor myself could attach much meaning. He said : " I have wished the sun to shine, and I have asked for day. Let it be so. I have spoken for myself. I am for peace. I cannot answer for others ; they may wish to fight ; who can keep them from mischief ? I know not what Heke's intentions are, and I care not. This I can say : I have done with him. If war comes again I will remain neutral. I will take no part in it. I have done with it. There are hidden places in houses which all men do not see. There are places in men's hearts which are not seen by all men. There are hidden spots in my heart ; there are wounds and grief and disappointment."

The old chief and his people are living on fern-root. We took them potatoes and fish, and it will not be difficult to imagine that we succeeded in our mission. Next day Kawiti came with his followers to the *pa* of Tamati Pukututu, where houses and every accommodation were provided for them. Kawiti proceeded the day after to Kororareka, where I witnessed the reconciliation between Waaka Nene and him. The meeting of the once hostile chiefs was most cordial, and I left them chattering to each other in the most friendly manner imaginable.

On the 29th January, 1846, Sir Everard Home, accompanied by two of his lieutenants, Johnson and Curtis, paid Kawiti and Pomare a visit at Kawakawa. The chiefs received the Captain most graciously, a cordiality which he reciprocated by rubbing noses with them. They talked freely, and after the conversation had exhausted general topics the sailor said : " Well, Kawiti, it is peace now." To this the chief replied : " That is for you gentlemen of the big guns to say. If you have had enough, we have. Then let it be peace." An answer which drew from the bulky mariner* the admiring remark : " You are certainly a splendid specimen of the New Zealand savage."

This character Kawiti retained to the end, though for several years he adopted a frigid attitude towards the white people and all their ways. He especially continued his obstinate resistance to the missionary efforts to induce him to accept the full measure of civilization, upholding the efficacy of his native gods against all persuasions until 1851, when he succumbed to the influence of Henry Williams, who was as a shepherd whose flock followed him into the wilderness. During a pastoral visit paid to Kawakawa by the missionary on the 27th October, 1851, Kawiti came to meet the Archdeacon, for whom, in spite of his native pre-dilections for heathenism, he entertained feelings of highest respect. Here he was induced to enter for the first time in his life a Christian church. The beauty of the service, the piety of the worshippers, the sincerity of the pastor, made

* On the 28th January, 1846, Sir Everard Home went over to the mission station at Paihia and there met Hone Heke, who was seated on a sofa smartly dressed in a frock-coat. During the early part of the conversation which followed Heke was inclined to be impudent, and said to Sir Everard—who was a man nearly 20 stone in weight—" You are like the King of Babylon. You are as big as a whale." This remark, fortunately, was not understood by the sailor, and the interpretation of it was skilfully evaded by Henry Williams.

During his stay in the north Sir Everard also visited Ohaeawai, where he met Pene Taui, to whom he was introduced by Mr. Burrows as the Captain who commanded the *North Star* during the attack on Ohaeawai *pa*. " Oh," said Pene to the missionary, " this is the Captain who supplied the shot we have lying about here." Giving a hint to a boy who was standing by, the lad immediately vanished and presently reappeared carrying a bag with something heavy in it. At a nod from Pene he emptied the contents on the ground, when half a dozen round shot rolled out. Pene, with a roguish twinkle in his eye, asked the sailor if he had ever seen them before. No one enjoyed the joke more than Sir Everard, who, on leaving, asked the chief if he felt the place to be his home again. With a rich diplomacy savouring of Erin's blarney Pene replied : " It is only now you have paid me this visit that I feel that I am on my own land."

so profound an impression upon him that on the following
Monday morning, before he left to return home, he made a
public speech to the people in which he announced himself
as a believer ; that he would hold out no longer, but would
lay aside his Maori *ritenga** and enter the Church. He
said he was satisfied the greatness of the *pakeha* was due to
their goodness, and that all their goodness was derived from
the Bible. He would therefore *whakapono*,† and as proof of
his sincerity he would go about among the people urging
them to attend upon the ministrations of the missionaries
and seek to know the truth.

That was the turning-point in sapping the foundations
of rebellion and in securing the adhesion of the turbulent
natives to the Crown. Kawiti's conversion gave a tremendous
stimulus to the cause of Christianity and to peace, for his
influence was unimpaired by his defeat, and his energy in
the interests of his new-found faith was untiring. Visita-
tions were made to Whangaruru, Ngunguru, Whangarei, and
Mangakahia, during which the erstwhile rebel made fervent
and successful appeals for the observance of law, the practice of industry, and the acceptance of the Christian faith.

In 1852, for the purpose of being nearer to Henry
Williams's ministrations, Kawiti removed to Pakaraka, whence
he continued to exercise a vigilant oversight of his people,
not all of whom followed his precepts or his example,
some remaining " hard as iron and as brass." After two
years of most exemplary life Kawiti was received into the
Church on the 20th February, 1853. The ceremony took
place at Trinity Church, Pakaraka, when he was baptized
under the name of Te Ruku, he having chosen the name of
Captain Duke as one that no other native had taken. There
was a great stir on the occasion. An encampment was
formed, and for three days the natives were collected under
both Christian and heathen chiefs, all of whom tendered the
greatest respect to their old leader, whose infirmities were
now pressing heavily upon him. " I wish I could have

* *Ritenga* = native customs and beliefs.
† *Whakapono* = believe—as a Christian.

sketched the scene in the church," wrote Mrs. Williams to her daughter. "The old chief, for the first time in his life, I should suppose, was dressed in a handsome full suit of black cloth, with frock-coat. He sat on a seat close to the pulpit ; behind him many respectfully dressed chiefs and teachers. David Taiwhanga came from Kaikohe for the purpose ; young Pomare, Te Haratua, and some from Hokianga. The church after it was full was packed and repacked, as more and more squeezed in. I trust the honourable old warrior has in sincerity and in truth become a soldier of Christ."

With Kawiti there came into the Christian fold, and consequently to the side of law and order, the Pomare family* and Te Haratua, the former lieutenant of Heke. This meant a valuable accession of strength not only to the mission, but to the Government, for henceforth the influence of these powerful people was all to be exerted in the interests of industry, husbandry, and of peace.

The crowning act of the great reconciliation between the two races, however, took place in January, 1858, when the flagstaff on Maiki Hill was restored by the voluntary act of the natives who had been engaged in the rebellion. Since the fall of Kororareka the staff had lain prone amongst the fern on the hilltop. The Government had been anxious enough to re-erect it, but never seemed to have both the power and the opportunity simultaneously. Colonel Despard had been instructed by Governor FitzRoy to see to its restoration on his arrival at Kororareka from Waimate, but the work was never done. Governor Grey commissioned Captain Stanley, of H.M.S. *Calliope*, to reinstate the staff. "I can very soon have one up," the Captain replied, "but who is to take care of it ? " Major Bridge, who was then in charge at the Bay, declined the responsibility unless supported by a thousand men. Upon the difficulty of the

* By this time the elder Pomare was dead. He died suddenly in 1851. Of him we are told : "He was always a formidable opponent of the progress of the Gospel until a year before his death, when he became a changed man, encouraging the due observance of the Sabbath, which had a salutary effect on the tribe."

situation being pointed out to him Grey did not persist, and in this he was wiser than FitzRoy, who might have had peace at any time had he been willing to respect the native prejudice against the staff. Grey did not strain a conventional point of honour in dealing with the Maori, and in framing his terms for acceptance by the rebels he discreetly refrained from insisting upon the immediate re-erection of the staff as a condition precedent to peace.* Time, however, was on the side of the Government, and after Grey had left the colony events began to move in such direction as to make the replacing of the staff not only possible but desirable.

In 1853 old Kawiti died and was laid to rest among the great men of Nga-Puhi. In his stead there ruled his son, Maihi Paraone Kawiti,† who had been a teacher in the back district of Mangakahia. He was thus already under the influence of the mission, and when he succeeded to his father's position in the tribe he naturally consulted with the mission leaders as to the most judicious policy to pursue. He was by them advised to cement the friendship with the *pakeha* by labouring to induce such of his people who had not already done so to abandon their feud with the Government. In the intervening years many of the old rebels had steadfastly held aloof, and no effort had been made by the Government to induce them to change their attitude. But now there was an economic pressure beginning to bear upon them with irresistible force. The friendly tribes had been reaping a rich harvest from their free intercourse with the settlers and traders, and the rebels slowly began to realize that their pride was perhaps, after all, a somewhat barren satisfaction. They were in want of money. There was still land to be sold, but to effect sales they soon discovered they must be *persona grata* with the Government, which they were not. This growing desire for closer intercourse with the Europeans fostered a wish for a better understanding with the Government, thereby rendering young Kawiti's mission

* As the war arose through the Government's insistence upon maintaining the flagstaff, and as they were subsequently not able to do this, there are those who argue that the Maoris won the war.

† Marsh Brown Kawiti.

on behalf of the law and the Gospel—the *ture* and the
Rongo Pai—more certain of success.

To his aid came yet another influence. The Waikato
tribe had set up their king, with Te Wherowhero as the
first occupant of the throne. As ambassadors of his cause
Waikato sent a deputation to Nga-Puhi, requesting their
co-operation in the new movement. As the price of his
assistance the King party offered to Maihi Paraone Kawiti
the governorship of the north and the second place in the
Maori kingdom, but Nga-Puhi remembered that they had
eaten Waikato, and in all probability they remembered that
Waikato had eaten them, and the overtures were declined.
They told Waikato they had no desire for a Maori king.
" Kuini Wikitoria " was their " Kingi."* They wanted no
other. Then it was, to mark the sincerity of these protestations of loyalty, the idea was conceived by young Kawiti
of re-erecting the flagstaff on Maiki Hill. This was to be the
voluntary act of those *hapus* who were directly concerned in
the cutting of it down, and at lengthy conferences, held late
in 1857, a division of labour was agreed upon which ensured
the collection of food to sustain the working-parties ; the
felling of a noble spar in the bush ; the preparation of it on
Kororareka Beach ; the dragging of it up the hill by four
hundred men specially chosen to represent every section of
the rebel tribes, no " friendly " being permitted a part or lot
in the undertaking. For several weeks the band of willing
workers toiled at their self-appointed task, and early in
January, 1858, the British flag, amidst the general rejoicings
of both races, again floated at the peak of a mast which
received the somewhat imposing title of *whakakotahitanga*.†
This happily has proved to be something more than a name,
for all through the intervening years the peace which it
commemorated has never been broken. The restored staff
has therefore remained, in fact as well as in spirit, the
symbol of Nga-Puhi " being at one with the Queen."

* Queen Victoria was their King.
† Being at one with the Queen.

APPENDIX.

WHILE compiling the text of this book the author was somewhat surprised that in the public records and contemporary prints he could discover nothing that would indicate the attitude assumed in the struggle between the Maori and the white races by Bishop Pompallier, head of the French Roman Catholic Mission at the Bay of Islands. The author did not doubt for a moment that the Bishop's influence would have been exerted on the side of law and order, and therefore the absence of documentary evidence to that effect was difficult to understand. He was advised that there was extant in the French language a copy of certain letters written by the Bishop at various times to the natives, and application was made to the owner for the privilege of perusing them; but this request failed to bear fruit, and so, had the letters been of any service, the opportunity to embody them in the main narrative passed. The author's attention has, however, been drawn to two letters written by Bishop Pompallier during the war period, and they are here included in the volume, even though it be at the eleventh hour. The letters were printed —the author believes for the first time in English—in the February number of *The Month*, a journal published in the interests of the Roman Catholic Church, at Auckland.

The first of these letters was written to Hone Heke, apparently on 31st January, 1845, after the flagstaff had been cut down for the third time, and conveys sound counsel of moderation to the chief, whose success, however, had by this period carried him far beyond the stage of reason. The second letter was written to Sir Everard Home, Captain of H.M.S. *North Star*, who, acting under instructions from Governor FitzRoy, had offered to convey the Bishop and his clergy to safety at Auckland, after the fall of Kororareka.

The letters are here printed as they appeared in *The Month*, and speak for themselves :—

To Hone Heke.
　　　　Greetings ! I learn from Father Petit that you are anxious to see me. This has pleased me very much, and this is what I have to say to you. For the present I send you my

Face p. 298.]

letter, which is my thought. You know that my words are not those of a chief vested with worldly authority. I love all the Maoris, to the exclusion of none—even those who are groping in the blindness of Protestantism and Paganism. But I love the foreigner too. I desire his well-being and happiness in Kororareka. That is why I feel sad at heart at the thought of war. I hear the flag has been torn down. You cannot resist the power of England. There are thousands of soldiers beyond the seas. You have not the ammunition. You have neither unity of thought nor unity of command among your chiefs. Well, if you do go to war, do not turn on the English, who live in peace : on women and children, else a great crime will be perpetrated before God and the nations.

If I were an Englishman living in New Zealand, if I had solicited you to cede to foreigners the sovereignty, you might ignore my advice. But I have never counselled you to submit to any stranger — English, French, or American. To do such things is not my mission. I am not sent by an earthly king. " Your sovereignty is your own affair " were my words at Waitangi. I will work for your salvation whatever happens. To you belong all worldly matters. My duty is to procure heaven for you. My being here is proof of my affection for you, for your children, and for posterity. My Marist Fathers and my catechists never cease to pray for peace and that true felicity might reign. Remember that " the pen is mightier than the sword," that justice is the foundation of true greatness, and that injustice involves its fall. Greetings to you and yours.

To Sir Everard Home, Commandant.

I am not insensible to your proffered kindness in suggesting that you transport us to a safe place away from the war-zone. But we have no one to bother about ; we have left everything, and the good shepherd gives his life for his sheep. I do not want to leave. Our safe place is heaven. All the efforts I could exert have been in the direction of peace. They will continue so during the war. When war is on political ground the voice of religion is foreign to the debate. The Maoris have, in spite of the calumnies uttered against me, understood the zeal and disinterestedness of our work among them. In the heat of the conflict they have respected my person and all and everything pertaining to my mission. Their respect for the Bishop, whose apostolate has been so decried, saved fifteen houses from destruction when all seemed doomed. Here is a circumstance which indicates that our presence is some guarantee of security for the inhabitants. Would to God that every European prejudice against the Catholic Church would be dropped. I fear neither pillage, fire, nor death so long as I can be of use to my flock.

INDEX.

ABERDEEN, Lord. Recognizes Maoris as independent nation, 1.
AUCKLAND. Site recommended by Rev. Henry Williams, 10; examined by Hobson, 11; fixed by Felton Mathew, 12; purchased and taken possession of by Lieutenant-Governor, 12; Major Bunbury recommends troops be concentrated, 17; garrisoned by 96th and 80th Regiments, 19; rumours of attack by Heke, 89; Bainbridge's description, 89.
AUCKLAND, Lord. City named after, 12.

BAINBRIDGE, W. T. Description of Auckland, 89; commandeering of drays, 147; recall of Governor FitzRoy, 215; arrival of Governor Grey, 217.
BALNEAVIS, Lieutenant. Believes *pa* deserted, 254; extract from diary, 258.
BARCLAY, Lieutenant. Commands 96th at Kororareka, 67; despatch to Governor, 80; court-martialled, 189.
BERARD, Captain. Arrives at Bay of Islands, 130; description of Kororareka, 130; participates in loyal ceremony, 131.
BRAMPTON REEF. How named, 146; *British Sovereign* strikes, 146; Pomare assists Captain Milne, 151.
BRIDGE, Major. Arrives at Auckland, 97; attack on Pomare's *pa*, 107; description of camp, 110; reconnoitres Heke's *pa*, 114; first experience of battle, 117; in command at Bay of Islands, 122; attacks Kapotai *pa*, 123; asked by Nene to attack Heke, 129; peace negotiations, 129; brings Heke's letter to the Governor, 134; commands 58th at Ohaeawai, 152; description of attack on *pa*, 157; induces Despard to postpone assault, 161; description of assault, 169; commands camp at Waimate, 191; superseded in command of 58th by Wynyard, 213; criticizes Despard's tactics, 239; description of skirmish, 244; commands camps at Victoria and Wahapu, 262; meeting with Heke, 287; recommends Governor to meet Heke, 288.
"BUFFALO," H.M.S. Arrives with detachment of the 80th Regiment.
BUNBURY, Major. Declares sovereignty over South Island, 6; opinion of Hobson, 9; commands 80th Regiment, 14; recommends increase of force, 17; the Major and the Frenchmen, 18; returns to Australia, 20
BURROWS, Rev. Robert. Intercedes with Heke at Kaikohe, 57; description of Kororareka, 76; advises Nene against precipitancy, 101; interviews Heke at Puketutu, 113; further interview with Heke at Ohaeawai, 132; attends to Heke's wounded, 143; receives troops at Waimate, 147; description of Ohaeawai *pa*, 154; observes its construction, 155; efforts to procure British dead, 174; interview with Heke at Titirangi, 203; letter to Protector of Aborigines, 203; further letter, 208.
BUSBY, James. Appointed British Resident, 2; assists in drafting Treaty of Waitangi, 5.

CAMPBELL, Ensign. In charge of blockhouse, 56; surprised at blockhouse, 68; despatch to Governor, 79; present at Puketutu, 116; court-martialled, 189.
CARLYLE, Thomas. English social conditions, 3.

302   NEW ZEALAND'S FIRST WAR.

"HERALD," H.M.S.   Takes Hobson to Waitemata, 7 and 10 ; takes Major
Bunbury south, 15.

HILL, Lord.   Limits troops in New Zealand, 15.

HOBSON, Governor.   Arrives at Kororareka, 4 ; negotiates Treaty of Waitangi, 6 ; stricken with paralysis, 7 ; establishes town at Russell,
9 ; selecting site for capital, 10 ; establishes Auckland, 12 ;
appeals for military aid, 15 ; becomes Governor, 21 ; his death,
21.

HOME, Captain Sir Everard.   Correspondence with the Governor, 98 ;
agrees to delay his departure, 99 ; treats Pomare kindly, 107 ;
explores Kawakawa River, 229 ; superintends delivery of supplies,
234 ; visits Kawiti, 293 ; meets Heke and Pene Taui, 294.

HONGI HIKA.   His last "word," 29.

HONOURS.   Conferred, 263.

HULME, Lieut.-Colonel.   Arrives in New Zealand, 20 ; commands force
against Heke, 40 ; accompanies the Governor to Waimate, 41 ;
takes Pomare prisoner, 105 ; abandons movement against Kawiti,
109 ; marches on Puketutu, 110 ; arrives at Okaihau, 112 ;
attacks Puketutu pa, 116 ; formulates new plan of campaign,
134 ; is superseded by Colonel Despard, 135.

HYMNS, Maori.   Morning and evening, 111.

JOHNSON, Lieutenant.   Description of march, 112 ; personal history,
160 ; lands gun at Kawakawa, 246 ; estimates of Heke and
Kawiti, 287 ; visits Kawiti, 293.

KAIKOHE.   Residence of Heke, 27.

KAPOTAI.   Tribesmen attack Kororareka, 67 ; their pa attacked, 122.

KAWAKAWA.   Navigable river, 33.

KAWITI.   His followers become troublesome, 43 ; his reasons for entering
the war, 46 ; becomes popular, 47 ; suggests fusion with Heke,
59 ; throws divining-stick, 63 ; attacks Kororareka, 64 ; fights
British at Puketutu, 119 ; builds pa at Ohaeawai, 132 ; resents
Heke's peace suggestion, 144 ; defends Ohaeawai, 145 ; responsible
for its lines, 154 ; peace negotiations, 200 ; begins to build
Ruapekapeka pa, 200 ; offers to make peace, 210 ; will not
surrender land, 211 ; refuses to make peace, 267 ; living at
Waiomio, 291 ; meets Waaka Nene, 293 ; becomes Christian,
294 ; death, 297.

KAWITI, Maihi Paraone.   Succeeds his father, 297 ; re-erects flagstaff,
298.

KERIKERI.   Made base by British troops, 112 ; troops return to mission
station, 121 ; Colonel Despard lands at, 146.

KORORAREKA.   Description of, 4 ; Hobson reads Proclamations, 5 ;
Government at, 7 ; Felton Mathew's advice, and disturbances
at, 15 ; social state of, 23 ; preparations for defence of, 55 ;
attack on, 64 ; town evacuated, 73 ; town burned, 78 ; troops
return to, 215 ; Grey addresses chiefs, 219 ; troops leave for
Ruapekapeka, 230.

LEGISLATIVE COUNCIL.   Not called together, 22 ; abolishes Customs
duties, 41 ; discusses fall of Kororareka, 84 ; passes Arms
Importation Bill, 229.

MAIKI HILL.   Flagstaff erected thereon, 2.

MAKETU.   Murders Robertson family, 31 ; chiefs decide to surrender him,
32.

INDEX. 303

W. A. G. SKINNER, Government Printer, Wellington.
[1,000/12/25—23272

Lightning Source UK Ltd.
Milton Keynes UK
UKOW040840160413

209288UK00001B/15/P